A WOMAN'S PLACE IS IN THE BREWHOUSE

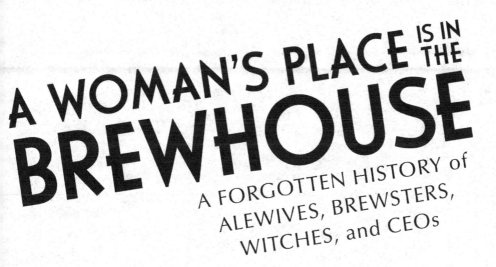

A WOMAN'S PLACE IS IN THE BREWHOUSE

A FORGOTTEN HISTORY of ALEWIVES, BREWSTERS, WITCHES, and CEOs

TARA NURIN

CHICAGO
REVIEW
PRESS

Published by Chicago Review Press Incorporated
814 North Franklin Street
Chicago, Illinois 60610
ISBN 978-1-64160-342-3

Library of Congress Control Number: 2021938739

Cover design: Sadie Teper
Cover illustration: Katie Skau
Typesetting: Nord Compo

Printed in the United States of America
5 4 3 2 1

For
Rose Ann Finkel
and my two grandmothers
Ida Rivin Nurin and Leonora Fleischer Roth

CONTENTS

FOREWORD

IN FAIRY TALES there's often an old wise woman who helps the heroine along her journey with clues or by sorting barley kernels from wheat kernels, or another such task. Author Tara Nurin is a young wise woman who is here with a book full of clues, and she's done all the sorting and sleuthing for you.

Perhaps you fell in love with beer because it is part of your family traditions? Or beer's long and deep history as part of human culture attracted your attention? Maybe you joined or follow the craft beer revolution because its fresh raw creativity and innovation captured your fancy? Somehow you found your way to beer, or beer found its way to you. And now you're ready to learn more about beer's rich lineage that goes back beyond recorded history, back to when our foremothers toiled over boiling cauldrons of brew, making beer.

Because beer was women's work then, and it still is women's work, and proudly so. Tara will introduce you to Sumerian priestesses brewing beer to honor Ninkasi, the earliest goddess associated with beer. She'll introduce you to my favorite ancient beer heroine, Kubaba, a brewpub owner and publican who was the first female king (yes, king) of Sumeria. She was the first woman ruler in recorded history and her legend grew to goddess status with shrines across Mesopotamia.

As you travel the coiled spiral of history you might wonder why women were the original brewers. While men hunted game and tended the farm, women tended the home and food preparation. Mothers, wives, and daughters threshed the grain, baked and brewed, prepped and cooked, and they made beer.

Some historians have postulated that civilization began when nomadic humans lengthened their stays at critical wild grain growing areas to successfully collect the precious kernels for beer fermentation. Beer had religious significance to ancient humans due to its intoxicating effects, which were considered a way to connect with their gods or goddesses. As brewers, women were spiritual conduits for this connection. Even today many religions incorporate alcohol or other intoxicants into their religious rituals.

This book is the key to the queendom. If you like women, beer, and history, as I do, then find a comfortable chair and pour yourself a tall frothy glass of fermented barley juice. The adventure you're about to embark on will open your eyes to the forgotten history of women and their role in the greatest civilizing event in history: beer.

Teri Fahrendorf
Pink Boots Society Founder
Portland, Oregon USA
February 18, 2021

TIME LINE

Dates are approximate and some dates are not conclusive.

4 million BCE	Hominid migration out of southern Africa
100,000 BCE	First rudimentary alcohol made by hunter-gatherers in Africa
13,000 BCE	Natufian grain beer found at Israeli burial site
8000–6000 BCE	Original pastoral settlements in Ethiopia and Egypt
8000 BCE	First grain-based civilizations, in Africa and Asia
7500 BCE	First evidence of alcohol, in Jiahu, China
4500–1900 BCE	Sumerian (Mesopotamian) empire
3500 BCE	Evidence of grain-based alcohol at Godin Tepe, in former Sumer/modern Turkey
3000–31 BCE	Dynastic period in Egypt
1800 BCE	The *Hymn to Ninkasi*
1800–1220 BCE	Babylonian (Mesopotamian) empire
1800–586 BCE	Biblical times
1200–400 BCE	Nomadic Celtic/Gaul/Germanic tribal migration into central Europe
800–31 BCE	Dominance of Greek civilization
500 BCE–800 CE	Iron Age in Northern Europe
27 BCE–476 CE	Peak of Roman Empire
0	Beginning of Common Era
500–1500 CE	Middle Ages
516 CE	Rise of ecumenical brewing in Germany and surrounding countries
1098–1179 CE	Sister Hildegard von Bingen
1346–1353 CE	Bubonic Plague (Black Death)

1438–1572 CE	Incan civilization
1453–1789 CE	Renaissance/Early Modern Europe
1486–1600 CE	Witch trials in Europe
1492–1892 CE	Spanish and Portuguese conquest and colonization of South America
Late 1400s CE	First shipment of hops from Flanders to England
1517 CE	Protestant Reformation
1607–1776 CE	Colonial Era in America
1692 CE	Salem Witch Trials
1775–1783 CE	US Revolutionary War
1820–1870 CE	High point of German immigration in America
1840 CE	First lager brewed in Philadelphia
1861–1865 CE	American Civil War
1865–1877 CE	Reconstruction
1877–1965 CE	Jim Crow laws in effect
1873 CE	Women's Temperance Crusade in Hillsboro, Ohio
1914–1918 CE	World War I
1919–1933 CE	Prohibition in the United States
1920 CE	Nineteenth Amendment ratified to give women the right to vote
1939–1945 CE	World War II
1978 CE	Post-Prohibition low point of US breweries (eighty-three)
1978 CE	Homebrewing legalized by President Jimmy Carter
2007 CE	Formation of Pink Boots Society
2021 CE	Eighty-five hundred US breweries

PREFACE

WHEN PINK BOOTS SOCIETY founder Teri Fahrendorf told me I should write the definitive history of women in beer, I felt at once exhilarated and overwhelmed. As the force behind the first organization dedicated to advancing women in brewing and related industries, Teri has pretty much had the first and last word on the subject.

No one has devoted a book to the full topic before, which strikes me as inconceivable considering humankind consumes more beer than any beverage besides water and tea. And though in the modern era we view it as little more than a social lubricant, women have brewed beer throughout history so their families would have what, in many cases, comprised the only potable, affordable drink available, and one that contained necessary nutrients to boot. Yet in almost every civilization—across thousands of miles and thousands of years—the forces of religion, politics, or economics have replaced women with men whenever this household chore has shown promise of profit or prestige.

Not anymore. Over the last four-plus decades, intrepid women have begun trampling the barricades that can no longer hold us back from reclaiming this proud heritage.

"So what," some ask. "It's just beer, not worthy of academic consideration."

I couldn't disagree more.

As Tiah Edmunson-Morton, curator of the Oregon State University brewing archives, explains, "Beer and beer production is the story of people! It is a food product and a terrific lens to look at culture, science, food, agriculture, economics, leisure, class, labor, gender, etc."

The complete telling of these stories also elucidates something else: injustice.

Throughout a decades-long crusade for social justice for women and disempowered populations that probably started around the time my mom took me to my first pro-choice march in Washington, DC, I've contemplated the patriarchal regime. Beer represents and parallels the myriad ways men have historically harnessed control of women.

Scientists believe the evolutionary ancestors to humans, who migrated out of southern Africa about four million years ago, lived in peaceful groups that valued both genders equally or distributed greater rights to women. Because these hominids didn't invent weapons for hunting large game until approximately ten thousand years ago, before then both binary sexes seem to have minded the children, gathered plants and berries for eating and, yes, brewing—and trapped rodents and other critters with their hands.

The late feminist author Marilyn French suspected the power structure shifted when men realized they fathered the children to whom women gave birth. Potentially wanting to benefit from the labor of their children, men began kidnapping and enslaving women from other clans to guarantee paternity of the offspring. French presents adultery as humankind's first codified crime—but only when practiced by women.

She suggests that when the bonds men formed as hunters weakened in the cultural transition to cultivating agrarian civilizations (to mass produce bread or beer), men instituted brutal puberty rites as a way to rip boys from their mothers and reestablish an exclusive sense of solidarity in opposition to women. If you think about it, the very act of farming implies domination over Mother Earth.

Sumer is traditionally credited as the first state to exist and also the first to sell beer. Formed in the fourth millennium Before Common Era (BCE) in modern-day Iraq, the civilization required armies to guard and enlarge it. Perhaps because so many societies seem to feel, at least symbolically, that those who give life should not take it away, women have not commonly fought in wars (though, certainly, exceptions exist). From Sumerian times to the present day, successful warriors have risen to leadership positions, and to the victor, they say, go the spoils. Male rulers concentrated power among their chosen disciples, and as statehood developed, smart leaders incentivized their winning troops by conferring them with status and wealth. In some cases, leaders forbade their soldiers from marrying.

As French writes in volume one of *From Eve to Dawn: A History of Women in the World*, "Since soldiers were men, the new rank was associated with males. A class arose in which women had no place at all; men did not need wives because of the invention of prostitution."

We can see the patriarchy evolve before our eyes in statues from ancient Egypt, credited as the first society to brew the type of beer we might recognize as such. Whereas the statues of queens and kings once stood at equal height, female royals start shrinking in relative size around 1200 BCE.

"By the time of Ramses II," writes French, "queens' statues stand no higher than the pharaoh's knee; [a] statue of the wife of Ramses I . . . stands in front of him, her head the size and at the level of his penis."

Keeping in mind that the rich get richer and power begets power, another truism applies here: history is written by the victor.

Women, too often illiterate through the ages and held captive by patriarchal customs and laws, have rarely gotten to document their own (her)stories. The very word *history* tells us everything we need to know.

With men conventionally dismissing women's lives as unimportant or not interesting enough to examine, our real-time histories haven't been written down. Where scant evidence of women does exist, as in legal documents or newspapers, we usually have to rely on the male record for wisps of information, which come bound up in the male perspective. Lamentably, the same can be said for the stories of African Americans and other marginalized populations.

Don't believe me? Here's Tiah Edmunson-Morton again.

> Archives and records repositories are spaces that reflect power and document the dominant narrative. Decisions are made by creators, by archivists, and by researchers about what to include and who to exclude—the result can be distortion, omission, and erasure. And so, for all the voices recorded in an archive, there are also many that have been silenced.

As anyone who has done historical research on women knows, their stories weren't actually hidden; more often they were simply not recorded. The history of women's work is often told through the story of husbands and sons. They were categorized as wives and mothers rather than business partners or owners.

Mercifully, an unprecedented number of female and BIPOC historians and archivists have emerged to laboriously recreate these missing first drafts of history. However, this problem doesn't relegate itself to the past. Reputable studies show women are still getting left out of news reporting and coverage.

When I started concentrating on writing about beer in 2005, after eleven years as a general assignment television, radio, and print journalist, female beer writers and brewers were rare, articles about them even more so. In service to surveying society in a way that proves productive to democracy, the environment, regional economies, and underrepresented voices (and, heck, because I've liked beer ever since my dad acquiesced to four-year-old me taking exactly one swig off every can of Bud he drank), I worked my way to becoming the beer and spirits contributor to *Forbes*.

I've cohosted a broadcast TV show about brewing, in which my coanchor and I intentionally overrepresented women as guests. I've given interviews and presented innumerable talks, workshops, and tastings (including the world's only weekly beer-and-chocolate class); earned titles from the Cicerone Certification Program and the Beer Judge Certification Program; and joined the faculty of a university to teach for-credit introductory courses on beer and spirits.

During all of this, I've kept women at the forefront. I've penned a regular women-in-beer column in the *Ale Street News* brewspaper and countless one-off articles that chronicle the successes and challenges of women entering the industry. I've founded one of the first educational groups for women interested in beer and volunteered as archivist and historian for Teri's international Pink Boots Society nonprofit along with cofounding the Philadelphia chapter.

Tiah writes in a blog post about these archival silences and how they relate to her research on Louisa Weinhard, wife of famed nineteenth-century Oregon brewer Henry Weinhard. She was able to locate Louisa's great-great-granddaughter, Lizzie Hart, and share her meager findings.

"Her [public] family story was the story of men," Tiah writes.

Tiah concludes her post by lamenting that she can't end with a quote from the deeply charitable Louisa because of the pitifully few mentions of her in the press and not a quote to speak of.

Instead, she closes with a note from Lizzie.

"What you are doing in your work—the recovery of women's stories, painstaking as it may be to grapple in the dark room of the dominant narrative—is such an important task to undertake on behalf of our futures," Lizzie writes.

It is with infinite humility and gratitude to the women in and around the beer industry—past, present, and future—that I contribute this book to the cause.

1 | THE REBEGINNING

SUZANNE STERN opened the door and peered in. The space wasn't much to look at, that's for sure. Dark, drafty, piled with dismembered airplane parts stored by the tinkering landlord, and located on an industrial patch of grape-growing land a mile from downtown Sonoma, California, the nearly windowless warehouse got Suzy's adrenaline going. It wouldn't be too long before she and her new friend and quasi-beau Jack McAuliffe would be churning out hoppy ales, porters, and stouts inside those thin corrugated-metal walls.

She didn't know what to expect, exactly. She couldn't have. No one had ever done what she was about to do.

But she loved new experiences and adventures; she was a divorced forty-five-year-old Vassar grad, music student, and bilingual former United Nations secretary who'd driven two of her kids from Chicago to start a new life close to her oldest son, who had enrolled at Stanford. Jack, whom she'd met through a friend, was charming, charismatic, and full of vision. So she'd agreed to put $1,500 plus full-time labor and use of her van toward trying to make her partner's grand experiment succeed.

If it worked, Jack assured her, they'd be legends. If it didn't . . . they'd be broke.

The space came together in 1975 and '76. Suzy, the city girl, poured concrete and tried her hand at carpentry. Jack—a welder, submarine mechanic, electrical

1

technician, and optical engineer—fashioned an office, factory floor, fermentation room, and a cubbyhole apartment he reached by ladder. Reading from nineteenth-century diagrams, they cobbled together a grain mill and salvaged a few fifty-five-gallon steel drums that Coca-Cola had used to store syrup.

On October 8, 1976, Suzy filled out winery paperwork to incorporate as New Albion Brewing Company, as no documents existed to license a small brewery. Jack called it New Albion to honor the name Sir Francis Drake had given to Northern California during the sea voyage that made him the first Englishman to circumnavigate the world.

As an Anglophile, Jack may have known the word Albion refers to England generally and to the famed white cliffs of Dover specifically. He definitely knew about the shuttered nineteenth-century Albion Ale and Porter Brewery in San Francisco. What he might not have known was that etymologists trace the word Albion to Albina, Etruscan goddess of barley flour and of the dawn.

On May 7, 1977, Suzy and Jack opened the doors to New Albion. In doing so, they ushered in a new day for beer with the first new brewery built in America since before Prohibition.

They didn't need to tell most folks what they were up to. Word had already spread through local gossip, a short blurb in the paper, and the occasional curious hippie who wandered into town to ask directions to a place he'd heard about but had trouble envisioning. People whispered, of course, and wondered who would possibly want to open an infinitesimally small hand-rigged brewery when no such thing existed anywhere else. Though per capita beer consumption was up, some historians posit the liquid was not drunk in fashionable circles. Extreme consolidation and closures of the old family-run regional breweries meant those who did enjoy beer could only access a few imports and a lot of light German-style lagers made by a dwindling number of producers.

But twenty-three-year-old Jack had drunk fresh British ale during his navy tour of Scotland and had taken up homebrewing to re-create those flavors. The pale ales, porters, and stouts he made had an essence he'd never tasted in the United States, and he knew he was onto something.

The partners welcomed visitors and took calls from press: reporters from *Newsweek* and the *Washington Post* wrote them up, and they hosted dignitaries like fabled beer writer Michael Jackson, *New York Times* wine critic Frank J. Prial, and crooner James Taylor. Ken Grossman—who would later open Sierra

Nevada, California's oldest surviving craft brewery built from scratch—came by a few times.

"I remember seeing that [Suzy] and Jack had a very challenging workload," Ken recalls.

University of California, Davis professor Michael Lewis, who led the venerable brewing science program since 1962, invited Jack and many an aspiring brewer to spend all the time they needed perusing his texts, and Michael regularly brought students to the brewery for field trips and sent them to work as interns or seek employment.

Don Barkley was one of those students.

"Jack was sitting at the desk and I said, 'I'd love to work for you here' and he just sort of looked at me and said, 'Get the fuck out,'" Don remembers.

But come summertime Don still needed something to do. So he went back and this time Suzy sat at the desk.

"I'll work for free," he told her. "She said, 'Sign here.'"

All summer long Don worked for beer—one case a week and whatever he could drink on the job. He pitched his tent on a nearby mountaintop, eating nuts and seeds and berries, shooing out the squirrels, and dating his girlfriend, now wife, Leslie. He brewed beer "like mad" and came back summer after summer until he finally earned a full-time job and a paycheck—$150 a week. He and Jack brewed three beers, just as Jack wanted. Don wrote the porter recipe; Jack dreamed up the pale ale and the stout.

The other original investor, Suzy's friend Jane Zimmerman, dropped in periodically to help fill twenty-two-ounce longneck bottles while Suzy managed the office work. Jack was gone a lot, driving to Sacramento and San Francisco and Marin County to buy grains, hops, and yeast and to peddle their very strange brew. The women spent some of those days dumping malt into the mash tun, monitoring the fermentations, and sitting at the top of the brewhouse steps talking about their lives and worrying about Suzy's daughter back in New York.

Don says an account in Berkeley bought two cases per week and some restaurants carried a little product too. The Associated Press reported that New Albion made the most expensive American beer on the market: $14.16 per case.

The partners lost $6,000 their first fiscal year, then almost broke even their second. In 1979, their output covered their expenses but not their growth, and in 1980 they finally reached profitability. They called together a board of directors, traveled to the Great British Beer Festival, and bought grain from Fritz Maytag down the road at the circa-1896 Anchor Brewing in San Francisco, which Fritz had rescued from near bankruptcy in 1965.

Jane and her husband hosted a cornucopia of dinner parties, and the crew formed a little family. Sal Guiardino, who drew the labels, and his wife hosted solstice parties. Don says Sal's sister-in-law, Lori Hillah, occasionally brewed alongside him.

The twentysomethings and Suzy may have had a lot of wild late 1960s nights but 6:00 AM came early, and the days and weeks felt never ending. Suzy and Jack never managed to pay themselves. Don contributed his college savings account to the business, and Jane left to pursue a career in marriage counseling and family therapy.

Though their ales were well received, in those days, as now, popularity didn't equal wealth. Don says they made ten cents on every bottle they returned to the Delray beer distributor, which was more than they made on the beer. In a scenario many modern brewers can relate to, the team put every dollar they earned selling beer into making more beer.

Truth be told, the people who worked with Jack agree he wasn't a nice man. He thought nothing of, say, throwing a bottle at a reporter who'd ventured in from Chicago for an interview. The grueling work combined with financial pressure made him more ornery than usual.

Both Don and his UC Davis classmate Brian Hunt tell the same story to illustrate Jack's often off-putting personality.

> Don: It was a hot day and no one was buying any beer.
> Brian: He kept a .38 or .45 under the seat of his truck.
> Don: He always carried a .45 with him.
> Brian: Jack had maybe a temper and maybe he had been drinking.
> Don: He shot the radio.
> Brian: It was only an AM radio.
> Don: He said don't worry about it.
> Brian: He shot through his radio.
> Don: I covered my eyes so I didn't get any shrapnel.
> Brian: That's the kind of guy he was.

Suzy, who worked as many hours as Jack did, took it upon herself to keep some sanity in the space. Calling her a class act, Don says she was the one who made it all work.

"She had an adventurous bohemian attitude," he says.

Complimenting Jack as a visionary, Suzy bought into his dream to open a brewpub, which would have made it the nation's first. They secured a site and applied for a bank loan. As so many of their successors would later learn, banks weren't keen on lending thousands of dollars to inexperienced mavericks who wanted to produce more of a dubious product that no one had manufactured on a small scale in decades.

So there was the small problem of funding, along with the big problem of Jack's stubbornness. He insisted on controlling the management and at least 51 percent of the business. He and Suzy asked everyone they knew for money: friends, family, friends of family, local merchants. But no one accepted Jack's terms, and as the 1970s rolled into the '80s, the business partners couldn't afford to stay small, they couldn't afford to grow bigger, and they definitely couldn't afford to build a brewpub.

Let's pause here to remember the 1980s, a decade that exemplified style over substance. America had preppies, yuppies, and an actor as president. "Shop till you drop" led to conspicuous consumption and vice versa. Credit card debt grew, individually and collectively. And other than domestic light lager, the public enjoyed neon blue cocktails that flair bartenders tossed showily above their heads.

Having finally woken up from the post-1960s hangover that was the '70s, Americans were readying themselves to become the me generation. They didn't want organic food, natural fibers, or handcrafted beer. They wanted *Miami Vice*, cocaine, and the stock market.

Boom time would come too late for New Albion. The early-Reagan 1980s suffered from the inflation and oil crises of the previous decade, and all was certainly not bullish on the banking front. The United States underwent a double-dip recession in January 1980 and July 1981. Interest rates skyrocketed, credit tightened, and unemployment shot to double digits for the first time since before World War II. According to data from the Federal Deposit Insurance Corporation's (FDIC) Division of Research and Statistics, between 1980 and 1994, a total of 1,617 commercial and savings banks failed. Those institutions held $206.2 billion in assets.

In 1982, Suzy and Jack closed New Albion.

Suzy remembers the end as sort of a gradual decline.

"We stopped brewing, we stopped delivering. Clearly it was a failing endeavor."

They sold their equipment to Mendocino Brewing (then Hopland Brewery), where Don got his next job. It would become California's first brewpub (and America's second) when it opened the following year. Jack worked there for a bit, developing a few recipes, including the flagship Red Tail Ale, then left.

Suzy never spoke to him after that. She says he declared bankruptcy without telling anyone and left her to repay an outstanding $12,000 loan with her own money.

Jack drifted for a few decades and then settled into a recluse's life in northwest Arkansas, not far from his sister and her family. He disappeared from the beer world for more than twenty years, unaware that by building New Albion, he'd fired the first shot in a revolution.

In 2011, with prodding from a daughter, Renee DeLuca, whom he had unknowingly fathered thirty years earlier, Jack resurfaced at the Craft Brewers Conference in San Francisco. Renee coaxed him onto the stage during a presentation and the crowd welcomed the surprised patriarch into the brother- and sisterhood with a standing ovation.

Father and daughter have attended festivals since, where appreciative attendees give him the full celebrity treatment. His homecoming solidified when he and Ken Grossman collaborated on a black barley wine to commemorate Sierra Nevada's thirtieth anniversary. They called it Jack and Ken's Ale.

In addition, Jim Koch of Boston Beer fame surprised Jack in 2013 by giving him the rights and recipes for New Albion that he'd bought from the public domain. Jim brewed the original ale recipe as a one-time tribute, and Renee, who received those rights as a gift from Jack, has kept his story alive by partnering with three breweries to recreate the ale yet again.

In 2019, Renee accompanied her ailing seventy-five-year-old father to Washington, DC, to accept recognition from the Smithsonian Museum of American History for his seminal influence on American brewing. That night, I leaned into his wheelchair to ask him some questions about Suzy and the old days, but he wasn't able to answer loudly or intelligibly enough for anyone within earshot to understand him.

Meanwhile, no one has offered Suzy or Jane these accolades. With the exception of one blog post from 2021, a book or two that mention their contributions, and two historians who interviewed Suzy at length in 2020, time has ignored their roles in mothering the first microbrewery of the twentieth century. Centuries after women forcibly gave up their ancestral right to brew, Suzanne Stern Denison and Jane Zimmerman replanted seeds that would blossom into vast fields of modern brewsters. But just as the narrative erased women from beer's timeline of the past two hundred thousand years, history has scrubbed these two women right out of the transcript.

2 | PLANTING THE SEED

"Alcoholic beverages might well have opened the human mind to new possibilities of thought."
—Dr. Patrick McGovern,
Scientific Director of the Biomolecular
Archaeology Laboratory for Cuisine,
Fermented Beverages, and Health,
University of Pennsylvania Museum
of Archeology and Anthropology

"I am reminded a lot that we are part of a lineage that's ancient. Beer has an archetypal quality to it and a wisdom/storytelling embedded in it."
—Kim Jordan,
Cofounder and Executive Chair
of the Board of Directors,
New Belgium Brewing

FRUIT FLIES, the scholar I call my ancient-beer advisor tells us in his landmark books, really like to drink. So do bees, howler monkeys, the Malaysian pen-tailed tree shrew, and myriad kinds of birds. German police once found a completely disoriented brown owl in the street, two bottles of schnapps by its feet. And the 1974 documentary *Animals Are Beautiful People* depicts a drunken jungle party attended by a Noah's ark of mammals that concludes with a couple of baboons getting it on.

It's likely the fermented sugar, found naturally in overripe fruit and artificially in processed hooch, that initially draws them, explains the author, Pat McGovern, who practices the archaeology of alcohol at the Penn Museum. But they stay, it seems, for the buzz.

Humans, too, are genetically and evolutionarily predisposed to enjoying alcohol. Between genetic and cellular evidence, the cranial structure of our prehistoric predecessors, and plain old common sense, Dr. Pat and his colleagues in the biomolecular sciences deduce that the preservative, digestive, nutritive, soporific, and social properties of ethanol helped our hominid ancestors survive.

"It doesn't take a great leap of imagination then to posit that early humans some one hundred thousand years ago in Africa were already acting in the role of *Homo imbibens*, making wines, beers, and mixed or extreme beverages with many ingredients, from wild fruits (maybe figs, dates, or palm fruit), honey, chewed grains and roots, and all manner of herbs and spices culled from their environments," he writes in the chapter he contributed to *Alcohol and Humans: A Long and Social Affair.*

In *Ancient Brews—Rediscovered and Re-Created*, Dr. Pat credits beekeeper Roger Morse for proposing that "mead making was the first biotechnology of humans." A Mesolithic or Neolithic honey hunter, Morse speculates, may have discovered a fallen beehive leaking honey into water puddled in the hollow of a dead tree. The sugar in the honey would have fermented into a potent and succulent beverage, and the hunter's honed instincts would have reassured him that the sweet scent likely indicated something safe to sample.

It's also plausible our forebears, given what Dr. Pat calls our "natural impulses to suck and chew," noticed that chewing on wild grains, tubers, or plants enhanced their sweetness. Because the enzymes in saliva could have converted the starches in those carbohydrate sources to sugars, these ancestors may have mixed the masticated material with water so that naturally occurring yeast in the air would land on the liquid and turn it into booze. Women in certain East African, Asian, and Latin American societies still make ceremonial alcohol using this method.

"Those who drank fermented beverages rather than raw water, which could be tainted with harmful microorganisms and other parasites, lived longer and consequently reproduced more," Dr. Pat surmises. Throughout the ages, those who drank high-alcohol holy water for spiritual rituals and otherworldly communions also hallucinated, spoke in tongues, and otherwise transformed their souls, whether for a few hours or a few lifetimes.

As divisions of labor formed along gender lines, perhaps with the gradual development of tools for hunting large game and weapons for fighting foreign clans, anthropogenists suppose beer making fell to the women.

"While men were out hunting, women were out gathering the ingredients they needed to make other foods and drink to go with the wooly mammoth or mastodon," Dr. Pat is fond of saying. "Women [were] the ones who [made] the household fermented beverages."

It continued this way off and on for the next one hundred thousand years, give or take.

But the fact is, there's a lot we don't know about beer—or human habits, for that matter—before the twentieth century. Although prevailing scholarship attributes both the formation of modern civilization and the intentional brewing of grain-based beer to the Mesopotamian empires that covered parts of the Middle East starting at the latest around 4500 BCE, newer discoveries suggest Ethiopians and predynastic Egyptians set up very sophisticated large-scale brewing systems before then.

As technology evolves, we increasingly find that beer's origin story appears to diverge from the narrative that dominated when I started researching it a little over a decade ago. Residue analysis conducted in 2015 tentatively places beer brewing in China millennia earlier than previously believed, and a startling discovery in 2018 seems to have unearthed chemical traces of wheat or barley beer at a burial site in Israel inhabited by the semisedentary, foraging Natufian people between thirteen thousand and fifteen thousand years ago.

Not only did a woman named Li Liu lead the Israel excavation, not only does the location in a cemetery fairly definitively connect ancient beer to funerary and religious rites, not only does this predate our next oldest physical evidence of beer by at least ten thousand years, but the discovery also places beer in roughly the same period as a nearby Natufian bread discovery. This lends credence to the argument that humans may have developed civilization to cultivate grains for beer instead of, or at least in addition to, the more commonly accepted notion of bread. Score another one for beer.

Though Israel isn't necessarily known as a hot spot for beer, the Bible and historians who study the region's early inhabitants have plenty to say about it. According to the book of Genesis, Abraham was summoned to the land (then called Canaan) from the city of Ur in Mesopotamia around 1700 BCE to unite the people who worshipped one God. It's conceivable these Jews learned to brew beer during their ensuing four-century captivity in Egypt, then brought that knowledge back to Canaan once they escaped the Egyptians, as recorded in the book of Exodus.

"Ancient Israelites . . . proudly drank beer—and lots of it," writes Michael Homan in *Biblical Archeology Review.* "Men, women and even children of all social classes drank it. Its consumption in ancient Israel was encouraged, sanctioned and intimately linked with their religion."

Eli Freedman, Philadelphia's best-known homebrewing rabbi, says religious Jewish texts directly link women with beer twice that he knows of. In the Talmud, which codifies Jewish law and theology, Rabbi Hisda (a brewer himself) warns his daughters "to avoid beer at night so they wouldn't fart in bed with their husbands." And in the book of Samuel the high priest, Eli, accuses Samuel's mother, Hannah, of being drunk on *sheichar.*

Rabbi Freedman says the Hebrew text uses the word *sheichar* as a noun twenty times. Though usually translated as strong drink and used parallel to wine, he believes it was "probably some sort of barley beer, maybe with dates and other additives; definitely no hops yet but maybe other bittering agents."

He notes that barley grew abundantly in Israel at that time. Archaeologists have found beer jugs with built-in strainers to filter out sediment, and *sheichar* relates to *shikaru*, meaning beer in Akkadian, the primary language spoken by Mesopotamians. Freedman says the word doesn't appear in the New Testament. However, many a historian supports the theory that Jesus would have actually turned water into beer, not wine.

These confusions frequently enter into the identification of ancient beer because the meaning of antiquated words can be imprecise to today's translators. It can also prove difficult to pin down definitions for thousands-years-old beverages.

Says John Arnold in *The Origin and History of Beer and Brewing,* "It is impossible to apply the modern conception and definition of beer to the ancient world, since there was nothing exactly to correspond."

I follow the general convention of classifying a drink as beer if it derives the majority of its fermentable sugars from cereal grains. (I call it ale if I'm referring either to beer fermented with ale rather than lager yeast or to the grain-based intoxicant brewed before hops entered the historical scene.)

Etymologists even disagree on how the words *beer* and *ale* derived. My favorite feminist author, Marilyn French, claims the word *brew* derives distantly from the proto-Indo-European kitchen vocabulary of *boil* and *broth*, which brings to mind the incantations goddess-worshipping women have recited for thousands of years over their magical frothing kettles, brought to life with ingredients born of the earth.

Whether a prehistoric pagan praising the moon for setting in the west African sky or a desperately poor medieval European mom toiling in the scalding sun, millions upon millions of women throughout history have cooked this critical liquid—typically when they could squeeze it in between gathering berries or farming, preparing meals, maintaining the homestead, caring for the kids, overseeing any servants, helping the husband with his cottage business or businesses, and taking on additional duties such as baking and sewing.

Along the journey of humankind, many of these brewsters, as female brewers used to be called, took to setting up ale service in their homes; thereby running a very informal alehouse while they attended to other chores in between pours. Fifteenth-century England applied the term *alewife* to these women, and if it weren't insulting enough to label them based on their relationship to a man, some seventeenth-century jokester gave a type of herring the same name because of its protruding belly.

No, history hasn't treated brewsters kindly, either in real time or in the record. But spirit-seeking women who brew hold sacred the belief that brewsters, as the ones who birth and tend the babies and the beer, guard the forces that preserve and perpetuate life. I like to think this deep connection to the past and future imbues them with an intuitive power, an innate knowing, if you will, of the mysterious essences of the earth.

All over the world, women with no ability to communicate or learn from one another have conceived of a similar agricultural process with similar results. And all over the world, in practically every single society, the abetting elements of economics, religion, and politics have jealously ripped women out of the groundwork they've laid.

But their roots remain. Mother Earth is patient. And her soil is fertile.

3 | RAINBOWS END DOWN THAT HIGHWAY

THE WORD I USE to describe Judy Ashworth is spitfire. At seventy-eight, a quarter century older than when she sold the East Bay, California, bar that earned her the nickname Grande Dame of Publicans, she still commands a room like a boss.

"Look at this," she instructs me at the start of an overnight visit to the suburban San Francisco home where she grew up and returned to when her elderly parents needed care. She's dragging me this way and that around The Oasis, her garage-turned-lounge, to show off a tin tacker of a defunct Golden State brewery, a poster announcing an event long since passed, and any number of the pieces of the breweriana that covers all four of the walls and ceiling.

"Try this," she insists, pulling an obscure locally brewed Polish-style beer from one of the three tap lines drawing from kegs in the beer fridge.

"Listen to this," she demands, as I read and she elaborates on newspaper articles in an album that chronicles her life as owner of the Livermore Valley's Lyons Brewery Depot from 1983 to 1998.

To give us quiet and my bestie Herlinda Heras, a radio beer-show host and international beer judge, more room to snap photos, Judy has already shooed away the girlfriends she invited over. Judy is accustomed to getting her way and making news, as she demonstrated every night at her pub, but none more so than that time she ceremoniously stopped selling Budweiser.

"Judy, you cannot do this!" exclaimed her dumbfounded Anheuser-Busch (A-B) sales rep when she informed him of her plans to sell only microbrews on tap from then on. "We don't want you to fail!"

Unperturbed, Judy invited the press to document her "Farewell to Bud" party as she poured out her last keg in what may have been the first expression of the now-common beer bar slogan, "No crap on tap." (She left Coors Light on about a month longer because she liked the delivery guy.)

The year was 1986, and Judy solidified her standing as one of the nation's very first craft beer bars when she replaced that Bud line with Lighthouse Lager from Santa Cruz Brewing, one of nineteen or twenty independent breweries in Northern California at the time.

Judy respected the consistency and technical perfection of Bud. She wasn't mad at it. She simply preferred to support the creative endeavors of her neighbors. It's a good thing, too, considering her appreciation for local innovation helped give some of the original craft breweries their start.

She doesn't recall ever meeting the crew from New Albion, which closed before she opened. But she does remember selling Anchor's full lineup, alongside Don Barkley's Mendocino beers and "Wild" Bill Owens's beers from Buffalo Bill's in Hayward. Few microbreweries existed outside of that part of California at first, and, given that she had to drive around to pick up their kegs, she wouldn't have been able to get them if they had.

———————

In Novato, fourteen miles southwest of New Albion, homebrewer Tom DeBakker and his wife, Jan, opened DeBakker Brewing around 1979 after taking what would become well-worn steps for brewers of their generation. According to beer historian Tom Acitelli in his seminal study of the US craft brewing movement, *The Audacity of Hops*, Tom and Jan toured Anchor, plied Fritz Maytag with questions, and accepted Michael Lewis's invitation to study the old brewing texts at UC Davis.

Zymurgy magazine reports that by the end of their first year the DeBakkers were bottling a pale ale and developing a porter and a pilsner. Just like New Albion, they filled a rented warehouse with repurposed soda drums and dairy equipment. They managed to secure two distributors and, according to Don Barkley, likely acquainted themselves with Suzy, Jack, and the scrappy entrepreneurs behind a few other California start-ups: California Steam Beer Brewing, opened by a commercial wine-making couple in San Rafael; Placer Brewing, in the capital of Gold Rush country; River City Brewing, in Sacramento; and Thousand Oaks Brewing, in Berkeley.

DeBakker, California Steam, and Placer all closed in 1981. Records and memories of this period's breweries are spotty but by most counts these three represented almost the entirety of the nation's pre-1980 start-ups and can thereby be considered victims of or actors on the very first craft beer shakeout. California Steam gained notoriety (and maybe a subsequent eviction notice) for crossing paths with Fritz, who sued over its use of the term *Steam*, which he had trademarked.

Though no one seems to remember much about Placer, it's more than likely this near-forgotten brewery withered from the same fate that crushed New Albion and so many of its successors: it reached the intersection of grow or die, and the recession economy at the end of the Carter era wasn't exactly favorable for loans to madmen starting strange breweries.

What Tom DeBakker couldn't achieve in business, however, he did accomplish in foresight. At the height of the first craft beer bubble in 1980, he told the *Los Angeles Times*: "I think tiny breweries like DeBakker and New Albion will be springing up all over the United States just as boutique wineries have in recent years. It is just a matter of time."

A matter of time it was. According to an *All About Beer* magazine survey by the late Fred Eckhardt, America's first beer columnist, fifteen microbreweries had opened in North America by 1982: eight in California, one in Colorado, three in Washington and Oregon, one in New York, one in Alaska, and one in Canada.

Despite the closures, 1981 proved seminal for the eventual success of the craft industry, especially in California. That year, Ken Grossman introduced Sierra Nevada Pale Ale as a showcase for the same Cascade hop that Fritz used to bitter his Christmas Ale and Jack and Suzy boiled into their pale ale. Considered the precursor to American—particularly West Coast—IPAs, Sierra Nevada Pale Ale has kept its position near the top of the sales chain ever since it was released.

Judy Ashworth says she knew nothing about beer until a few years into her tenure as Lyons's owner, when she took a road trip with some friends to a "little brewery in Chico" that turned out to be Sierra. She definitely hadn't planned to become an avid advocate or even a bar owner. But the divorced single mom had clerked at a beer distributorship and, while surviving on earnings from a janitorial service she started, she volunteered to help her friend Frank Lowven restore his 1860s-era Lyons Brewery Depot in the frontier town of Sunol.

The bar's name derived from the fact that Western Pacific Railway workers used to unload kegs there from the old Lyons brewery in Hayward for distribution to miners via horse and buggy. According to *Celebrator Beer News* cofounder Julie Nickels in an article she wrote about her close friend Judy in a different publication, the depot housed shops throughout much of the twentieth century. Judy boasts about its stint as a Hell's Angels hangout and a longneck cowboy bar.

That's until the grande dame of publicans came along to clean it up.

A Lyons regular named Bob Hufford taught Judy how to homebrew with all grain and what she needed to know about beer styles, glassware, and other craft beer finery. As she got deeper into homebrewing, she joined a club near Santa Cruz, and the two traveled the region to judge competitions.

That's how she started meeting brewers and visiting breweries. She quickly learned to admire "the enthusiasm and excitement these young brewers had."

Foremost among these young brewers was the gentle and genteel Mark Carpenter, who spent forty-three years as Anchor's brewmaster. In yet another of the infinite examples of Anchor generously sharing its resources to nurture the craft beer movement, Mark championed Judy from her first day to her last, forever supplying her with beer and introducing her to other brewers.

Two days before Christmas 1987, a fire that ignited in the feed store next to Lyons burned the bar to the ground. The story Judy emphasizes from the experience isn't the tragedy or the economic loss or even the friends and regulars who rushed in to help her recover and clean up the smoldering mess. It's Mark Carpenter, striding down the street, unannounced, with sales rep Bob Brewer, each carrying a case of Anchor for Judy and her volunteers. He also spearheaded a fundraiser for a Lyons Brewery Depot part two.

———————

Within a year, Judy was back, presiding over a cozy British-style pub in the town of Dublin that doubled the size of her old place. There she implemented astonishingly advanced tools and rules that most beer bars don't even utilize today.

She not only installed a cold room and an unheard of thirty draft lines, she appropriately set different temperatures for different beer styles and kept the tubes short between keg and tap to minimize the distance the product would have to travel unrefrigerated. Inspired by a trip to England, she served her draft ale the classic British way, using nitrogen, instead of CO_2, which she made herself with a reverse osmosis machine.

In a passionate effort to teach every patron about these newfangled ales that held unfamiliar intrigue and didn't come from a Bud, Miller, or Lowenbrau plant, she banned smoking, which incensed some of her patrons but allowed them to smell and taste the beers cleanly. She also pioneered now-commonplace concepts such as meet-the-brewer nights, Christmas in July, a chocolate and stout fest, and the blending of two craft beers in a glass, similar to a Half and Half, but better.

"I had to teach every single person how to drink my beer," she says.

It was worth it to her. Once they understood, they'd tell everyone they knew.

Judy never remarried after divorcing the father of her three children. That made her patrons' wives worry whether she was or wasn't a "little charlatan." Judy swears she never crossed the line.

That said, she did control her bar like the matron of a no-nonsense household. Even at its busiest, Judy kept Lyons meticulous, going so far as to place vases full of flowers between the urinals and telling construction workers to knock the mud off their boots and the bike gangs to leave their colors outside. Without being asked, the construction workers did one better by walking around in socks.

The apologetic guy who put a cigarette out on the floor surely never made that mistake again after Judy demanded to know—an inch from his face—if he'd dare do that at his mother's house. And the "patriot" who told Judy he could curse as he pleased because this is a free country got shown the door and schooled on the fact that at Lyons, Judy's rules superseded those of God and Uncle Sam.

It's plain to see why nearly no one in the industry treated Judy like a "poor little woman," as she calls it, but occasionally a stray man would wander in to do business without being forewarned.

"Bob Stoddard came in and wanted to sell me Palo Alto Brewery's beer," she grins. "I'm buffing the floor or something and he says, 'What time does the owner get in?'"

Judy asks why he wants to know. He says he wants to sell him some beer. She says OK, sit down in that booth.

Forty-five minutes pass.

Judy slides in.

"You're looking at her."

"Ohhhhh, shit," he says.

At age fifty-six, Judy had a heart attack; her kids made her sell the pub. In a rare display of acquiescence, she agreed, reluctantly, given she'd already suffered through breast cancer—twice. (She survived, her breasts didn't.) Though few beyond the old guard of California beer geeks recognize her or her advancements anymore, she carries on her engagement as a high-level homebrew judge and cheerleader at local beer events and breweries.

Staying happily ensconced in her childhood home surrounded by physical reminders of days gone by, it would be easy for Judy to wrap her emotional self in sentimentality. But that's not her style. She enjoys reminiscing, obviously, but instead of getting wistful, she chooses to embrace and promote new endeavors, new takes, new ideas.

This is the attitude that helped me finally settle an argument with myself over where to stand on the debate over novelty beer. Does glitter beer count as "real" beer, whatever that is? What about pastry stouts? Milkshake IPAs? I couldn't decide, and I hate holding ambiguous positions.

So I asked Judy's opinion. We were standing in The Oasis beside what I adamantly, yet mistakenly, remember to be a bobblehead of Judy's dear friend Pete Slosberg, founder of Pete's Wicked Ale. We were drinking from a small glass of excellence produced by yet another of Judy's favorite under-the-national-radar breweries. When she answered, I honestly wondered why I ever entertained any other view.

"I drink all styles of beer," said the septuagenarian with complete earnestness and certainty. "Why wouldn't you want to support creativity and innovation?"

One can credit Mother Earth for blessing California with its agricultural bounty, but other forces also conspired to place the womb of craft beer in the Golden State. Nova Albion, as Sir Francis Drake christened it, embraces its frontiersman ancestry, prospecting mentality, anticorporate philosophy, and beatnik and hippie legacy. It's where Alice Waters seeded the locavore movement at Chez Panisse in 1971; it's home to America's first homebrew club; and it inspired Fritz Maytag and Michael Lewis to pass through its golden gates to build pilgrimage sites for the first generation of craft brewers.

And of course, California has wine.

4 | THE *HYMN* TO *NINKASI*

"You are the one who holds with both hands the great sweet wort, Brewing [it] with honey [and] wine"

—*Hymn to Ninkasi*

NINKASI.

The Sumerian goddess of beer sure must have had a good publicist. Four thousand years after the civilization that worshipped her died out, her name lives on as the most recognized in the history of women and beer.

Ninkasi, you are the one who pours out the filtered beer of the collector vat,
It is [like] the onrush of Tigris and Euphrates.

Ninkasi did actually have a good publicist. Though we don't know his name we know we have a poet to thank for etching the *Hymn to Ninkasi*, the first known written beer recipe, into cuneiform tablets in 1800 BCE near modern Turkey. The *Hymn to Ninkasi* is a repetitive poem, probably sung, that describes the Sumerian process of beer making. It's believed to have been orally passed down from brewmaster to brewmaster until our poet friend committed it to clay after the downfall of Sumer. The empire inhabited the Middle Eastern alluvial plain, known as the Fertile Crescent, between the Tigris and Euphrates rivers in modern Iraq from the fifth to the third millennium BCE.

Chanters of the paean, which is believed to be a combination of two drinking songs, were reminded to mix a barley bread called *bappir* with honey and dates, then bake it twice and cool the bread on reed mats. They were then instructed to mix the finished bread with water and wine and put it into a vat to ferment. After fermentation, brewers would filter the beer and pour it into ceramic jars, which were typically placed on the floor between drinkers and slurped through long strawlike reeds. Pictograms from the era show women partaking this way.

The *Hymn to Ninkasi* is notable for several reasons, including that it has immortalized women's fundamental place in brewing the Sumerians' most relied-upon and revered beverage—used for everyday drinking and religious ceremonies—in what may have been the world's first political state. Sumer is critical to the study of beer, as it's the first place we know for sure humans settled into agrarian civilizations and deliberately brewed beer.

That women reigned over civilization's original beer creations is both a win for women and astonishingly predictive of every major society that followed. While early Sumerians endowed women with a much higher social status than they'd enjoy in later millennia, a series of wars that erupted after a massive regional flood gave rise to a hierarchy that put men in a position of power they still haven't relinquished.

Before then, Sumerian goddesses such as Ninkasi, Siris, and Inanna controlled the goods. The citizenry worshipped Inanna as their primary deity, and some historians believe women managed the processing and distribution of crops stored under her temple until religion privatized and came under the rule of the male city administrator.

According to myth, Inanna assumed ultimate power from the god of wisdom, Enki, who gets so drunk with Inanna that he gives her the sacred laws of humanity. Enki gets sick and fathers Ninkasi and several other goddesses with the Mother Goddess, Ninhursag.

Ninkasi means "lady who fills the mouth" but she's also known to have been born of sparkling water and, as her mother tells her father in the poem *Enki and Ninhursag̃,* is the daughter who satisfies the heart. She is both the goddess of beer and the beer itself.

Her position makes her responsible for ensuring that the liquid tastes as pure and delicious as possible—a weighty duty given that Mesopotamians thought gods created beer to make humans happy and that consuming beer and bread "distinguished them from savages and made them fully human," Tom Standage writes in *A History of the World in 6 Glasses.*

The *Oxford Companion to Beer* tells that Ninkasi had nine children, each named after an intoxicant or the effect of ingesting one—The Brawler and The Boaster among them—and also reigned over grain, the harvest, drunkenness, fertility, sex, seduction, and war.

In real life, Ninkasi's priestesses brewed beer for temple functions, and common women brewed beer at home for their families, just as they would for many ages to follow.

This excerpt from an unnamed Sumerian literary piece reprinted in *The Oldest Cuisine in the World: Cooking in Mesopotamia* by Jean Bottero extols the virtues of a good brewing wife: "The house where beer is never lacking, she is there."

In a society where Mesopotamian scholars deduce that silt, salts, animal refuse, and litter from travel and economic activity probably filled the waterways, and edible foods were limited and rudimentary, beer, with its carbohydrates and other nutrients, quickly became a critical means for survival.

The artistically and architecturally sophisticated Sumer was founded on the basic staple of grain. Early settlers came in off the proverbial road when they discovered thick stalks of wild wheat and barley growing in enough abundance to pick and store for a year. These cereals thickened their soups into gruel, which, left outside for a few days, would become inoculated with airborne yeast and naturally fermented into a fizzy beverage that tasted OK and made the settlers feel cheerfully buzzed.

They taught themselves to cultivate barley, wheat, spelt, millet, rye, emmer, and einkorn and attracted droves of wanderers to the area, some of whom would have had the intellectual liberty to invent nonfarming jobs in craftsmanship, writing, trade, and eventually, municipal administration. Villages and towns grew up around farming centers, and by 3000 BCE the Sumerian people built cities, including Uruk, the world's first.

The empire developed, sometimes united under one king and other times conducting business as a network of city-states. Through it all, Sumerians depended on beer.

Malting preserved the life-sustaining grains, and fermentation increased their nutritional value. Through trial and error, Sumerians improved on their favorite beverage, learning how to filter and potentially inventing the straws that archaeologists believe helped them avoid residual sediment. They invented cuneiform as the first system of written language, which they used to communicate and record transactions for the beer trade.

The earliest written documents are Sumerian wage lists and tax receipts, in which the symbol for beer, one of the most commonly used words, was a clay vessel with diagonal linear markings drawn inside.

Beer and bread were currency used to pay all classes of workers; the temple paid a standard daily rate of beer and bread for one day's work but the amount varied depending on an employee's status. Ladies of the court received three *sila* (approximately two US pints each) per day, versus one for menial laborers and five for senior officials who ostensibly spent the surplus on tips for workers. Women and children took home beer rations for a few days' work at the temple, and female and child refugees received their rations monthly.

Sumerians used specific words such as *ikaru, dida,* and *ebir* to refer to classifications such as light, dark, amber, sweet, and specially filtered beers. Cuneiform tablets show us the birth of the concept of a dowry, with *bride-price* as a forerunner to the early European *bride-ale* (the origin of *bridal*) payment of beers from a bride's family to a groom's.

"Grain was edible money," says Standage.

Grain was also medicine, as we see in a cuneiform tablet that prescribes rubbing a mixture of beer and saffron on a pregnant woman's abdomen to ease labor pains.

In 1992 a team of biomolecular archaeologists led by Dr. Pat McGovern of the University of Pennsylvania Museum of Archaeology and Anthropology identified beer stone (calcium oxalate, a by-product of brewing) in a clay jug decorated with diagonal lines. It was discovered in Godin Tepe in modern-day Iran, dated to 3500–3000 BCE as the earliest evidence of grain-based alcohol at the time. Godin Tepe was an outpost on the far reaches of Sumer along the trade route that would become the Silk Road.

Around 3300 BCE a branch of the Euphrates dried up, dispersing its dwellers. Clans warred over property, with the winners declaring themselves the world's original kings. A new class structure emerged to honor the wartime triumphs of men while the temple buildings took on dual roles as centers of political, no longer public, power. Priests accepted food offerings to the gods and used them to enrich themselves with authority and build transportation and irrigation infrastructure for their complex urban systems.

At first, elite women shared power, with wives of city rulers helping to manage the municipality, temple, and household. Although most girls did not attend school and their mothers stayed home to care for them, many women did work outside of the home. Making and selling cloth and producing food and drink occupied most of them, though women could run businesses and buy and sell real estate. Even after Sumerians started worshipping male over female deities, the sisters and daughters of rulers served as high priestesses who oversaw and kept records of religious sacrifices.

A single queen may have ruled in a long line of kings. It's hard to separate fact from fiction in the story of Queen Kubaba but the famed cuneiform King List mentions her name and occupation: tavern keeper. Depending on who's doing the explaining, tavern keepers—usually women—were either respected middle-class businesspeople or brothel madames. Putting together the pieces, it seems tavern managers and owners occupied a relatively esteemed class while her barmaids did not.

Kubaba may have worn the crown or she may exist only in myth, and in that realm, women's positions shrank. In early legends, Inanna controlled everything on earth, from birth to death. A later poem exalts a male god as equal to her and an even later one places the god Enki atop a newly created bureaucratic hierarchy in which he snubs Inanna by assigning just two lowly offices to goddesses. After she protests the sexist slight, he names her to some indecipherable position, and in subsequent writings she falls even further: from goddess of love and war to liaison to the ruling male gods to goddess of prostitutes. It's speculated that Sumerians invented the oldest profession.

We see the sex trade arise as a theme again in the circa 2700 BCE saga—and earliest example of written literature—*The Epic of Gilgamesh*. To summarize the plot, the temple harlot, Shamhat, seduces the ruffian hero, Enkidu, away from his friends and shows him how to behave in polite society by teaching him how to drink beer properly. Later, the barmaid Siduri advises Gilgamesh to give up his quest to identify the meaning of life and to basically chill out and have a homebrew.

Marilyn French writes, "In early Sumerian myths, goddesses created every-thing, and Siduri, one of the most prominent, reigned in paradise. Later, a sun god usurped her realms, goddesses were demoted, and by the later epic of the legendary king Gilgamesh, Siduri was a barmaid."

————————

Late in the twentieth century and early in the twenty-first, a few male craft brewers independently paid homage to Ninkasi. In 2006, two friends founded the well-respected Ninkasi Brewing in Eugene, Oregon, the thirty-eighth-largest craft brewery in the United States in 2018.

In 1988, Fritz Maytag added to the scholarship of ancient brews when he recreated the recipe from the *Hymn to Ninkasi* by following each step as closely as possible. He brought it to a brewers convention for a special tasting where participants sipped the liquid through straws from communal jars. In 1992, Fritz adjusted the recipe and brewed it again.

But he never released it commercially.

"Exploiting the name of the goddess doesn't sit well with me," he told the *New York Times* news service after the second batch. "This is above that."

When I asked him about the project at a 2019 Smithsonian event to honor an all-male group of pioneers in craft brewing, he answered, "Women were really the key to brewing for thousands of years."

> *Ninkasi, you are the one who soaks the malt in a jar,*
> *The waves rise, the waves fall.*

5 | THE BIRTH OF BEERVANA

"Let us study our wine, friends, and accompany its drinking with beautiful songs."

—Anacreon, sixth century BCE, Greece

WHILE IT'S SAID that wine is produced by nature and beer is made by (wo)man, both processes rely on the work of agriculture, fermentation, and aging to coax flavor, aroma, and body out of the liquid. At the end of the 1970s and beginning of the 1980s, three California-bred winemakers seized on the similarities and transitioned from making wine to brewing beer. Of the three, only California Steam rooted itself in the state's lush landscape. The other two followed the grape trail to Washington and Oregon, which is where we find Shirley Coury and her husband, Charles.

Chuck and Shirley Coury, née Cartwright, had migrated from La Jolla, California, to Oregon in 1965, the year Chuck became one of two vintners to fertilize the Willamette Valley's famed wine industry by planting its first profitable crop of pinot noir grapes. Despite running the Charles Coury Winery and making groundbreaking biochemical advancements in wine, Chuck dreamed of opening a small brewery. When the outspoken, domineering scientist unceremoniously left the wine business, he and his industrious, nurturing wife opened Cartwright Brewing in Portland—Oregon's first modern brewery.

Their son Charley, a college student at the time, remembers buying malt with his dad and watching his scrappy mom, a registered nurse from Cornell University, do the grunt work.

"She enjoyed working," he says. "She was never afraid to roll up her sleeves and make it happen. I can picture her now inside these stainless steel milk vats they used to make beer—washing them out."

Charley admits his dad was more skilled at wine making than brewing and had trouble filtering and stabilizing his beer. By the time the Courys made the decision to sell their beer unfiltered—an eccentric and unpleasant idea at the time—the couple had run through their savings. Without the ability to secure a bank loan, they turned to friends to fund what Charley calls a Hail Mary business plan. It wasn't enough.

"They commercialized too fast before proving out their basic beer formula," he says, remarking on the fact that his parents rented a big space and bought a bottling machine before Chuck quite had his recipe down. "My dad was a visionary—and with that sometimes comes an overconfidence that all obstacles will be easy to overcome."

The Courys closed Cartwright in 1981, the year after they opened. They moved back to California, settling in Calistoga, where Shirley renewed her nursing license and took care of sick people until she died of a stroke in 2005.

Chuck, ten years her junior, passed the year prior.

When I approached Charley to recount memories of his mother, he e-mailed, "It was an honor to think of someone asking about my mom. They always ask about my dad."

Though California Steam and Cartwright didn't last, the brewery conceptualized by their competitors Nancy and Dick Ponzi did. The fellow winemakers and transplanted Californians founded Columbia River Brewing (now BridgePort Brewing, sadly closed as Oregon's oldest craft brewery in 2019) in Portland in 1984. Though they sold BridgePort eleven years later, Nancy remains a fixture in the state's brewing scene.

She's known, among other things, for convincing the brewing brother pairs Widmer and McMenamin to lobby the statehouse to legalize brewpubs in the 1980s, something Chuck Coury had failed to accomplish. Believing they needed a permanent voice in the statehouse, Nancy hosted the meeting to establish the Oregon Brewers Guild at BridgePort, as it was centrally located for the other three breweries that were sited in what brewer Karl Ockert's wife, Carole, calls the "slimy" unpopulated district they nicknamed the Brewing District (now the trendy Pearl District). According to Cascade Brewing founder Art Larrance, they set up the the Oregon Brewers Fest around the same time.

Nancy and Dick, who helped pioneer the Willamette Valley's wine scene along with Chuck and Shirley, had some things going for them that their predecessors didn't. They held enough capital to hire the academically trained Karl as their brewer, and they entered the nascent industry a few years later than some of the like-minded entrepreneurs who were similarly establishing a toehold in the curious community coalescing between Portland and Seattle.

The U.S. Brewing Industry: Data and Economic Analysis guidebook counts more than one hundred aspiring brewery owners who'd contacted Fritz for advice by 1983. At that point, Anchor, as he'd restructured it, was coming up on its twentieth anniversary, and Michael Lewis was celebrating more than two decades leading the brewing program at UC–Davis. President Jimmy Carter had legalized homebrewing four years earlier—not that its illegality had ever stopped anyone.

Tom Baume, like many of his peers, had been a homebrewer. When he and his wife, Beth Hartwell, decided to follow the lead of a very few others in opening a small brewery, they found a home for Hart Brewing in a rickety one-hundred-year-old building in the old logging town of Kalama, Washington, thirty miles north of Portland.

"Everything about it was not going to work," says Beth.

They leased, then bought the building anyway, putting in sweat equity to rip up the elevated wood floors, pour concrete, and build a cold room for their open fermenters. Beth says there were no closed tanks for breweries any smaller than one of the state's nineteenth-century legacy breweries, Olympia.

Throughout the 1980s Beth and Tom formed a loose circle with a list of acquaintances that reads as the who's who of Oregon and Washington brewing: the Ponzis and Karl and Carole Ockert; Art Larrance (Cascade Brewing); Fred Bowman (Portland Brewing); Mike and Brian McMenamin (McMenamins); Kurt and Rob Widmer (Widmer Brothers Brewing); Mari and Will Kemper

(Thomas Kemper Brewing; Chuckanut Brewery); Mike and Kathleen Hale (Hale's Ales Brewery); Bert Grant (Yakima Brewing & Malting Co., AKA Grant's Brewery Pub); Irene Firmat and Jamie Emmerson (Full Sail Brewing); Paul Shipman and Starbucks cofounder Gordon Bowker (Independent Ale Co./Redhook Brewing); and future Wyeast Laboratories founders Jeannette Kreft-Logsdon and David Logsdon.

Members of the brewing community taught themselves and one another how to brew, leaning on Karl for his knowledge. They ordered malt in bulk and stored it at the F.H. Steinbart Co. homebrew shop. They also pitched in to interpret the manual that came along with the Italian champagne filler Beth and Tom bought once they earned enough money to forego the dairy or soda tanks and buy family-sized European equipment unavailable in the States. Life would get slightly easier—or at least easier to read—once Don Jones's JV Northwest manufacturing plant in Oregon started supplying miniature stainless steel fermentation tanks to the indie brewing industry. Little by little their experiment in small-batch brewing grew a little more professional.

Carole tells Oregon Hops and Brewing Archives curator Tiah Edmunson-Morton in a recorded interview, "Passionate isn't the right word from my perspective. They were just enthralled. Yeah, people [thought it was] weird and they [didn't] necessarily think it [was] going to go anywhere but . . . it [was] such excitement."

The mostly twentysomethings borrowed necessities like sugar and hops from one another, hung out after intense fourteen-hour workdays, swapped beers, and partied together. As hardworking young spouses and parents, they encouraged their significant others to keep up their support by including families and children in work and social affairs.

Carole remembers clipping baby seats onto bars, feeding little mouths under linen-covered restaurant tables, and entrusting the teens to watch the younger ones at conferences. She feels this set a precedent for craft beer to become a family-friendly space.

"I certainly didn't feel left out and maybe part of that was because I had the privilege of having someone who wanted to have his family included," Carole says. "And he was the guy in charge."

Though technical advancements, along with trial and error, helped these family businesses professionalize a bit, professional didn't equal easy. But no one could accuse this generation's beer women (and men) of lacking the entrepreneurial spirit or gutsiness to do hard labor.

They entered adulthood in the 1970s, after women had joined the workforce in record numbers, and many came from male-dominated and physically demanding professions such as logging, ski patrol, and landscaping. More than a few boasted mothers and grandmothers who'd been business owners or managers.

For Irene Firmat, Beth Hartwell, and the handful of women blazing their beer trail through the Pacific Northwest in the 1980s, running a brewery literally meant working almost around the clock at the brewhouse, traveling to make supply runs and sales calls, and trying to raise a young family.

"I did every job in the brewery," says Irene, who traveled out west from a fashion-buying job in Manhattan before conceiving of Full Sail (originally Hood River Brewing), bringing in investors, and marrying the head brewer she hired. "I was the general manager, I helped brew, I cleaned the bathrooms, I cooked in the pub. The only thing I really never did was drive a forklift. I'm a very bad driver."

"I stood on a bottling line with a baby on my back for thirteen hours," seconds Beth, mother of two. "I was going 136 miles to Seattle a couple times each week to do tastings and thirty miles to Portland to chase parts. There was always work to be done."

Beth had grown up in San Diego as the daughter and granddaughter of entrepreneurs. After graduating from Oregon State University she went to Proctor and Gamble, where middle-aged men instructed her to sell by talking instead of listening.

"We'd sit in the parking lot and they'd say what are you going to sell and I'd say, 'I don't know; I haven't even talked to them yet. It's called listening.' It was that way everywhere. It was just the times."

From there she became the first female paper mill foreman in the logging town of Longview, Washington, even though the company, under pressure to hire women, didn't know where to place a young female employee with a business degree.

Her boss told her he'd never put a woman into management. Three days later his bosses put her into management.

Sadly, transferring to the beer world didn't give empowered women like Beth and Irene much of an advantage. They insist their male colleagues never treated them with any inferiority, but these businesswomen couldn't muster much credit from men outside their circle. Assuming she was "just" somebody's wife, a photographer once asked Beth to step out of a picture capturing her cohort.

Irene refused to sell to anyone who told her they didn't "take orders from ladies," and Beth had a similar reaction to bar owners and notoriously chauvinistic wholesalers who told her to come back with her husband.

"Where's Tom?" they'd ask.

"Brewing," she'd answer. "Someone's got to do it."

––––––––––––

Gender assumptions haven't disappeared since the 1980s. So many contemporary beer women report similar treatment, though more often from clueless customers and vendors rather than industry insiders. But back then, the intense pressure of misogyny may have felt even weightier landing on shoulders already hunched from a sales routine that was much, much more arduous than now.

"It was really challenging for anybody in the 1980s trying to explain why [what we were doing] mattered. There wasn't any sense of why you'd want to have a brewery when there were so many breweries already," Irene says with no disregard to irony. "Being a woman just added to the general confusion. I wasn't doing this for a husband or boyfriend. I just really love beer and saw a different path, an opportunity to make American beer expectations better than they had been for a long time. That was very unexpected."

––––––––––––

Records list ninety-seven American breweries in 1984, the year Irene incorporated Full Sail in the distressed timber town of Hood River, Oregon, and took her business plan to the bank. Regardless of the groundbreaking nature of her idea, Americans laughingly believed Bud, Miller, and Stroh made enough beer to go around, and she was turned away repeatedly.

It took three years, countless friends and relatives, and a start-up funding package from the Small Business Association for Irene and a few business partners to raise enough money to start production inside the vacant Diamond Fruit canning plant. Microbiologist Jeannette Kreft-Logsdon invested along with her husband, David Logsdon, who signed on as brewer.

When Full Sail opened in September 1987, Irene joined five women in the brewery founders' club: Beth, Rosemarie Certo of Philadelphia's Dock Street Brewing (1985), Mellie Pullman of Wasatch Brewery in Utah (1986), Marcy Larson at Alaskan Brewing (1986), and Carol Stoudt, the famed Queen of Hops at Stoudts Brewing, ninety miles outside Philly (April 1987). It never bothered her that she missed out on being first. In fact, Irene didn't think much about gender differences in the workplace at all. Other than refusing to do business with the myriad contractors who told her they didn't take orders from ladies, she never really encountered reason to.

After a doctor ordered bed rest for Jennie Kreft-Logsdon, who was pregnant with triplets, husband Dave had to stop spending eighty hours a week brewing at Full Sail in order to mind the couple's start-up lab. Irene brought in Jamie Emmerson, whose résumé boasted an organic chemistry degree and a masters in brewing science, for a trial period. It was quite a bet at this point considering brewmasters with this kind of training only worked for big breweries.

With Jamie's passion for beer, he took the challenge. He fell in love with small-scale brewing and he and Irene fell in love with each other. His expertise helped the brewery work through their first bottling line, an Italian wine-bottle filler they nicknamed the "torture machine," given the temperamental piece of metal was, after all, intended for still wine, not carbonated beer.

Raising a family while managing a rapidly growing company kept Irene mostly grounded in Hood River despite becoming politically active. She holds the title of first female member of the precursor to the independent brewery trade group the Brewers Association and was one of the first female board members of the Oregon Brewers Guild.

At the brewery, Irene set precedents too. She and her managers pioneered ecofriendly systems that have become industry standard, and as leader of a staff of more than one hundred, she was the first to adopt rewarding workforce policies. Though she believes "the best thing is to be treated as if there is no gender," some of her company's personnel policies reflect a compassion that sometimes gets attributed to female sensitivity. Under Irene, Full Sail adopted a four-day work week and provided full benefits and generous family leave time. If you ask Irene if that's a feminine thing, she answers that it's a human thing.

As with most women in the brewhouse—both then and now—she did her best to balance work and life but, for better or worse, the entrepreneur couldn't let her own family stop her from doing everything that needed to be done. There was simply too much to do. Trying to relieve some financial pressure, Irene sold the company to its employees in 1999 and Full Sail became the first majority employee-owned American brewery.

"Some of our employees have been here for more than twenty years. We raised families together," Irene says.

Until a few years ago, Irene and Jamie still ran operations as CEO and executive brewmaster, respectively, though in 2015 their employee-owners voted to sell the brewery to a private equity firm. At the time of the sale, the Brewers Association (BA) named Full Sail the twenty-fifth largest brewery in the United States.

For their part, Beth and Tom found themselves too stuck in the grind to keep moving. Despite continually, as Beth says, "shedding equipment and getting new equipment," they remained woefully unable to keep up with demand, borrow money, or reduce their work hours. She says the stress, plus the fastidiousness that led Tom to flawless beer, frustration, and anger, left them both exhausted. They sold their brewery to a group of investors and eventually divorced. Both left the business, though their endeavor, renamed Pyramid Breweries, Inc., lives on.

6 | OF GODDESSES AND HIGH PRIESTESSES

RIGHT AROUND THE TIME the circa 1800 BCE poet was scratching his hymn to Ninkasi into handheld tablets, Babylonian King Hammurabi was consolidating power in his city of Babylon. Babylon lay in south-central Mesopotamia, the area that blanketed parts of modern Iran, Kuwait, Turkey, and Syria. It included the ancient state of Babylonia; the former Sumerian empire, which had been conquered a few centuries earlier; and assorted city-states. With Hammurabi's influence, Mesopotamian culture assimilated under Babylonian rule until the Assyrians vanquished it around 1220 BCE and moved the capital outside of Mesopotamia, effectively ending Earth's first experiment with civilization.

Beer played just as much a role in Babylonian life as it did in Sumer. Its beer making and drinking customs can confound archaeologists because they both overlapped with Sumer's and picked up where Sumer's left off, making it hard to know who invented what. At the same time, Babylonia was forming close ties and sometimes sparring with Egypt, which was developing into its own great civilization. Though some historians argue it went the other way around, most attribute a good bit of Egypt's beer culture to Babylonian influence. Reality probably lies somewhere in the middle, making the Babylonians a bridge between the Sumerian and Egyptian empires, at once extracting from and contributing to the region's evolution of beer.

Women didn't enjoy as many rights in Babylonia as they did in Sumer, though it appears they, too, brewed for money and ran taverns for a public just as obsessed with beer as its predecessors. With its bigger cities and top-down kingly leadership, Babylonia's women participated in an economy that had become much more structured, geographically far-reaching, and patriarchal than Sumer's had. And they had to contend with government-owned industrial breweries that served bland, cheap swill to the masses.

Women ran or at least worked front of house at the *bit sabiti* (taverns) that served "discerning clientele" from the "leisure class" as William Bostwick puts it in *The Brewer's Tale*. Setting up a pattern that played out in many civilizations that followed, the women who managed these taverns used them to sell extra beer from the batches they'd made for their families.

And there was just so much beer. Seventy varieties, in fact.

Taverns did serve some low-end beer but also spiced—and priced—things up with flavorings such as saffron, pepper, radish, mandrake root, resinous sap from the acacia tree, savory, thyme, and coriander. The rarer the spice, the more special the beer.

Depending on the grains used, beer colors ranged from white to red to black. Black cost the least as it contained no spelt, only barley. Precision mattered to Babylonians, who categorized and sometimes labeled their brews by quality, ingredients, color, taste, and processing. Processing referred to whether the beer had been strained.

Babylonians named their beers very literally, ordering, say, a "sweet mixed beer," a surprising "one year old beer," a "20 qa [liquid metric] beer," or even a "beer to lessen the waist," which means US breweries probably didn't invent light beers in the twentieth century as some, like Miller Brewing, disingenuously claim.

But all was not well for keepers of the brew. Not only did early kings disparage taverns as sanctuaries for sex, crime, and insurrection, but Hammurabi, in his eponymous code of laws, also fixed strict prices so taverns couldn't undercut his macro-beer monopoly. As Bostwick describes, violators were "prosecuted and thrown into the water." That means drowned.

Hammurabi meted out severe punishments to keep order and influence, and at least in the realm of beer making and selling, those punishments came down hardest on women. He warned: a tavern keeper who doesn't turn in anyone planning rebellion in her establishment will face death; if a priestess drinks in a tavern or opens a tavern—drinking with commoners—she will be burned to death.

Perhaps, then, it's a fitting irony that in 2018, a female archaeologist named Elsa Perruchini, with the help of two other women, made what might be one of ancient Babylonia's biggest beer discoveries. Perruchini used gas chromatography out in the field for reportedly the first time to separate the chemical compounds coating the inside of dainty cups and jars found at the Khani Masi excavation site in northern Iraq. She compared her findings with modern beer brewed at Philadelphia's Dock Street Brewing, owned by craft brewing pioneer Rosemarie Certo, to conclude that the compounds found inside the drinking glasses came from barley residue. Though some archaeologists remain skeptical, together with her study coauthor, Claudia Glatz, Perruchini proved with more precision and certainty than ever before that Babylonians did, in fact, drink beer.

7 | DECENTRALIZATION

THE LOWEST POINT for breweries in the United States came in 1978. Of the eighty-three that operated, a couple of conglomerates owned them all, save a few legacy family brands left over from the nineteenth century. August Schell Brewing is one, home to matriarch and former special projects director Jodi Marti. Sprecher Brewing is another. Pink Boots Society communications director Anne Sprecher managed marketing communications there until she and her husband sold it in 2020.

But with the influence of California and Pacific Northwest prospectors spreading throughout the country, the sun would soon rise on the world of artisanal brewing. In 1979, Boulder Beer Co. opened as the first microbrewery east of the West Coast. Eleven years later, it would become Colorado's second brewpub when restaurateurs Gina Day and Diane Greenlee bought in, saving the company from bankruptcy and running it for two more decades.

By the end of 1983, at least fourteen small, independent American breweries were actively brewing beer on the West and East Coasts, as well as in Colorado, Montana, Idaho, Iowa, and Arkansas. Before the next decade, women would put Utah and Alaska on that map, and two sisters-in-law would help turn Colorado into the brewing powerhouse it is today.

Mellie Pullman was a homebrewer, engineer, construction worker, and restaurant employee in Park City who, upon spotting a business plan for a brewery lying on a table in a friend's condo, decided to quit her engineering job to invest and run its operations. The man behind the plan, Greg Schirf, knew Tom Baume at Hart through some mutual friends and encouraged Mellie to spend a few months learning to brew commercially in Kalama. When she returned to Utah, she and Greg opened Schirf Brewing (better known as Wasatch), the state's first post-Prohibition brewery and the company behind the widely recognized Polygamy Porter.

In a division of labor that's still so uncommon as to be practically nonexistent, Mellie headed up brewing while Greg worked the administration and sales side. In addition to the usual wars with insubordinate yeast and testy equipment, Mellie fought battles on several fronts. In order to sell her product, she had to help Greg push the drinking public through an onerous era of mass-produced light lagers. They dueled with politicians to modernize Utah's extremely restrictive brewery laws. And she confronted gender discrimination. A lot.

"I wasn't the role model [visitors or locals] expected because I wasn't the stereotypical German brewmaster," she says. "It wasn't a good ole' boys' club but it was a boys' club. There was a struggle for credibility."

To even things out, Mellie did something no one had done prior: she hired an equal number of women and men. It was a novel move, sure, but in a village full of energetic women who worked ski patrol in the winter and construction and landscaping in the summer, it wasn't unfathomable.

Mellie claims just a little bit of credit for the fact that when Squatters opened as Utah's second small brewery five years later, owners hired a woman as brewer, then brewmaster. Jennifer Talley, who'd learned about beer and homebrewing from Mellie during breaks from her bartending shifts at a joint across the parking lot, not only stayed at Squatters until leaving for Russian River Brewing in 2013, she's considered nothing short of a legend among the second wave of American craft brewers.

Out on the Alaskan frontier, Marcy Larson has also made a point of hiring women as leaders since she and her husband, Geoff, opened Alaskan Brewing in 1986 as what their website calls, "the 67th independent brewery in the country and the first brewery in Juneau since Prohibition." Chief operating officer Kristi McGuire, for instance, started as a brewer after interning on the canning line at Anheuser-Busch (now AB InBev) in college. Over the next five years at Alaskan Brewing, she moved up to quality assurance manager, then operations manager. She left Alaskan to get married, worked her way into top executive positions at AB InBev, then returned to Alaskan in 2014 to assume her current role.

In Marcy's experience, brewery women work hard, unafraid to stir a steaming mash kettle, shovel grain, wear rubber boots, and sweat. She led by example, initially getting the brewery off the ground by doing all the paperwork and cleanup, helping with beers, shoveling malt, working the bottling line, giving tours, and "chasing everyone around making sense of everything." In 2021, she took over as CEO from a woman named Linda Thomas.

What's more, the sixty-three-year-old who spends leisure time training search-and-rescue crews to use dogs to save avalanche victims reads voraciously about beer, subscribing to every possible brewing publication and devouring practically every book she can find. Though she makes clear she's not a brewer by trade, she, like Kristi, has earned her Beer Judge Certification Program (BJCP) credentials and leans on that knowledge to judge the most prestigious competitions.

Kristi teasingly chastises her boss for too much humility as the elder woman lays out her former responsibilities to me. Kristi credits Marcy's efforts to protect the brand and research the historical recipe that inspired their flagship Alaskan Amber as fundamental to their success.

Sisters-in-law Wynne and Corkie Odell, who established Odell Brewing in Ft. Collins in 1989, at least had a third leg of the stool to balance out their job duties: Doug Odell—Corkie's brother and Wynne's husband.

The two women correct the record when overwhelmed younger women get the false impression that they've spent their adult lives as co-owners of one of the nation's most successful, award-winning, sustainable, and beloved breweries, simultaneously working sixty hours a week, flying five thousand miles a year, raising kids, and playing active roles in the community. They haven't, and they don't think others can or should, either.

The three Odells retired from brewery operations when they sold to employees in an Employee Stock Ownership Plan (ESOP) in 2015, but they kept majority ownership and seats on the board. Believing firmly that, when possible, one spouse should take time for kids and community, the women each tried to limit their workload to an average of thirty hours a week, even when they occupied the C-suite.

They've done their best to provide that same balance to their workers. They say they paid them fair wages and benefits, gave them time to volunteer and pursue activities that bring them joy, and instilled them with a sense of ownership long before they actually sold the company to the workforce that had stewarded it so conscientiously. Wynne and Corkie say they could provide that luxury to themselves and their employees in part because they prioritized good, solid beer above all else—never rushing growth or chasing the almighty dollar.

Over their tenure, they say they paid attention to creating a pipeline of empowered, entry-level women and, with some assistance from a diversity, equity, and inclusion (DEI) specialist, concentrated on making it a place women wanted to be. They express disappointment that they left management without getting the brewery to one-third female employment, but Wynne comes to terms with that during our interview by reconciling, "We were able to get the system and ethos into place so that now it's positioned to move into that much more quickly."

As board members and majority owners, they intend to keep pushing for more female inclusion, as when they fought the board to get the woman who runs all of Odell's taprooms a seat on the heavily male executive team.

"The taprooms are an enormous marketing arm and a serious revenue generator but it's like restaurant work so it wasn't considered as meaningful," Wynne says. "I'm actually embarrassed to be telling this story but we were able to get this woman on before we stepped out."

Though Corkie gets frustrated that strangers inevitably ask her unaffiliated husband about the brewery when she's standing right next to him, both Odells, as well as Marcy Larson, speak gushingly of their male partners. They describe theirs as highly accepting, nonhierarchical partnerships where everyone naturally finds their fit. Both big-name brewers, Doug and Geoff, without ego, have fully included them in national brewing circles and shared all manners of credit and praise.

"It's always been about the both of us," says Marcy.

Not so for Mellie, who left Wasatch in 1989, having philosophically parted ways with Greg. She appears nowhere in Wasatch's lengthy online history, which lovingly details Greg's role. What's worse, almost no one knows that she served as the very first female brewmaster of the last century.

In fairness, Mellie's tenure lasted a mere three years, and after a short stint as a brewery consultant, she retired from the beer world, going on to earn advanced degrees and impressive job posts in unrelated subjects at top universities. She reemerged at Portland State University in 2005 to apply her extensive expertise in supply chain logistics to create the first certificate program emphasizing the business side of craft brewing. Though she doesn't brag about her unique status, she does quietly feel young women are avenging history's misogynistic memory.

Maybe that's because women comprise 40 percent of her students.

8 | BREW LIKE AN EGYPTIAN

CLEOPATRA. Quite likely the most famous female ruler in history, we associate the ancient Egyptian queen with international and sexual affairs and makeup (well, I do, anyway). But Cleopatra VII also has a lot more to do with beer than most people realize, and the history of the beverage in this most awesome of civilizations boasts more real and mythical women in positions of power than any other.

Beer, as in Sumer and Babylonia, dominated Egyptian life. *Hekt,* a common word for beer—some historians argue barley beer, specifically—was the staple food of lower-class Egyptians, and beer in general (*zytum,* similar to the Greek word *zythos)* was used to pay or feed workers, from the enslaved and nonenslaved female and male builders of the pyramids to scribes, artisans, and bureaucrats. As in most civilizations, beer was used for religious rituals, nonsecular ceremonies, and the all-important funerary rites, not to mention social and daily drinking. Though ancient Egyptians generally frowned on drunkenness, special occasions called for higher octane party fuel, as became customary across much of later time and space.

Egyptian medical healers prescribed beer to remedy more than one hundred different ailments. A thirty-five-hundred-year-old medical text at the University of Copenhagen directs pregnant women to urinate on two bags—one containing wheat and the other containing spelt. According to some translators, if the wheat sprouted first, she carried a boy; spelt—a girl.

So when Cleopatra imposed a tax on the barley beverage to help fund her sprawling empire and war with Octavian's Roman faction at the end of Egypt's tremendous thirty-one-hundred-year reign, it contributed to the downfall of both the legendary queen and the Egyptian empire itself. History's first beer tax was so shocking and unpopular that one modern observer likens it to a tax on water. Cleopatra claimed she wielded it as a necessary weapon to combat drunkenness.

Evidently, it didn't help her military cause. She lost to Roman troops and appears to have committed suicide to spare herself an undignified death at the hands of her conquerors.

Sixty years later, Christianity had completely vanquished the great African empire. It would mean the end of Egypt's devotion to goddesses, including those who governed beer.

According to myth, Osiris, god of cereals and agriculture, taught ancient Egyptians the art of brewing (more likely it was southern Africans, Babylonians, or an indigenous wellspring of knowledge). Osiris delegated ongoing oversight to Tenenet, the goddess of beer, who, like Ninkasi, supervised brewers to ensure they followed the recipes and made the best beer possible.

Hathor (also called Sekhmet), another goddess of the brew, didn't enjoy quite so sunny a reputation at first. Ra, the almighty sun god, sent Hathor to earth to punish humans for forsaking him in his old age. But she carried out his order to annihilate the whole of humanity so thoroughly that other gods warned Ra that he was losing his source for sacrifices. So he sent slaves to mix up crushed barley, fruit, and human blood and dump the resulting beer into a river. Hathor paused for a drink and got so drunk she forgot about her mission before she could complete her slaughter. One of Egypt's most popular annual celebrations, the Festival of Drunkenness, honored this event.

The multitude of beer goddesses and Hathor's revered role as a mother of the divine kings hints that women were, initially, very active in the production process, both making beer at home for their families and selling it for profit. Throughout much of Egypt's history, women enjoyed some of the greatest civil rights among literate peoples in the ancient world, and unless they were very poor, had the ability to divorce; own property and commercial enterprises; conduct their own legal affairs; earn equal pay for work, including brewing; and achieve immortality.

"Although," says (Welsh) Swansea University's Egypt Centre curator Carolyn Graves-Brown, "Women had those rights in theory; in practice, men had the most wealth, were more likely to initiate divorce, etc."

The status of women and men appears roughly equal, at least in earlier centuries of the empire, and for many, many years, queens ruled and women warriors fought with equal supremacy (and bloodshed) as their male counterparts. Kings won legitimacy though royal marriage; their lineage passed down matrilineally. It was truly a uniquely golden age for women.

Marilyn French writes that equality carried the day in civil society until, "Suddenly, near the end of the fourth millennium [BCE], images show one man towering over the others as they dig a canal or kill adversaries."

No one can definitively explain the shift, but we simultaneously witness the appearance of the word *king* (pharaoh) around 3100 BCE, when the presiding pharaoh unified Upper and Lower Egypt into one state, centering his kingdom, administration, and temple in Memphis.

Future pharaohs' Great Royal Wives served as high priestesses, their married sisters as advisors. Gradually, priests of major temples consolidated power by calling in regional priests and assimilating and submitting their gods and goddesses under one overarching deity.

Right after King Tutankhamun's death, in 1327 BCE, an unrivaled period of reigning queens ended abruptly when his daughter, along with Queen Nefertiti, got caught trying to ally herself with the enemy. Authors used the betrayal as an opportunity to wage a satirical smear campaign against all women.

In the ensuing period of war, soldiers rose in prominence and a swollen percentage of the population was enslaved. Male slaves could earn their freedom but not women, who could only perform less physical, menial duties.

The soldier Ramses I became a powerful king who not only relegated priestesses to singers and dancers in the temple but efficaciously professionalized society and cast aside kin connections.

Says French, "In societies where a man names his family as administrators (hoping for loyalty), female kin have a chance to function politically. Without that entrée, women are shut out of the public realm."

When it came to financing the kingdom, Egyptians undoubtedly had enough barley, rye, spelt, and sorghum at their disposal. The Bible calls Egypt "the granary of the ancient world," and the soil's abundance made for a rich, joyful population that loved to sing, dance, and drink.

John Arnold writes in *Origin and History of Beer and Brewing*, "Sweet beer, iron beer, sparkling beer, perfumed beer, spiced beer—cold or hot, beer of thick, sticky millet. . . . The beer-houses contained stores of as many varieties of beer as of different qualities of wine."

Arnold says women labored as maidservants in these beer houses (taverns), greeting patrons, sometimes with song, leading them to comfortable seating arrangements, and encouraging them to drink up. Women, including those attending university, also did their turn as imbibers, partying at private gatherings called houses of beer. Bostwick says a funerary painting depicts two women, "One of them paying her tribute to nature, being full of drink, while the other renders her kind service."

Egyptians worked hard to make high-quality beer, teaching themselves through trial and error that, for instance, they could improve consistency by reusing the same vessels for mashing and fermenting. Like the Babylonians and probably the Sumerians, they drank beer through clay or reed straws conceivably used to push through layers of thick sediment and/or hygienically reach into the shared, undecanted vessels. It seems they also filtered some beer and poured it from pitchers into ceramic cups.

Beginning around the start of the Middle Kingdom, and even more so under the rule of Ramses II a millennium later, around 1300 BCE, temples, castles, governors, nobles, and upper-class landowners all possessed their own breweries, where they employed professional brewers and provided beer as payment to vast numbers of slaves, laborers, soldiers, and craftspeople.

"Although beer was produced daily [by women] in most ancient Egyptian households, there was also large-scale production in breweries for distributing rations to town-dwellers, taverns or 'beer houses,' wealthy individuals, and state employees," writes Helen Strudwick in the *Encyclopedia of Ancient Egypt*.

Pat McGovern says in *Ancient Brews* that he and Dogfish Head Craft Brewery cofounder Sam Calagione joked while filming the *Brew Masters* television episode about their Egyptian beer amalgamation, Ta Henket, that, "The rise of Egyptian civilization was on the line, and mass-producing beer was necessary to make it happen."

Brewmasters held positions of high esteem, as evidenced by the elaborate tomb of one of Luxor's official brewmasters, Khonsu-Im-Heb. According to the *Atlantic*, this gentleman would have also taken charge of the city's beer warehouse, a prestigious job duplicated dozens of times over for every imaginable commodity.

Despite all of those goddesses who oversaw and received offerings of beer, women's role in brewing shrank after 2100 BCE, at the very latest.

A few statuettes removed from tombs of this general period represent women, perhaps servants, engaged in the act of milling grains, sifting flour, and kneading dough with their feet. They're generally accepted to be brewers, not bakers, though the roles sometimes overlapped, and breweries and bakeries usually shared space. They indicate the presence of women in the production of commercial grain-based beer.

They, along with a brewery/bakery complex excavated at Giza from circa 2550 BCE, also strongly suggest that Egyptians of that era made beer by rolling crushed grains and baking them with water to make dough. We do know that brewers fermented their wort with chunks of yeasty bread and preserved and bittered it with the lupin plant, which hops expert Stan Hieronymus says is puzzlingly not related to the *Humulus lupulus* plant otherwise known as hops.

Some suggest these statues help construct a narrative that prior to the Middle Kingdom era (2055 BCE) the creation of social classes almost definitely precipitated the demotion of women to mere assistants in the craft of brewing. In other words, as brewing grew more hierarchical over the lifespan of the Egyptian empire, each brewer increasingly had a specialty, and eventually, each important brewer also had a penis.

9 | THE GREAT EASTWARD MIGRATION

"LET ME HAVE SOME OF ED'S BEER."

That's how men in Carol Stoudt's rural central Pennsylvania community ordered Stoudts' German-style lager beer in the 1980s.

Ed Stoudt is Carol's husband. But while he made for a popular local figure as the owner and operator of the Black Angus Steakhouse, which served Michelob and Dortmunder Actien Brauerei on draft plus bottles of Yuengling and any German imports they could acquire, the beer in question was most certainly not his.

The beer belonged to Carol. She not only sold and promoted it, but she also brewed it, and she owned the company.

Until Carol, every woman to own a brewery in post-Prohibition America had done so in partnership with a man, usually her husband. Besides Mellie, none had managed the brewing side. Nevertheless, the thirty-eight-year-old former schoolteacher offered to establish and operate Stoudts Brewing sixty-nine miles northwest of Philadelphia once Ed learned that Pennsylvania law prohibited him from owning a brewery in conjunction with the restaurant.

Had they waited a few months for the commonwealth to legalize brewpubs, Ed could have probably done it. But then Carol wouldn't have gained recognition for being what her eponymous company calls "the first woman in America to oversee the design and development of a craft brewery from start to finish."

Carol didn't want Ed to abort his plan. So despite knowing less than zero about beer making when she brewed her first commercial liquid in April 1987, she went for it.

The mother of five says, "The youngest was going to start going to kindergarten in the fall. I thought, 'Maybe I can do this.'"

Carol made her historical and life-altering decision around eight years after small brewing migrated back to the Eastern Seaboard with Marie and William Newman, who incorporated the Wm. S. Newman Brewing Co. in Albany as early as 1979. According to Tom Acitelli, they served their first beer in February 1982—a pale ale—which they fermented in the cask and poured at cellar temperature according to British custom.

Time magazine included Newman's ale in a July 1983 feature on microbreweries that ran under the headline "Small Is Tasty." Boston Beer founder Jim Koch worked there for a stint and presciently remembers, "I could see there was an opportunity to brew a richer, more flavorful beer . . . than the pale and bland mass domestic and import beers that were ubiquitous at that time."

Like their peers out west, Marie and William succumbed to money problems. Carrying a heavy debt burden, they closed down their facilities sometime between 1987 and 1990 (reports differ) but continued to brew on a contract basis at an outside facility for several more years.

The history of that time period tells of scattered East Coast endeavors that, like some marriages, didn't last past the honeymoon phase.

Other reverse wagon trainers, however, live on, notably in New England, which became the center for East Coast microbrewing in the 1990s. Thanks to fortuitous geography and timing, I was introduced to craft beers (through a boyfriend with a fake ID) as a senior at suburban Boston's Tufts University in the middle part of the decade.

The region's first craft brewery to incorporate is also the oldest one east of the Mississippi to survive: D.L. Geary Brewing, in Portland, Maine. Karen and David Geary incorporated in October 1983, then David shipped off to England to perfect his craft while Karen stayed home to write a business plan. Without a bank loan, it took the couple eighteen months to raise $300,000 in start-up funds, and they sold their first pints of Geary's Pale Ale on December 10, 1986, at a local pub owned by the self-titled Indiana Jones of Beer, adventurer and author Alan Eames.

The Gearys brought legendary Englishman Alan Pugsley over to manage production. With him traveled a strain of yeast from the Ringwood Brewery, whose descendants still define the profile of a traditional New England ale. Younger brewers often cite Geary as an inspiration, and David still worked there, along with the couple's daughter, Kelly, and son, Matt, until David sold it in 2017. Karen passed away seven years ago after losing a long battle with breast cancer.

Thanks to David's travels and the scarcity of West Coast beer, former brewer and journalist Lauren Clark writes in her *Crafty Bastards* history of New England brewing, "It's no exaggeration to say that the early years of New England craft brewing were influenced more by what was happening on the other side of the Atlantic than what was happening on the other side of America."

Up in Vermont, it took Nancy and Greg Noonan from 1985 to 1988 to persuade state lawmakers to legalize brewpubs, a change that allowed them to open Vermont Pub & Brewery in Burlington. Well ahead of their time, Nancy used to re-create colonial beer recipes and share them with guests while telling drinking stories about New England's foremothers and fathers. She also paired beer with chocolate and explored the beers of Belgium—both supremely novel ideas in the 1990s.

Years after the Noonans' divorce and Greg's death from lung cancer in 2010, the Vermont Brewery, now a dated landmark on Burlington's Church Street Marketplace pedestrian mall, remains a pilgrimage site for history-minded beercationers like me.

In 1987, Janet Egelston convinced her brother, Peter, to help her open the Northampton Brewery in Massachusetts. After five years of co-ownership, with Peter handling brewing operations, the pair set sights on New Hampshire, where they founded Portsmouth Brewery as the state's first brewpub.

Two years later, Peter set up Smuttynose Brewing, which he ran as a respected regional brewery with conservative approaches to styles and beers until he auctioned it in 2018. Peter still owns Portsmouth, not with Janet, who went back to Northampton full-time, but with his longtime romantic partner,

Joanne Francis. In 2017, Joanne released a beer called Libeeration, made with herbs, such as mugwort, stinging nettle, and motherwort, to alleviate the symptoms of menopause.

Though she didn't own a brewery or brew beer, it's critical to mention another New Englander who proved monumental in directing the course of craft beer: Rhonda Kallman.

Before Stoudts, before Vermont Brewery, before Northampton and Portsmouth and before Geary's released its seminal pale ale, there was the Boston Beer Company (BBC). Since its founding in 1984, the company that's dominated the craft brewery size hierarchy for decades has been majority owned and operated by fourth-generation beer man Jim Koch. Rhonda, an executive assistant he brought over in her twenties from the corporate world, was there at the start.

Rhonda and Jim hit the streets with Sam Adams Boston Lager in April of 1985, and though it took some time for the idea of a flavorful amber lager to catch on with Boston publicans, their lager grew to such distribution heights that it represented many Americans' introduction to craft beer until around 2013.

Rhonda stayed with BBC as founding partner and executive vice president for fifteen years, helping to lay the foundation for what has become a more than $11.5 billion company—by far the most successful start-up craft brewery to date. But it was far from easy. Rhonda traveled constantly to visit her customers, hired and trained what she says is regarded as the best sales force in the United States, and raised two children. All the while she faced near-daily discrimination, from customers to bar managers to other brewers.

"It was very chauvinistic," she says. "People would ask me, 'Are you a promotional girl? Are you Jim's wife?'"

In 1985, she says, after Sam Adams was voted the "best beer in the room" at the Great American Beer Festival, "There were rumors that I was exchanging sexual favors for votes!"

Undaunted by this behavior from competitors (and continued grumblings from old guard West Coast brewers who accused Koch of stuffing the ballot box), she brought more women into the company. She says she simply took advantage of a large pool of untapped talent—the more than 50 percent of the population that's female whom no one was hiring. When she left BBC, women comprised more than 55 percent of the sales force.

Rhonda went on to invent beer styles at a new endeavor, New Century Brewing, which became infamous for its caffeinated beer, Moonshot 69. The 2009 documentary *Beer Wars*, written, produced and directed by corporate consultant Anat Baron, centers around Rhonda's efforts to fight the Food and Drug Administration and once again create a market for an unknown product. After losing a protracted legal challenge against the government agency, she left the beer industry.

But her exit doesn't negate the awards she's won: the Institute for Brewing Studies' Recognition Award for being a "pioneering woman in the beer industry," *Draft* magazine's Top Ten Innovator award, and *Beer Business Daily*'s sought-after Maverick Award.

Not one to stay down, the serial entrepreneur went full circle to launch the Boston Harbor Distillery in 2015, before craft distilling had truly caught on.

Speaking of her Sam Adams days in a way that translates to her role today, she says, "There was no ladder to climb so I built one."

––––––––––––––

Rosemarie Certo, who opened Dock Street Brewery & Restaurant as Philadelphia's first craft brewery in 1985, echoes Rhonda when she says, "I had the pleasure of being in an industry that was nonexistent."

Rosemarie descends from a line of no-nonsense women who controlled the family's olive and grape orchards in Sicily. So when she and then-husband Jeff Ware decided to transition from homebrewing into this nonexistent industry, they drew from her strong will to fight for what they needed.

Fight they did. First they successfully lobbied Pennsylvania lawmakers to legalize wine and spirits sales at brewpubs. Then when high tariffs and unfair trade practices made the cost to export Dock Street beer to France almost prohibitive, they protested . . . in a big way. They printed upside-down bottle labels and stamped the word "protest" across each. The neck labels communicated their reasoning.

Rosemarie and Jeff encouraged their customers to boycott foreign beers and to ask their federal representatives to impose equally high tariffs on imported beer and other goods. These efforts got the attention of the feds, who invited the couple to represent the entire brewing industry at negotiations for the General Agreement on Tariffs and Trade in Washington, DC. The *Today Show* and the *Wall Street Journal* took notice and gave them positive coverage.

By the late 1980s, Dock Street had grown into one of the top ten largest craft breweries in the country. But some skeptics don't give Rosemarie proper credit because even though she was a full half of the force behind the business, she and Jeff decided it best to avoid potential sales and approval problems by leaving official ownership in his name.

It sounds unfathomable now but sadly made sense at the time. After all, it wasn't until 1974 that Ruth Bader Ginsberg's legal work led the Supreme Court to prohibit banks from denying credit to women on the basis of sex.

(When Janet Johanson, forty-two-year-old owner of the BevSource contract brewing company, learned her computer engineer mother couldn't sign legal financial documents as a young married woman, she asked dumbfoundedly, "In my lifetime you had to have a man sign a loan?" Her mom replied, "Yes, Janet, your dad had to sign for our mortgage.")

After the Certo-Ware union dissolved, Rosemarie put her name on the company's documents and sold Dock Street. A few years later, she repurchased it and brought the contract-brewed beer back from New York to Philly.

She now employs her daughter and son, co-owns a tequila company in Mexico, runs three Dock Street locations, and keeps making national news by commissioning exclamation-worthy beers, like one that fermented while Wu Tang Clan songs played and another produced with smoked goat brains to celebrate the TV show *The Walking Dead*.

Despite that, Rosemarie still considers brewing a macho industry that harbors suspicion of women.

"Women are still not trusted to know as much as men," she says.

An hour's drive from Dock Street, Carol Stoudt didn't trust herself at first. She calls her younger self a wine and "girlie cocktail" drinker who appreciated beer for the first time on her honeymoon to Germany and Austria, followed by an educational bus tour to the breweries, hop farms, and malthouses of the West Coast led by Brewers Association founder Charlie Papazian.

That said, Carol secured a small bank loan and sold half of the equity in the Stoudt homestead to her husband. Then she asked each of her kids' godmothers if they wanted to invest. Carol says she did all of her own research, paperwork, and purchasing; oversaw construction; and traveled to Louisiana for two weeks to apprentice with Karl Strauss at Abita Brewing.

She'd already fully established the company by the time she brewed her very first beer.

That start-up phase marks the most discouraging period of Carol's life. Account managers who took her phone calls told her "no thank you" and the ones she met face-to-face informed her that her German-style beers were so bad they'd offend the Germans. In her mind, she'd failed as a salesperson and failed as a brewer.

Her bad luck broke for good when Philadelphia restaurateur and internationally renowned sustainability advocate Judy Wicks read about Stoudts (which back then carried an apostrophe) in an article and called Carol with a demand.

As Carol tells it, Judy said, "Listen. You are going to sell beer to me."

After protesting that she didn't sell beer all the way in Philly, Carol relented and loaded two kegs into her station wagon. Judy gave Carol a standing draft line at her landmark White Dog Cafe and helped her sign distributors. Some declined to list her beers in the price sheets they gave to accounts, and one refused to sell Scarlet Lady ESB because the artistic belle epoque drawing of a lady on the label made its decision makers squirm.

Ten long years after her first Philly sale, she nailed her first account close to home, selling Stoudts Gold to the Lancaster Dispensing Company. On the menu, someone printed "Ed Stoudt's Lager."

Moving forward, she traveled occasionally for industry conferences and judging at Charlie Papazian's annual Great American Beer Festival in Colorado, though otherwise she almost always made it home to tuck the kids into bed. When she couldn't do that, she'd have her cleaning lady babysit.

At those conferences, she remembers introducing herself to Mellie and Jenny Talley from Utah and master brewer Teri Fahrendorf from Steelhead Brewing on the West Coast. But Carol and the others say they were too busy doing their jobs and raising families to think about trying to connect on any sort of deeper level or notice whether they were or weren't the only women in the room.

As recognition of Carol's brand grew, so did her family's business. The Stoudt property draws tens of thousands of people to its annual Oktoberfest and still houses the steak house and beer garden, a bakery, and an antiques mall. Following in the steps of "The Beer Hunter" Michael Jackson and other Gen Xers and boomers who've given themselves beer nicknames, she has assumed the crown of Queen of Hops.

Now everyone notices when Carol Stoudt walks into a beer room. Commonly misidentified as the nation's first modern female brewmaster, she's royalty among royalty. But as a soft-spoken grandmother who favors traditional (read: old-fashioned) styles and believes all beer should be local, her renown isn't nearly enough to keep the stodgy Stoudts Gold Lager gushing in a river of sought-after limited releases and hype.

She announced her retirement in late 2019, promising to participate in collaborations and events that call to her septuagenarian sensibilities. Instead of spending any more of her life chasing sales and changing minds in today's trend-obsessed marketplace, the Queen of Hops is happily reigning over her family's destination property and enjoying the children of the children she raised while polishing her crown atop the kingdom of beer.

10 | WHAT'S PAST IS PROLOGUE

THE MORE WE LEARN about the scattered geography of prehistoric brewing, the more we wonder whether the domesticated production of the fermented beverage we might call beer might not, in fact, have sprung forth in the so-called Cradle of Civilization between the Tigris and Euphrates Rivers but rather may have been birthed by the discoveries and collective consciousness of women, who across the globe had, at varying times, reached similar phases of human development.

Not nearly enough attention is paid to beer brewing in the Africa, South America, or East Asia of the past; even less so to the women who likely made it happen. American beer scholars have a passing knowledge of chicha, an alcoholic drink that varies greatly by culture. Its commonality comes from the fact that Andean and Amazonian women have for millennia chewed up and spit out carbohydrate sources such as maize or fruit to activate the fermentable sugars within.

But that's pretty much it.

Other than Egypt, western beer historians tend not to poke around Africa, where contemporary women are doing their best to revive the beer-brewing traditions of the greatest of their grandmothers. And though we recognize the discovery of the earliest fermented beverage known to (wo)man in Jiahu, China, we don't realize that women almost assuredly invented Japanese sake.

Admittedly, East Asia doesn't have too much of a native beer culture that we know of but the other two continents do, and English-language resources about them remain pitifully scarce. Regrettably, much of what I've found so far comes from North American men. I suspect and hope that the emerging class of New World (more technically, Old World) craft brewsters will take further deep looks into the legacy they inherit and add widely to our understanding of this noble history.

Africa

Much of what we know about old-time African brewsters comes from those who now retread their path. Historians believe that outside the international macroproducers who set up shop there, the vast numbers of Africans who homebrew and sell on a small scale—to balance out the priciness of corporate beer—typically do so according to ancient traditions.

So it's mainly by working in reverse that we can deduce what once was.

"Every occasion and gathering except religious ones always have crates of beer present," e-mails Peace Onwuchekwa, brewer and quality control supervisor at Bature craft brewery in Nigeria. "Before the advent of beers, we had the likes of palm wine, burukutu (sorghum and millet beer), etc. . . . that were all locally brewed."

The importance of beer, both past and present, can be ascertained instantaneously upon entering some traditional African villages: the brewery sits at the center. I've had numerous African brewers linguistically roll their eyes as they tell me that like always, the women brew and the men drink.

"When women brew the beer men stay at home. They don't need to go anywhere," laughs Leo Sawadogo, an immigrant from Burkina Faso who co-owns New Jersey's Montclair Brewery with his Jamaican American wife, Denise.

John Arnold puts it more seriously, writing in 1911 that "all labor devolves anyway upon the women, and more especially the work of brewing."

All About Beer reported in 2001, "In the Johannesburg gold mining hostels, the call for sorghum beer is so great that mine unions order that the women be accommodated near them to provide the inimitable, indigenous homebrew."

Though non-Egyptian Africans didn't grow barley until much later than their eastern neighbors, the continent is rich with naturally growing grains. Sorghum and millet dominate, and a band called the Sorghum Beer Belt follows the line of the Sahel semiarid region that stretches across all of North Africa and separates the Sahara Desert above from the tropical savanna below.

"Sorghum beer," says McGovern in *Ancient Brews*, "besides its nutritional value, was and continues to be central to the economic, social and religious life of the eastern Sahel. You can still see women chewing the grain and spitting it out in the age-old method of making the beer."

Not to dismiss its nutritional value, however, McGovern writes in an article about African brewing, "In Africa, fermented alcoholic drinks, especially those made from cereals, are estimated to provide today more than half of the energy needs of over a billion people."

Sorghum contains no gluten. As such, it gives worldwide sufferers of celiac disease an option for drinking beer and distinguishes itself from the bread that so often goes hand-in-hand with beer making in other ancient civilizations.

Women, particularly those of the Zulu and other Bantu ethnicities, have historically brewed myriad types of beer across southern Africa, and Zulu people highly revere the fertility and agriculture goddess, Mbaba Mwana Waresa, for teaching humanity to make beer. It's said that Inkosazana, another fertility goddess, can absolve someone of blame if they follow her command to make beer and pour it over a mountain.

The real-life brewers of southern Africa favor a fermented combination of maize and sorghum called *umqombothi*.

All About Beer says, "Neither commercial nor illegal and brewed by individual households, this smooth, rich and slightly sour indigenous sorghum beer is made by adding sugar, water and corn to soft-cooked sorghum-meal porridge, allowing it to stand, then repeating the process to taste."

South African brewer and owner Apiwe Nxusani-Mawela grew up drinking *umqombothi* at family functions. After getting interested in the sciences in college, Apiwe went to work for South Africa–based SABMiller. Now that the entrepreneur can brew what she wants, she's bringing back the old foodways by using homegrown ingredients such as sorghum, rooibos, hibiscus, and South African hops.

Repeating a lament uttered frequently by African craft brewers, Apiwe, who learned to brew from her grandmother, says, "I was busy mastering the art of Western brewing, while knowing nothing about what we as Africans have been brewing for generations. It's time we claim it back. Our foremothers have been doing it, we're doing it, our granddaughters will be doing it."

According to Arnold, who credits a researcher named Dr. Loir at the turn of the twentieth century, Bantu-speaking Ndebele women in Zimbabwe have, since time immemorial, brewed beer that takes several weeks. He describes their process of combining malted and unmalted maize, sorghum, and/or millet in a hefty clay pot, soaking it for twenty-four hours, then packing it in bags or between blankets heated with hot stones for forty-eight hours to let the grains germinate. Then they dry the resulting malt in the sun and the actual brewing begins.

"Flies and other insects sip of the fluid and drown in it, thus adding yeast material," he writes. "It is sour in taste, and quite refreshing because of the carbonic acid in it, and is not unlike cider mixed with water."

In Tanzania, both women and men participate in the harvest, and women homebrew and sell *pombe*, a millet beer that local beer blogger Matthew Van Dis writes comprises 90 percent of beer consumed in the country, as corporate beer can cost six times as much.

Up north, women in Burkina Faso have spent the past fifty-five hundred years fermenting sorghum into beer called *dolo*. The nation's ethnic Dogon goddess Yasigi frequently appears in artistic renderings dancing with a beer ladle because she spoons out woman-made beer to drinkers gathered for ceremonial rites.

Leo learned to brew at the knee of his mother, who brews for family, neighbors, and friends at Christmastime. Many women brew *dolo* regularly, in clay pots, to sell to male buyers who pass around a communal calabash outside the house in a makeshift beer garden.

These women, who've formed an informal continentwide collective, hold a great deal of power, he says, because they sustain a large chunk of the economy. They also know that a man with a belly full of beer doesn't tend to stray too far.

"Women brew beer to keep all the society together," he says.

East Asia

One of China's closest connections to beer also emerges from legend. The ancient Chinese believed rice beer, as well as all alcohol, came to them via instruction from Yi Di, wife or consort of the mythical King Yu the Great. The story, as usual, changes according to the storyteller and some versions replace rice beer with *baijiu*, China's national spirit.

Throughout the earlier dynasties, the Chinese treated alcohol as sacred—fundamental for funerals, female and male ancestral worship, and offerings to Heaven and Earth—and thereby required special ministries to manage its production, storage, and service. Until very recently, historians believed that alcohol took its place in ordinary life only as modernity crept in with later dynasties and international exposure.

However, scientists working in the mid-2010s have pieced together very strong evidence of barley beer brewed at a dig site that resembles breweries found at Godin Tepe and in Egypt from around the same period—3000 BCE, fifteen hundred years before the first confirmed dynasty. Because barley didn't grow natively in China at that time, researchers conclude that the brewers at what they're calling a microbrewery would have imported it via trade routes, along with some brewing know-how.

This is astonishing for several reasons: it suggests that predynastic Chinese people may have enjoyed beer in their nonritualistic lives; it upends the theory that before they turned to rice, early Chinese brewers solely made their *huangjiu*, or "yellow wine," from millet; and study leader Jiajing Wang tells *National Geographic* magazine that this represents the earliest discovery yet of barley in China.

"The finding of barley was a surprise, because we really didn't expect to find barley dated that early," she says.

———————

Ancient Japanese people attributed the origin of alcohol to a goddess who chewed and spit out rice to break down the starch.

Gastro Obscura writes this would have fermented "the rice from a sober grain into an effervescent elixir, puckery-sour, lively with yeast, its alcohol content enough to bring her worshippers to ecstasy."

The reality is slightly more sobering. Daimon San, sixth-generation head of Osaka's Daimon Brewery, says more than likely both women and men helped make rudimentary forms of rice-based booze in Shinto temples and at home for consumption and sale.

And written records don't specify gender to track the production of sake, Japan's national beverage (which more closely approximates rice beer than the frequently misattributed rice wine), once it emerged in temples as an offering to the gods, then made its way to royalty, aristocracy, and, eventually, the masses.

Considering they may have financially relied on the sale of their wares, medieval Japanese alewives were known to assert themselves in the busy marketplace. A fictional literary collection from around 1500 CE tells of a brewster interrupting a vendor hawking pots on the street.

"First," yells the brewster, "Buy some sake!"

Even though the Japanese eventually cut women out of ownership by passing down their businesses from father to son, a few Japanese women are starting to make international names for themselves as sake masters. Miho Imada, *toji*, which translates to "master brewer," at Imada Shuro and Nanami Watanabe, who won one of Japan's biggest sake competitions at age twenty-two in 2018, are two to watch.

South America

The disparate tribes who populated the Andes before the Incas conquered and consolidated power in the 1400s worshipped goddesses and led lives of relative gender parity. The Incas . . . not so much.

When the Incas defeated an enemy, they would celebrate by drinking chicha—out of the decapitated heads of the people they vanquished! So you can imagine that they couldn't leave the production of chicha to just anyone. No, Incan rulers, who controlled every aspect of female sexuality, relied on the empire's most beautiful young women—virgins groomed for the role since childhood—to make the ceremonial liquid.

According to fifteenth-century Spanish scribes, male imperial agents removed attractive girls from their families around age ten to spend their lives as *acllas*, or "chosen women." These *acllas* grew up sequestered in houses of the chosen women, in the capital of Cuzco, Peru, or in provincial capitals, married to the sun god, learning religion, weaving, cooking, and brewing chicha, which varies tremendously from culture to culture but loosely refers to corn-based beer.

Marilyn French writes that the *acllas* "were reserved for one of three roles: to be celibate servants of the gods and to officiate in rituals; to be second wives or concubines to royal or official men; or, if they were physically and morally perfect, to be sacrificed in important state rituals."

The girls who got married off were given as a reward for loyalty or achievement. The ones who got sacrificed lived their last moments in Cuzco, as described by a seventeenth-century witness and paraphrased by French: "He saw the golden Inca throne, statues of the gods, the pouring of the chicha, and the slaughter of a hundred thousand llamas for the feast. Then the [four girls, aged ten to twelve], were lowered into a waterless cistern and walled in alive."

11 | RELAX, DON'T WORRY, HAVE A HOMEBREW

I FIRST MET NANCY RIGBERG at the Ladies' Beer Tea she hosts every year during Philly Beer Week. A few dozen ladies fill up the Belgian Cafe's side room to catch up, sip beer, nibble on dainties, and compliment one another on how nicely they clean up in floral dresses and semi-ironic Easter hats. Nancy launched the novelty beer tea before almost anyone had heard of women grouping together to drink beer, and in their garden party finest, no less.

But the more common place to find sixty-three-year-old Nancy, when she wasn't home doing office work, was with her longtime husband, George Hummel, at Home Sweet Homebrew, the Center City Philadelphia brewtique they bought in 1989. Nancy is short, never wears makeup, and can be spotted by her frizzy grey hair. They're both curmudgeons. Sarcastic and cynical. Madly articulate. Insightful. And hilarious.

Their storefront, which they gave up when they semiretired in 2019, was a relic: cramped and covered in yellowed photos of friends-turned-famous-beer-personalities, with a short L-shaped glass display case for them to both store and act on product, paperwork, and lunch. It was also the last time I visited, devoid of customers.

Through a decade of interviewing and socializing with Nancy, the hippie-at-heart has shown me that when it comes to some male homebrewers' expectations of women, the more things change, the more they stay the same.

"It's really nice there are a lot of female brewers now," she says, "but sexism is as rampant as ever."

Nancy and George bought Home Sweet Homebrew from microbiologist Pam Moore and her husband, who'd opened it three years prior. Nancy once told me new customers in the 1990s would be polite to her face then ask George if "the girl knows anything." When I asked her a few years later if this was still the case, she replied that new customers did know better than to refer to her as "the girl" but they still directed questions to George if he was around. Now, she says, new customers, with their noses in their phones, don't greet either of them.

Chances are high that most of these disinterested young hobbyists know little of homebrewing's subversive past. Now commonplace, though subject to volatile market vagaries, the act of homebrewing was not just counterculture but illegal when microbrewers first put malt to metal. Somehow, the authors of the Twenty-First Amendment that repealed Prohibition neglected to remove the language that criminalized homebrewing.

Luckily, the feds rarely enforced that restriction. Most wine-making shops covertly carried brewing supplies, and intrepid Northern California merchants such as Ken Grossman and Byron Burch opened true homebrew shops in the mid- to late-1970s.

It's thanks in large part to a New Englander named Nancy Crosby that President Jimmy Carter signed a law to decriminalize homebrewing on October 14, 1978, and thereby legalized the number one pathway to a career as a craft brewer for the first time since 1920.

Nancy, a former bookstore clerk who dreamed of owning a business, signed on as partner to a mail order wine- and beer-making supply shop in Connecticut in 1972 and, as day-to-day operator, helped turn it into one of the most far-reaching brick-and-mortar home-supply merchants in the nation. Nancy and her business partner, Pat Baker, founded a homebrew club called the Underground Brewers in 1975, making it the second or third club in the country after the Los Angeles Maltose Falcons. Unafraid of raids that never came, Nancy and Pat formed the Home Wine and Beer Trade Association for their fellow shopkeeping felons, and under Nancy's leadership, steered the group to join with the American Homebrewers Association (founded by Colorado homebrew instructor Charlie Papazian in 1978) and a Maltose Falcons member to lobby Congress for legalization.

With assistance from California senator Alan Cranston, they got it done. But Nancy wasn't finished. According to Lauren Clark's *Crafty Bastards*, she, along with Pat, his wife-to-be, Betty Ann Sather, and another brewer pored over Michael Jackson's *World Guide to Beer* to catalogue dozens of beer styles so that homebrew competition coordinators could categorize entries. Those style guidelines formed the basis for an intense exam to certify beer judges for competitions that went on to become the Beer Judge Certification Program, which informs the Great American Beer Festival, World Beer Cup, and National Homebrew Competition, along with thousands of smaller competitions every year.

In 2013, veteran competition judge Annie Johnson became the first woman to win the AHA's Homebrewer of the Year title in thirty years and the first African American.

"I had to be three hundred times better to get recognized that I was good," Annie told me in 2020. "I had to win that. I had to. For right now that's the way it is in the beer industry."

Generally, she reports that before winning the title, a high percentage of her male colleagues—including her own brewing partner—would grill her for hours then reject her advice. This, despite winning gold in the first homebrew competition she ever entered then going on to spend ten days brewing at Pilsner Urquell in the Czech Republic and at the Guinness brewery in Ireland.

Award-winning homebrewer Lee Hedgmon says as former competition coordinator then the first female president of the Oregon Brewers Club, she made it a priority to make herself visible at beer festivals to encourage women to enter competitions and claim their wins.

She says in an oral history preserved at the OSU archives, "It's important for women's names to be on the board. People will see your name and see that you are winning."

But visibility can have its setbacks on a stage where almost no one looks like you. If earning homebrewing cred as a woman seems hard enough, Lee says try adding black skin to the mix of underrepresentation and prejudice.

Though they look nothing alike, Lee says someone once confused her for Annie. She recalls that she responded, "Nope, sorry, I'm the other Black woman who homebrews."

The lack of awareness—and, in many cases, respect—matters. The vast majority of today's craft brewers and owners start as homebrewers, and if women don't fill the homebrewing pipeline, fewer will enter the trade. Lauren

Clark says Jim Koch bought his homebrew starter kit at Crosby & Baker, which had moved to Massachusetts by then.

Nancy Rigberg counts the owners of Yards, Flying Fish, Victory, Oxbow, and Dogfish Head as former customers who learned to brew on equipment she sold them. It's telling that the first four breweries she mentions were founded by pairs of men, and most people don't know that Dogfish's celebrity owner, Sam Calagione, bought the brewery with his wife, Mariah, who managed several departments, both then and now.

One homebrewer who defied the odds by going pro is Gretchen Schmidhausler, who owns the cozy Little Dog Brewing at the Jersey Shore. She started her career as the state's first female commercial brewer by working at a homebrew shop. She stayed on as brewer when it turned into Red Bank Brewing and spent over twenty years after that brewing in the central part of the state.

Despite her success, she felt isolated from other women, saying she'd find it very unusual when a woman would come into the brew boutique. She found comfort in her friend JoEllen Ford, who in the late 1990s opened the Brewers Apprentice homebrew shop in central Jersey with her mother, Barbara Hamara, and sister, Penny van Doorn.

JoEllen, a former teacher whose ex-husband turned her onto porters and stouts, says she and Gretchen "clung to each other" through their first few decades in business as Gretchen worked her way up through the testosterone-heavy ranks of brewing and JoEllen interacted with a mostly male clientele.

Not only was homebrewing "pretty much a sausage sport," as George Hummel describes homebrewing in the 1990s, it could be a brutal business too. In 1995, Suzy Rizza and her husband, Tim O'Leary, opened the first "U-brew" facility in Montana, where people came to brew small batches on site.

Things at the KettleHouse U-Brew started out wretchedly and never improved. For one, the couple suffered through a social situation dreaded by practically everybody in the civilized world: no one came to their grand opening.

"Like your worst nightmare," Suzy cringes.

Though popular nationally, brewing on-premises proved to be a novelty fancied by groups of friends who'd occasionally replace, say, a golf outing with an afternoon at the U-brew. Suzy and her husband saw little repeat business and found it difficult to take walk-ins because they had to prep customers' yeast in advance. Admittedly, they couldn't afford to advertise and didn't know how to budget for the lean times.

On top of that, Suzy worked nights at KettleHouse after spending her days at a newspaper job. She'd race home, make sandwiches for dinner, staff the store until nine, sweep up, then wake up and do it all again. Suzy says 99 percent of their friends and role models in the business were men, though it never occurred to her that they and/or customers might be sexist. Probably because, she says, she was too busy and tired to notice.

Since then, homebrewing hasn't put on much of a more feminine face.

Though Nancy Crosby cofounded it, the Beer Judge Certification Program had only had one female board member as of 2017, and until recently, the AHA didn't reach out to women or even collect official gender data. In 2012, the AHA estimated its female membership at 6 percent, and former spokesperson Barbara Fusco e-mailed me at the time to explain that the AHA didn't target specific demographic groups in its membership campaigns.

"I'd say it's a '[homebrew] love is blind' type of approach," she wrote.

But AHA staff did proclaim itself aware of the problem. When the organization announced Annie's big win it wrote, "At some point in history, brewing beer became synonymous with the Caucasian male."

Make that a lot of points in history. At least former AHA director Gary Glass acknowledged to me at the time that homebrewing had a lot of ground to make up.

Happily, the AHA has made progress. In the intervening years, the group— a subsidiary of the Brewers Association—has consciously included more photos of women in its media and marketing materials, has booked more female speakers at its annual convention, and has hired more women as writers for its website and magazine. Female AHA membership had risen to 11 percent by November 2018 and according to an AHA survey, women currently comprise 16 percent of local homebrew club membership. Last year, women held a staggering eleven of fourteen seats on the AHA's governing board.

Glass has told me that he believes anything that helps bring more women into homebrewing is a good thing.

Sadly, perhaps, none of the women mentioned in this chapter still work full-time in homebrewing, though a few have transitioned to bigger and better. Nancy Crosby has passed away. Gretchen quickly turned pro brewer then owner, and after three years keeping the U-Brew on life support, Suzy and Tim shut it down to establish KettleHouse Brewing in Missoula. Their flagship Cold Smoke Scotch Ale has won ten national awards; its Bongwater series, five.

Annie lost her job as chief recipe developer and brand ambassador at a homebrewing equipment manufacturer called PicoBrew during the COVID-19 pandemic. JoEllen quietly closed Brewers Apprentice during a bleak period for older brick-and-mortar homebrew shops in 2019.

After giving up their lease, whose price tag they say had skyrocketed over the years, Nancy Rigberg and George started taking phone orders to sell and deliver homebrew supplies from home. The people and neighborhood have changed, they lament, and millennials buying the new $2 million condos that have risen around them showed no interest in spending a day homebrewing two cases of beer when they can easily sample so much of the latest and greatest at any number of nearby bars and bottle shops.

The most frustrating part of the loss, says Nancy, is that even the customers they did get lacked interest—interest in learning about the hobby's history or the reasons homebrewers of previous generations needed it to access decent beer in the first place.

I find the most frustrating part of this chapter to be how few women homebrew even now. A lot of guys I know take it as a day off from the family, leaving their wives to mind the kids while they sit around for eight hours drinking beer and potentially boasting of their beer-making prowess. When women did it, it was work. When men do it, it's leisure.

I hope they're home teaching their daughters to brew on the one day a year we women gather to dress up in feminine frills and toast our ancestral homebrewing mothers during Nancy's Ladies' Beer Tea.

12 | IT'S A SAHTI PAATI

THE LEGENDARY FEMALE BARTENDERS at the Coyote Ugly chain of saloons have got nothing on the female settlers of Northern Europe. Sure, they strut all over the bar tops half-naked, pouring liquor straight from the bottle into mesmerized patrons' mouths, and generally run the show with their confident, sexualized version of femininity.

But at certain pagan festivals of yore, Nordic women not only partook in "licentious beer-drinking and general unrestrainedness," as describes Finnish beer journalist Jussi Rokko, but "ate, drank, and behaved carnivalistically, undressed their lower body, and went around the village where they seized men, stripped their trousers off, and criticized their sexual virility based on what they saw."

Size-shaming aside, women and beer played such a significant role in first-millennium Finnish life and folklore that the *Kalevala*, the epic national book of poems that put Finns' orally transmitted songs and tales on paper in 1849, devoted two hundred lines to the creation of the world and four hundred to the creation of beer. Also, beer's creator, as you may have guessed, is female.

> *Osmotar, the beer-preparer,*
> *Brewer of the drink refreshing,*
> *Takes the golden grains of barley,*
> *Taking six of barley-kernels,*
> *Taking seven tips of hop-fruit,*
> *Filling seven cups with water,*
> *On the fire she sets the caldron,*

Boils the barley, hops, and water,
Lets them steep, and seethe, and bubble
Brewing thus the beer delicious.

Early Finns, along with others in northern Europe, hosted many a ritualistic beer fest; the Ukon Sakat—celebrating Osmotar's first brew, which succeeded thanks to the inadvertent help of a bear—among the most well known. Hunters drank beer out of a bear skull, and women, as noted by Jussi, led in the beer-drinking and jolly-making. At the conclusion of the festival, tribespeople and villagers would bring the bear's skull and remains back to its den, repeating the international ritualistic theme of death and renewal. Some students of religion compare this to the story of Jesus.

Women hosted their own parties too. Translating folklore expert Satu Apo's analysis in her Viinan Voima book about the cultural role of Finnish drinking fables, Jussi says women celebrated Katrinan kahjakset on what is now St. Catherine's Day by brewing a communal beer to recognize women's chores, particularly animal husbandry.

"Beer and porridge were on offer, later even spirits. Matrons might take the beer and porridge to the cattle shed and savor them there," he says.

Likewise, Lithuanians, Latvians, and Prussians honored the mythical brewster Ragutiene with intoxicated annual feasts on the autumnal equinox. Along with her husband, Raugupatis, and Raugo Žemėpatis, god of fermentation, she brewed at the Holy Brewery Ragutis. Archaeologists have discovered an altar stone to Ragutis in Vilnius, Lithuania, that visitors can see for themselves.

And in Norse mythology, Ægir, god of the seas, brewed for the gods with the help of his nine daughters.

"They were portrayed as beautiful maidens dressed in white robes and veils and always helped their father brew the beer," writes Patricia Monaghan in *The New Book of Goddesses and Heroines.*

Despite the Finns crediting women for beer and the Norse and Baltic people sharing godly brewing duties with nine fair maidens and one fair goddess, the same strict superstition used to show up time and again across the 950-mile divide between Estonia and western Norway: women entering the brewhouse meant sour beer leaving the brewhouse.

"The belief was that if a woman somehow happened to intervene or step in to help in the brewing process, the beer would go bad," writes Lars Marius Garshol in *Historical Brewing Techniques: The Lost Art of Farmhouse Brewing*.

I attribute this to rigidly patriarchal societies' view of menstruating women as unclean. Male-dominant societies, writes French, teach girls their bodies are powerful but contaminated.

"A girl learns she has power—to pollute: in such cultures menstrual blood is a source of horror and fear."

Conversely, in some parts of Estonia, "There are farmsteads where women always do the brewing and men are not even allowed to watch," e-mails Garshol.

Inexplicable brewing superstitions ran rampant through Northern Europe during the era when it appears both women and men first brewed fermented grain-based beverages there, potentially dating as far back as around 500 CE and lasting until the late second millennium. But the division of labor on the local level calcified so solidly that populations would have likely reacted with alarm at the suggestion that brewing could be done by either gender.

Extraordinarily scant evidence exists to patch together conclusive patterns in this region's early brewing. Generally, women of the day probably worked as the default household brewers but exceptions punctured this general rule so frequently that these responsibilities could vary from village to village and principality to principality.

Taking a high-level view, one can sketch out a rough map that shows men brewing more often in the eastern parts of the territory, namely in pieces of eastern Finland, Estonia, and Russia, and more women brewing in the western reaches of Finland and Scandinavia. (Despite conventional wisdom, the Nordic country of Finland does not join Sweden, Norway, and Denmark in the political union that is Scandinavia.)

Overlaying maps and timelines, beer historians extrapolate that women in the far corners of Northern Europe were simultaneously needed for important domestic duties while both getting excluded from certain highly valued endeavors and taking blame when things went wrong—like when the men accidentally brewed contaminated (sour) beer.

For instance, Lars doesn't believe it a coincidence that the places where men brewed are the places where grain ran scarce.

"Are these remains of a time when grain was so holy that the main grain products, bread and beer, had to be made by men? It's possible," he writes.

Finland's *sahti*, which survives in present day as the best known of all the rustic Nordic and Baltic brews, exemplifies these complexities. Sahti is a notoriously hard-to-define, high-ABV, low-carbonation concoction generally made with some combination of malted and unmalted barley, rye, juniper, and baker's yeast and heated with hot rocks instead of a boil. American craft drinkers may recognize it from Dogfish Head's two retired sahti-inspired ales: Immort Ale and Sah'tea.

Despite oral and leftover traditions indicating that eastern sahti brewers may have skewed male, beer-savvy Finns understand farm women typically attended to brewing as a household chore while men tended to outdoor tasks.

"You can't be working the fields, felling trees in the woods, doing building work, or be gone hunting for days and at the same time take care of the brewing," explains Jussi. "Of course, if there was a man in the household who couldn't do those 'man chores' anymore (because of old age, weakness, injury), he might be the brewer then—if he was any good in brewing."

But sahti historians do argue that healthy men likely made at least some of the liquid, as it was a special drink for feasting, not regular consumption, and they theorize men could have probably taken a few days off from farming to do it.

What's more, though brewers did produce low-alcohol "ladies' sahti," they brewed regular sahti of up to 9 percent ABV for particularly celebratory or mournful gatherings. So as opposed to an everyday beer that would have probably gotten lumped in with the daily kitchen chores, a sahti brewer would have had to occasionally haul around a relatively high volume of heavy ingredients to brew a lot at a time.

As it concerns the malt needed to brew the sahti, Finnish brewery owner Pekka Kääriäinen surmises that although women and children helped dry the malt in the ubiquitous wooden saunas that form a major part of Finnish culture, malting was mostly the work of men.

"It was very heavy to carry the malt out of storage, bring it to the water, and back to the place where the malt could grow to one centimeter in height then get taken to get dried in the sauna," says Pekka, who brewed the world's first commercial sahti with his wife, Sirpa, at their Lammin Sahti brewery in 1987.

Without the efforts of Pekka and Sirpa, rural sahti may have disappeared completely during the late nineteenth-century Industrial Revolution when commercial breweries began brewing *olut* (beer) instead of sahti in Helsinki and other urban areas. A few families quietly carried on the legacy until the 1960s, when it all but died out.

Pekka, who sells sahti at the Bryggeri Helsinki he owns in the city of the same name, brewed sahti growing up in the Lammi district near southern Finland's Päijänne Tavastia region (Lake District), the closest thing that exists to a modern-day sahti stronghold. In his book *The World Guide to Beer*, beer critic Michael Jackson calls sahti "a glass of anthropology." At the time, he said only Lammin produced sahti for (legal) sale and only one pub sold it.

Mika Laitinen, author of *Viking Age Brew: The Craft of Brewing Sahti Farmhouse Ale*, counted six commercial sahti breweries in the late 2010s. Marjokaisa (Kaisa) Piironen, Finland's official ambassador to the European Beer Consumers Union (EBCU), makes sure to let her countrymen and women know about as many of them as possible.

Every Friday the thirteenth, the joyfully affable Marjokaisa leads the mostly male membership of Sahtipäät (which Kaisa translates to "The Association of Sahti-people in Capital Area") on an exuberant crawl to a dozen Helsinki pubs to drink sahti late into the night. It's just one fun way she promotes her national drink, to which the European Union granted a Traditional Specialities Guaranteed appellation in 2002. This designation protects its production method but not its place of origin.

"With sahti came a whole new world for me: ALL the nice and funny sahti brewers and drinkers. When we gather together there is never a sad face and never any arguing. More talk, laughter, dancing, and going to sauna. Oh boy, how I love sauna, sahti and dancing!" e-mails Kaisa, who learned sahti making from her late husband's uncle, the same homebrewer who taught Michael.

Kaisa, who delights in sharing sahti from her traditional double-handled wooden *haarikka* drinking vessel, brews all kinds in her suburban Helsinki winter brewery (her garage) and summer brewery, which consists of a simple backyard homebrew setup behind the lakefront hut that houses her sauna. Twice a year, she invites the public to a sahti brewday, and on other days she hosts Sahtipäät meetings during lulls in a regularly scheduled group brew.

I think I was made an honorary Sahtipäät member when I visited Kaisa's house in September 2019 and followed along to two stops on the crawl. I bailed out early to rest for my morning flight home; the middle-aged Kaisa e-mailed later to tell me she'd stayed out drinking sahti and dancing until 4:00 AM. In my defense, my nervous system may have still been shocked from spending the afternoon skittishly naked—as is custom—in my brand-new friend Kaisa's backyard, alternating between lying in the hot sauna and jumping off her dock into the frigid lake.

That's after she "beer-pressured" me into snacking on a salted cricket (I could feel its dead little legs in my mouth—gag) and washing it down with two of her sahtis, showing me around her house and describing her business plan to run a sahti-centric inn there.

I assured her I'd stay with her when I return in 2022 to judge the national sahti competition, as she and others invited me to do. I told her I'd bring my bestie and international beer judge Herlinda, along with Teri Fahrendorf, who reminds me of Kaisa and has a husband of Finnish descent.

Forever in pursuit of spreading her sahti gospel, Kaisa tells me she happily succeeded in creating a spectacle during the three times she's loaded her equipment onto a wagon to brew wort while leading a merry band of sahti brewers through the streets of Helsinki and two smaller Finnish towns. She's also helping the VTT Technical Research Centre of Finland research various strains of baker's yeast to augment the one that almost all twenty-first-century sahti brewers use.

She says, "Maybe we will get even more different sahtis in the future? Like we used to have."

13 | SLOW FOOD, SLOWER BEER

"EVERYBODY EATS WITH THEIR EYES," says beer cookbook author Lucy Saunders, who employs the tagline "Beer Is Food." "Having the food presented really nicely is important, along with staging a ritual of appreciating beer by pouring it into a glass rather than serving it in the bottle."

By displaying beer this way Lucy and her peers have been able to evoke an idealized version of Europe's relaxed, communal dining lifestyle that inspires so many older craft brewers to do what they do. Not surprisingly it's from within Europe that American beer connoisseurs like Lucy, Brooklyn Brewery Brewmaster Garrett Oliver, his boss Steve Hindy, Dogfish Head owner Sam, and representatives from the Association of Brewers (now Brewers Association) discovered and imported the Slow Food movement that neatly packages this ethos for consumption.

Along with the American Institute of Wine & Food and specialty beer importers from Merchant du Vin and VanBerg & DeWulf, these ambassadors brought beer to America's tables and found synergy with the Slow Food organization, founded by Italian Carlo Petrini in 1986 after a protest against the impending construction of a McDonald's at Rome's Spanish Steps. At the turn of the millennium, they helped form Slow Food USA and used its methodologies to win over Americans who weren't necessarily lovin' it where fast food or beer was concerned.

Slow might have been the goal for these Aquarian-age proponents of pleasurable eating and drinking, but it certainly wasn't the pace they would have chosen for the public to buy into their message. Almost unimaginably, they'd age ten to twenty years before the American populace would truly begin to embrace the idea of local, sustainable foods and handcrafted beer. Despite these advocates' work and travels, the concept of fine beer paired with fine food lodged stubbornly in the public's throat while the stuff that went down easy came packaged as mass-market cheese, pretzels, and tailgating fare—salty, handheld foods that matched the American light lagers so prevalent in the day.

The sluggish timeline both frustrated and motivated Rose Ann Finkel and Wendy Littlefield, two specialty drink importers on opposite coasts who'd been preaching the beer gospel to chefs and food purveyors as far back as the late 1960s. By living abroad or traveling extensively enough to come into close contact with the family beer, wine, and food producers of Europe, both women had absorbed the Old Country culture that finds languid gratification in a handcrafted meal where the inclusion of table wine or beer is as assumed as the setting of a plate.

Rose Ann, who grew up appreciating the cooking of her native New Orleans, says she rediscovered "the pleasure of the table" when she accompanied her newlywed husband, Charles, on his professional wine-buying trips to the Continent in the late 1960s. The younger Wendy, speaking with awe of her own early-1980s train trips through Belgium with her husband, Don Feinberg, marveled at discovering, "Every town had a brewery and their beer was nothing like the town next door."

Separated by more than a decade and the thousands of miles between Wendy's former home in New York and Rose Ann's in Seattle, the women worked independently but with parallel purpose to educate American restaurateurs and inquisitive drinkers as to the elegant mealtime possibilities of beer. At first, the response they received reflected a deep vein of epicurean indifference, regardless of whether it was projected in the 1960s, 1970s, or 1980s.

"Nothing about it allowed for curiosity," recalls Wendy, who thinks of herself as a cultural ambassador working through the medium of food and drink.

Wendy, a former advertising executive who founded Vanberg & DeWulf with Don in 1982, recounts, "We'd go to prospect restaurants in New York to proselytize for the beers and we'd get, 'Are you kidding? I don't want to talk about beer and I don't want to convince someone to drink a glass of beer instead of wine.'"

So they would circumvent the dining room for the kitchen, where chefs understood quality and would share beers with one another.

Through the 1990s, former Rogue Ales sales and marketing rep and food connoisseur Sebbie Buhler ran into the same circumstance when she'd pitch her product to restaurants in New York City and along her Eastern Seaboard territory. The chef would get it but the front-of-house manager would complain he didn't have enough space to stock anything new.

"It was very difficult to go beyond, 'We already have Brooklyn [lager].' Kind of ironic, right?" she says.

But Sebbie, like the other two, kept at it. For twenty years the Rogue rep, whose last name may look familiar because her brother David cofounded Elysian Brewing in Seattle, funneled her sales efforts through food. Chef Waldy Malouf, senior director of food and beverage operations at the Culinary Institute of America, first showed her the possibility of pairing beer with fine dining. She attended the James Beard Foundation's second-ever beer dinner, leveraged her relationship with Iron Chef Masaharu Morimoto into an appearance on The Food Network, and climbed high in the ranks of the world's top cheese societies. An early adopter of pairing beer and chocolate, her face graced the Rogue Chocolate Stout bottle until 2018, and she used to blog about beer pairings on her website, roguechocolatestout.com.

Rose Ann, who instinctively grabbed a piece of chocolate the first time she tried stout, also understood that it took an improvisational mind to work any and all avenues. A Renaissance woman who later founded a branding agency with her husband, they started out together as wine importers, bringing small-batch West Coast wine to the mainstream and coining the term *boutique winery* in the process.

In 1977, Rose Ann opened a gourmet grocery called Truffles with two other women. Charles helped modernize the Washington wine industry by overhauling Chateau Ste. Michelle and turning Seattle's suburb of Woodinville into the state's top spot for winery tasting rooms. Meanwhile, Rose Ann sold impossible-to-find German and Czech imports along with Bass Ale and Anchor Steam (that era's version of what beer geeks now call whales) and garnered a mention in *Time* magazine for operating one of the nation's best specialty edibles boutiques.

In 1978, Rose Ann and Charles founded Merchant du Vin, the first importer to bring in family-owned, independent beers from England and Germany and the first to import any beers from Belgium. As COO, Rose Ann worked tirelessly on both sides of the Atlantic to properly brand clients' beers in Europe and educate diners and restaurant staff at home.

As a woman who recoiled at beer labels splashed with the too-common bikini-clad women, she felt other women would also find them offensive. So she tried new approaches to appeal to craft beer skeptics.

One tactic: she wrote the first beer menus and drink lists in the United States. Another: At one early beer fest, she and her team set up an eye-catching display that looked like a British pub and didn't fill attendees' cups until they repeated—and repeated again—foreign-sounding names of brewery clients, such as Lindeman's.

"That was the first exposure a lot of people had to beer, especially women," Rose Ann says.

She named Samuel Smith's classic Winter Welcome, and as she "sat around one night with Michael Jackson," as she tells it, she named what might be the world's most famous doppelbock. Once the name Celebrator brought global attention to the six-hundred-year-old Ayinger Brewery in Bavaria, she licensed its worldwide use to her friend and client, coproprietor Angela Inselkammer.

Unlike most of her peers in the United States, Angela held a considerable amount of influence over her family's beer business. Like many of her German colleagues, Angela married into the sixth generation of the brewery and has run its guesthouse and restaurant ever since.

"That's what we don't have," muses Rose Ann of the US brewing industry. "The tradition of women running the business."

Not the case at Merchant du Vin. Rose Ann and Charles hired a woman named Elizabeth Purser as their original vice president of sales. Rose Ann remembers Elizabeth as the first US female beer rep of the modern age and ascribes her success to the same qualities that account for the success of many of the era's beer women.

"She was smart and insightful," Rose Ann says. "And nobody else was educating the public about beer."

Nobody else, really, except Wendy and Don, and they came years later. They started their company by introducing Duvel to America, then enlarged their all-Belgian portfolio to include what Wendy calls "the best indigenous example of every beer style brewed in Belgium and produced by an independent, family-run brewery."

Their portfolio expanded to fifty-two beers from Affligem, Boon, Dupont, Moortgat, Rodenbach, and others, plus beers they blended themselves and honorary Belgians from French Flanders, the United Kingdom, Italy, and Iceland—all of which adhere to the Belgian tradition of making beer to drink with an exquisite meal. Over the decades they've worked with progressive minds at trendsetting culinary institutions—Mildred Amico at Manhattan's venerated James Beard Foundation is one—to elevate the place that beer holds as an ingredient and partner to fine food. They've educated chefs and restaurateurs such as Rick Noonan, Emeril Lagasse, and Danny Meyer about the enjoyment of quality beer, and they developed foundational beer dinners with the likes of Leslie Revsin, the first woman to serve as executive chef at the Waldorf Astoria.

Wendy and Don published the first US edition of Michael Jackson's seminal *Great Beers of Belgium* in 1977 when his usual publishers rejected it on grounds that it was too arcane for a mass audience.

In 1997, the pair founded Ommegang Brewery on a former hop farm in Cooperstown, New York, as the first Belgian-style brewery in America to package 750 ml bottles sealed with corks and the first to follow the tradition of adding yeast to the bottle to further ferment the liquid in a process called bottle conditioning.

In an indication of what makes her most proud, Wendy writes on her résumé that she's "credited with championing gastronomy à la bière with serious chefs . . . connecting brewing in America with the farmstead tradition . . . and revitalizing the rural economy by celebrating its food heritage." It's a big part of Ommegang's raison d'être and it's basically a list of the attributes that summarize the intentions of Slow Food International, an organization that started four years after Wendy and Don plotted their own course to the same destination.

Rose Ann and Charles helmed Slow Food USA's original Seattle convivium (chapter) and, in typical progressive fashion, hosted beer dinners that spotlighted local farmers long before the term *farm-to-table* described menus, other than jewels like Alice Waters's legendary Berkeley restaurant, Chez Panisse. By the time the US Slow Food contingent celebrated its first anniversary in 2001, Rose Ann and Charles had already judged and presented at two international Slow Food gatherings in Italy.

In a 2003 *All About Beer* article, Fred Eckhardt writes that Carlo Petrini has called the American microbrewery movement the "purest expression he's seen of the slow food concept in action."

We have people like Lucy, Rose Ann, Wendy, and Sebbie to thank for making the connection. Like everything in the independent beer world, it's been nothing if not a labor of love. Despite efforts that started with Rose Ann in 1968, the concept of a beer dinner remained mostly foreign outside Manhattan and the major West Coast cities until approximately 2010.

Sebbie says her coastal Oregon bosses and coworkers didn't really understand what she was up to in New York, though Rose Ann, who opened the Pike Brewing Co. in Seattle's Pike Place food market with Charles in 1989, never quite understood what there was to understand.

"Beer is liquid bread. How do you separate the two?" Rose Ann asked me once, rhetorically.

Rose Ann kept promoting the connection between beer and food into her seventies, when, instead of slowing down, she and Charles opened a casual fine dining spot to showcase local seafood and local wine above the brewery and pub, which Charles has outfitted with nine thousand pieces of historical brewing memorabilia. Beer is served, too, of course.

Rose Ann didn't get to enjoy the restaurant for very long. In the fall of 2019 she underwent a bone marrow transplant for a rare form of cancer and never fully recovered. She isolated at home for five months—doctor's orders—before the rest of the world joined her in COVID-imposed lockdown. In the spring of 2020, she checked back into the hospital to reverse a decline in her health but the plan backfired. With visitors prohibited by coronavirus restrictions, the normally active and social Rose Ann declined. After a few weeks, the Finkels decided it was time for her to come home.

Throughout Rose Ann's convalescence and hospice, Charles kept his bedridden patient as occupied and engaged as her health and immobility would allow. The Jewish couple watched documentaries and listened to online books about Black civil rights, discussed the increasingly terrifying political news of the day, and worked a bit from a makeshift desk positioned to let Rose Ann look through a large window onto her flowery, hilly neighborhood below.

Prepandemic, the Finkels managed to host a Chinese New Year dinner party for a dozen people and a *From Russia with Love* wedding party for fourteen. As time grew more precious and Rose Ann more delicate, the parties tapered off but the Finkels did break their strict quarantine once, at the end, to savor the company of dear (mask-wearing) friends who bid their farewells from six feet away. Charles cooked meals for his "sweetie."

In a series of e-mails Charles sent to update me on Rose Ann's status, he told me they never got bored or tired of each other, and in fact, enjoyed "the best time anyone could have while dying."

When I posted the *Forbes* obituary I wrote for Rose Ann on my social media pages, countless acquaintances and admirers shared the tribute and wrote in to collectively grieve the loss of this ambitious, creative, charitable, loving, and infinitely kind go-getter who made such an impact on so many. Sebbie posted on my Facebook wall, "So so so sad to get this news—Rose Ann Finkel inspired me and many others."

Charles, who's been finding solace tending his garden, returning to work, and a taking a daily walk with a friend, e-mailed afterward to say he'd been answering hundreds of letters, e-mails, texts, and calls, and that he hoped COVID wouldn't keep him from inviting a few loved ones to the garden for a memorial service within a few months to stand in the stead of the funeral he didn't get to hold for his wife.

Throughout the time I've known the Finkels, I've observed that Charles, who always takes care to share full credit with his wife, has received the majority of recognition from colleagues and ink from the media. He has a Wikipedia page and Rose Ann doesn't. Maybe Charles captained grander projects or Rose Ann took more time for the kids. Maybe society overlooked some of the achievements of the female half of the power duo. I wasn't around them long enough to know.

But I do know that their adult daughter, Amy, e-mailed a comment to me that continues to at once soothe and disturb me. After she wrote to thank me for the obituary and we discovered we both call our moms Mumsy, she repeated almost verbatim what Charles Coury had written about his mom, Shirley, who'd passed almost twenty years prior.

She said, "Thank you for bringing attention to my mom. For as long as I can remember, people have mentioned my 'dad's business,' and I've corrected them."

14 | B(EER) IS FOR BARBARIANS

YOU KNOW THAT JOKE, "Wine drinkers spit, beer drinkers swallow"?

For my mom, who spent my childhood weekends leisurely sailing around Annapolis, Maryland, with our family, the expression goes more like this: sailboaters sip wine, powerboaters slug beer.

Nearly twenty years into my beer-writing career, I'm still pleading with her to change her haughty mindset. I blame the ancient Greeks and Romans for this.

According to conventional wisdom, the Greeks likely learned beer brewing from the Egyptians and, showing little interest in the process, promptly sniffed at it condescendingly and dumped it in favor of wine. Most of that is true, except for the issue that they might have picked it up from the Mesopotamians, and they would have known their early neighbors, the Thracians, who lived around Macedonia, were also brewing barley beer.

The point stands. The Greeks had easy access to grapes and more than a passing whiff of superiority toward beer-guzzling Thracians and, later, their voraciously imbibing Celtic and Germanic Central European neighbors. The snooty Greeks tarnished the barley beverage's reputation so devastatingly that the repercussions ripple out to aesthetes to this very day.

We know from ancient Greek scribes that women and men who lived in Thracia loved to get drunk at social gatherings, causing one writer to scorn them as "addicted to drinking and laziness and every sort of intemperance, disregarding all good habits."

Plato writes, "Both the women and all the men . . . spill [drink] all over their clothes and think that they are maintaining a very honorable practice."

It's speculated that the pre-Greek Minoan and Mycenaean peoples who inhabited Greek lands gradually stopped drinking fermented cereals so that by the time the classical Greek civilization developed, writers ascribed beer only to foreign cultures such as Egypt, Thracia, and the Germanic tribes. Though written evidence of Greek beer consumption almost entirely fades out, University of California, Davis brewing legend Charlie Bamforth writes in *Beer: Tap into the Art and Science of Brewing* that the lower classes, who've been overlooked in the record, would have almost certainly continued to partake.

We find our earliest derision of beer in the works of Athenian playwright Aeschylus. In his *Lycurgeia* tetralogy he explores the cult of the wine god Dionysus, who is ridiculed by a king for his effeminate appearance. Throughout the plays and those that follow, Aeschylus repeatedly mocks beer drinkers as unmanly.

Indicating that beer drinking is a literally fruitless, unfilling, quick fix, Greek herbalist Dioscorides compared beer versus wine to the sexual relationship of an adult man and teenage boy rather than the enjoyment of a reciprocal relationship with an adult woman.

Dramatists such as Aeschylus and his disciples steadily reinforced this stereotype, especially when they wrote in the context of Dionysus. I suspect a financial impetus may have been at play. Land for growing grains was scarce and better suited to grape cultivation. Someone from the wine lobby or the agriculture department may have gotten to Aeschylus and persuaded him to discourage people from drinking cereal-based beverages. (Wink.)

This gives us a rare opportunity to mock the Greeks, who unequivocally brought tremendous value, along with some serious misogyny, to the world. It seems, says Max Nelson in *The Barbarian's Beverage: A History of Beer in Ancient Europe*, that although they categorized both beer and wine as intoxicants, Greeks didn't understand that the two shared a common intoxicating denominator: ethyl alcohol, which, in both cases, is formed by the interaction of yeast and sugar.

Basing their speculations on the "science" of Hippocrates, the "father" of medicine, medical practitioners believed that the processing of cereal for beer—but not bread or porridge—turned male drinkers into girly-men.

It appears that, according to Nelson, "since the process of malting is basically a sprouting and kilning of grains, the process of fermentation in beer was logically seen as a subsequent decomposition of the cereal. . . . It is striking here that it was believed that beer had to decompose, that is be subject to yeast, while wine was not seen as arising in the same way."

The rationale likely arises from the perceived differences in temperature between beer and wine. The Greeks viewed grains, when used for beer, as damp and chilly while wine was considered hot. Nutritional guidance at the time put forth Hippocrates's notion that men were naturally hot and dry, and thus superior to women, whose cold and soggy biochemical makeup made them inferior. By the transitive property of Greek-invented geometry, beer made men effeminate.

Even the wise Aristotle bought into this cockamamie temperature theory, suggesting in his *On Intoxication* that, says Nelson, "Old men are most susceptible to drunkenness, young men fairly susceptible, and women least so, due to the natural heat of each (the hotter being the more susceptible)."

This leads me to wonder if we might find here the origins of the later creed that women, who supposedly didn't get drunk as easily, should act as a moral, steadying counterbalance to men, who couldn't necessarily control themselves under the influence of alcohol.

Ancient Romans had even less use for beer than the Greeks. When Italians wrote of beer—which Bamforth says the lower classes also drank here—they did so only in the context of the Celtic, Gaul, and Germanic peoples who inhabited most of continental Europe at varying times between around 700 and 200 BCE. Because these Iron Age Europeans hadn't yet developed a written language, we must rely on Greek and Roman chronicles of their customs.

These pale-skinned beer drinkers would have done better to find a different source to document them. Writers of the Roman era consistently describe these "Barbarians" as warmongering, quarrelsome, brutish, gluttonous, excessive overdrinkers who liked to fight and—women included—lie around naked.

Julius Caesar levels this analysis of the Gauls, who are often written about interchangeably with the Celts: "The whole race is madly keen on war, brave and impetuous, and easily outwitted."

It's assumed that the sturdy blonde women who migrated, marauded, and sometimes settled into fertile farming communities with their Celtic and

Germanic men brewed for the homestead and inspired fear in Roman soldier and historian Ammianus Marcellinus, who writes, "A whole troop of foreigners would not be able to withstand a single Gaul, if he called his wife to his assistance, who is usually very strong, and with blue eyes."

Upper-class Celtic and Germanic populations sometimes imported wine from the Romans, though wheat beer with honey; smoky, brown, and slightly sour ale; and other grain-based beverages made for their definitive staples. Wine wasn't just expensive; in the latter part of the Roman empire, Caesar writes in an ironic reversal, "They absolutely forbid the importation of wine, because they think that it makes men soft and incapable of enduring hard toil."

Any potential lack of wine may not have mattered too much; Gauls were master brewers. Historians are coming to realize that those who lived in modern-day Spain and France may have harnessed the possibilities of yeast and hops, or at least the lupin plant, hundreds of centuries and hundreds of miles from what we typically credit as their source.

Roman naturalist philosopher Pliny the Elder (whose name you may recognize as one of Russian River Brewing's most famous masterpieces), writes that astoundingly, "The Spanish provinces have by this time even taught us that these [intoxicants made from water-soaked grain] will bear being kept a long time."

These same Celtiberians, he writes, may have somehow figured out some rudimentary form of fermentation. Later historians credit women, who would have been baking the bread. "When the corn of Gaul and Spain of the kind we discussed is steeped to make beer, the foam that forms on the surface in the process is used for leaven."

Say what? Though we know that even the earliest brewers understood that some force was turning their sugar water into an intoxicant, most beer historians attribute the discovery of yeast's mysterious methods to Louis Pasteur, working at Denmark's Carlsberg brewery in the late nineteenth century. And conventional beer history informs us that twelfth-century German nun Hildegard von Bingen first wrote about hops' ability to preserve beer.

Ian Hornsby ponders in A History of Beer and Brewing, "What, I wonder, was the method that some of the Celtiberians used to preserve beer? Did it involve the use of hops? Pliny's observation . . . suggests that the technology might have been developed independently by a multiplicity of Indigenous peoples in this part of Europe; maybe European brewing know-how did not necessarily emanate directly from Egypt and Mesopotamia."

Here we get to again cite renowned beer writer and hops expert Stan Hieronymus in speculating that these brewers were using the lupin plant, unrelated to the lupulus (hop) plant, to preserve and flavor their beer. The plants have so much in common and were discovered and used for the same purposes by two groups of people who didn't know the other existed.

15 | THE LAST OF THE FIRST CRAFT BREWERY WOMEN

HOW IS KIM JORDAN SIMILAR TO CHER, Madonna, and Adele? In the brewing world, the cofounder of New Belgium Brewing in Ft. Collins, Colorado, requires just one name. She's so "beer famous," as they say, her identity is assumed.

She still sets standards in the industry more than thirty years after joining it, which places her among the last of the old-guard female owners. Each of the women who followed her established their breweries with romantic partners in the 1990s and have earned their own celebrity by captaining their companies to the crest of the industry.

A small handful of nonproprietor brewsters also entered the field at this time. Racking up awards and achievements, they set a lot of records in their own right and were familiar faces and respected influences on the brewers of their generation. Now between fifty and sixty years old, give or take, they're each pouring their expertise into new endeavors.

Not only was Kim the second woman after Irene to join the Association of Brewers, her peers elected her the first president of the Brewers Association, which formed in 2005 from a merger between the Association of Brewers and the Brewers Association of America. But her political activism isn't what gives Kim status as a household name.

After opening New Belgium Brewing in 1991, then splitting from her husband and taking over all of New Belgium's operations in 2009, the former social worker has emerged as an international model for environmental sustainability and progressive workplace policies. Kim follows Irene's lead in providing employee-friendly benefits such as generous time off and 100 percent medical insurance coverage. She famously gives workers a bike on their one-year anniversary and a trip to Belgium on year five.

She says that at the foundation of her leadership style is the assumption that all of her people do good work so she builds a culture where they know it's OK to take projects and run with them. She believes that kind of culture makes people feel valued.

Because she thinks people want to be connected to something bigger than themselves, some sort of tribe or community, she encourages collaboration. This requires effective communication.

Kim doesn't disagree that these might be labeled feminine or soft skills. But she also harnesses so-called masculine traits like competitiveness and assertiveness when she needs to.

"We believe in good communication, but we also believe in winning and we believe in really trying to kick ass," she says. "I think I set the standard that we're going to be excellent and we're going to be loving. Then I get out of the way," Kim says.

Plus, she can empathize with working moms in a culture that doesn't make much space for them. Early in New Belgium's history she took her four- or five-month-old son to a meeting to sign up a distributor.

"I breastfed him while we were sitting there, and ten years later they were still telling that story."

At the dawn of the 1990s, Deb Carey decided it was time for a change. Corporate beer life was feeling old to her husband, the highly educated and decorated brewer Dan Carey. So she offered to start up a brewery and hire him.

His reaction? "Yeah, right."

She showed him she was serious. While living in Colorado, Deb wrote a business plan and raised $225,000 to open New Glarus in her home state of Wisconsin. She negotiated for used dairy tanks, bought a shuttered pub out of foreclosure, sold their house to finance the purchase, and hired Dan as her brewer.

"I came home and told Dan, 'Put in your notice,'" she remembers.

The two of them did everything themselves to turn the abandoned Vietnam-era building into a small brewery. They cut floor drains and hauled in pub equipment bought out of foreclosure, "cleaned the dead bodies and filth," as Deb jokes (I hope), and lived hand to mouth with Deb writing out their accounting longhand and saving up for a dot matrix printer. Their kids roller-skated around them as they toiled.

"I made a commitment to help him run it for two years yet I'm still here twenty-three years later. It turns out actually I'm pretty good at this."

"Pretty good" is a pretty modest way of putting it. The United States Small Business Association (SBA) has recognized Deb as runner-up for the best small business person in the nation, while Wisconsin's SBA named her the best small business person in the state, and Ernst & Young designated her a regional entrepreneur of the year. In 2012, President Barack Obama and Vice President Joe Biden invited her to talk business with them at the White House. Dan, who's studied at the world's top brewing programs, has won practically every brewing award imaginable.

With this pair charting the course, New Glarus's business figures are the envy of the industry. Deb and Dan's team produces 240,000 barrels per year, putting them in the top twenty in the nation, and they don't sell a drop outside Wisconsin.

Lost Coast, which opened in 1990 in Eureka, California, as the first brewery owned by a pair of women (and a completely silent male partner), sells beer in twenty-three states and eight foreign countries. Barbara Groom had home-brewed practically forever but still spent three years studying the science of brewing before launching with her then-partner, Wendy Pound. A few years ago Lost Coast moved to its third facility, where Barbara oversees as many females as she can hire who have the capacity to fill 1,000 kegs and 135,000 bottles per day. For each capital upgrade, Barbara holds firm to the region's historical brewing roots.

"When Mendocino had their grand opening—the moment I saw it, that's when I knew that's what I wanted to do with the rest of my life," she says.

In 2013, Kim sold the company to her employees, as did Irene before her and the Odell family after. In the first half of the decade employee stock ownership plans (ESOP) appeared to be a developing trend but never gained traction. It's possible that the Full Sail's employee-owners' sale to a private equity firm in 2015 scared would-be followers off.

In 2015, the fifty-eight-year old who *Forbes* estimated was worth $225 million stepped down as CEO of New Belgium to chair her board of directors. She left operations to president and COO Christine Perich and a deep pool of female execs.

Pretty much everything Kim does still makes national news. When she and her longtime boyfriend, Elysian cofounder Dick Cantwell, helped friend Dave McClean out by taking over majority ownership of Haight-Ashbury's long-standing Magnolia brewpub—national news.

And when New Belgium followed what is a trend with legs by steering the sale of the brewery to Japanese brewing conglomerate Kirin at the end of 2019—international news.

But for all the headlines Kim has commanded over the decades, she leaves one enduring legacy that few outside of craft brewing history circles know or will remember. As a practically permanent member of the BA's board, she proposed the idea of funding a craft brewing collection for the Smithsonian's National Museum of American History. The BA helped fund a curator named Theresa McCulla for three years, which it then extended. Theresa has proven herself extraordinarily interested in unearthing and amplifying the stories of women and has contributed unique information and extraordinary support to this book.

Four months after celebrating with Theresa and about a dozen of craft brewing's most iconic (male) pioneers as the curator unveiled the inaugural artifacts in the museum's permanent craft brewing display case, I had the pleasure of flying to California to interact with Don Barkley, who worked at New Albion with Jack—who attended the Smithsonian event—and Suzy, who did not.

It was my first time meeting Don, and I couldn't have been more ecstatic to spend a few hours with him and his wife at Hopland Tap in Mendocino County, courtesy of my virtuoso Northern California concierge, Herlinda Heras. Hopland filled the old Mendocino Brewing building where Don spent twenty-five years after leaving New Albion. Lagunitas Brewing's former director of sales and marketing Ron Lindenbusch bought and rechristened the site with its original name and contracted Don to supply it with Red Tail Ale, which Jack invented during his short stint there and I drank obsessively when I spent a year out of college in San Francisco, knowing absolutely nothing about this story.

To my disappointment, Don wasn't able to get a keg of Red Tail to the bar in time. But it didn't diminish how incredible it felt to relax with him and Ron in the mothballed brewhouse around the back of the building and spontaneously dance atop the picnic tables in the empty courtyard on a balmy mid-March afternoon.

Over a lunch spent talking about NorCal beer women, Ron chimed in with the names of two women he counted on every day at Lagunitas after it opened in 1993: Carissa Brader and Robin McClain.

Carissa was married to Tony Magee, who founded the Sonoma County brewery. At first, she'd come in to have lunch with her husband during breaks at her volunteer recycling job. But once when she spotted Ron loading a truck by hand, she offered to help.

"I know how to drive a forklift," she told him. Before he could register what was happening, "Zoop, zoop, zoop, she started working there that day. She was the silent force, the one nobody ever knew about," he says.

She took on the role of brewery mom, Ron remembers, cooking steak lunches (hot dogs when times were tough) and lending money to employees. She ended up running production for the next ten years, "juggling bowling balls with a sword in the middle," as he says.

She hired Robin as a powerhouse comptroller by offering, "How about fifteen dollars an hour and you don't steal from me?"

Perhaps because of Carissa and Robin's influence, Lagunitas has championed female leadership from the start. To wit: Rebecca Newman, whom Ron calls a "freaking legend," runs quality control. The Heineken-owned company installed AB InBev brewing veteran Mary Bauer as head brewer and then plant manager at its satellite Chicago brewery, then put her in charge of international brewing operations. Most recently, Lagunitas lost its female CEO, Maria Stipp, to Stone Brewing in San Diego, where she holds the same position.

"Nope. They hired my brewers away all of the time," Denise Jones replies when I ask if she's ever worked at Lagunitas. As a rock star brewmaster who started brewing in 1992 after leaving the postal service, she's won ten Great American Beer Festival awards, and she studied at the American Brewers Guild, Siebel Institute of Technology, and with the Master Brewers Association of the Americas. She also signed on as head brewer for the short-lived attempt to reopen San Francisco's Albion Ale and Porter Brewing Company, which didn't survive Prohibition. She's trained so many brewers at so many NorCal breweries that she jokes she felt like she was running a brewery puppy mill for the Bay Area.

To me, Denise presents as a central casting California cowgirl, with dusty boots, a strong work ethic, and a mouth that drops f-bombs left and right. She's a legend in California brewing circles.

Annie Johnson, the AHA award-winning homebrewer, says when she homebrewed in the San Francisco area, Denise, then at Third Street Aleworks in Santa Rosa, would remind her not to let the guys make her doubt herself.

"She was the best," Annie says. "Her focus was never about tearing down others. She didn't have to because her beer was so good."

Denise earned her national reputation brewing under Brendan Moylan at the eponymous Moylan's from 2006 to 2013, winning medals for her flagship Scotch Ale, Kilt Lifter.

At Moylan's, she trained Alexandra Nowell, now making a serious name for herself with Lynne Weaver at Three Weavers in Los Angeles, as well as April Anderson, who recently started brewing at Tomoka Brewing in Florida, co-owned by none other than Don Barkley.

Denise says Brendan, who remains a close friend, hesitated to hire the two women. Though he staffed his pubs with women, Denise says she thinks he preferred guys for their muscle; brewing is nothing if not laborious and women were invisible to the brewing world.

"Evolutions of thought can be a long time coming for some. He hired me because he had seen my work ethic at Santa Rosa and knew that I was a proven force," she says.

Fellow California girl Jennifer Talley has that same focus and drop-dead honesty to her. Coming from the same brewing generation as Denise, she co-owns, brews, and bartends at 1849 Brewing in Gold Country. Talking to me by phone during two bartending shifts as I marveled at how she can simultaneously tell me her life story and warmly take orders from every "Honey," "Sugar," and "Sweetie" who comes to the bar, I ask why she says it's a smart idea to bartend for a while at one's own brewpub. She stops her dual conversation for a beat, then two, then three, and I know what's coming.

"Isn't that obvious?" she asks.

"Yes," I say. "But I need to hear it from you."

"You're learning how to make money by getting to know your customer."

That's what I thought.

Jen was bartending in Park City, Utah, in 1991 when she got into brewing. She worked across the street from Wasatch and would ask Mellie questions about beer during her breaks. Mellie says she'd like to think she had a little something to do with Jen getting hired as a brewer at nearby Squatters, which opened a few years later.

If so, Mellie has much to be proud of. After working as head brewer there for many years, Jen migrated back to California to work under Vinnie Cilurzo at Russian River, whom she credits as a mentor, then she won the coveted Russell Scherer Award for Brewing Innovation. She's the first of two women to win it so far.

Maybe there's something in the California water that gives the final brewster in this triad the same hilariously irreverent, outwardly sure-of-herself, tell-it-like-it-is attitude. Gwen Conley worked her way up the brewhouse and quality assurance ladder at Flying Dog Brewery, moving cross-country with the company when it left Colorado for Maryland. She then crossed the country again to lead quality control at Lost Abbey, then Ballast Point, both in San Diego.

Gwen now joins a steadily increasing number of brewers leaving beer for spirits. Trudiann Branker, master distiller at Mount Gay Rum, and Abby Titcomb, head distiller at 3 Floyds Distilling, are examples, as is Denise, who keeps feet in both realms.

Gwen followed Ballast Point founder Yuseff Cherney to the spirits side when he sold the brewery to Constellation, picking up somewhat where she left off as the recipe developer and sensory goddess at Cutwater Spirits. Though her spirits have won 481 awards in seven years, she says she took some grief from craft brewing friends who feel she abandoned them for an industry that has an uneasy kinship with their own.

It's a little odd that the decade's five most prominent nonowner brewsters clustered in just two states—California and Massachusetts. With Boston dominating the East Coast craft brewing scene of the 1990s, it mostly makes sense to find Lauren Clark and Jodi Andrews there. Lauren isn't as well known as Jodi, because she left the industry a long time ago for journalism, founding blog Drinkboston and writing *Crafty Bastards*.

Jodi, on the other hand, remains well known in certain circles for three reasons. First, from her perch as longtime brewer at Boston Beer Co., she mentored and inspired a fair number of New England's young and aspiring brewsters—Boston Beer's Megan Parisi and Vilija Bizinkauskas, head brewer at Middlebury, Vermont's prominent Drop-In Brewing, among them. Second, she's won a very impressive eleven GABF medals. Third, she married, had a child with, and divorced Eddie Stoudt, son of Carol and Ed. She left beer in 2019, suing her last boss for sexually harassing her in front of her subordinates.

"Forty-nine years old and I was told to give a hand job to the packaging supervisor. Pretty classy," she says.

Beer's loss makes for marijuana's gain. She's currently working in cannabis research where she feels much more respected. Though hardly any women have left beer for cannabis yet—BrewDog USA's former CEO Tanisha Robinson as perhaps the most prominent exception—it is, like beer once was, the new frontier. Because it's getting its legal start four hundred years into American beer's lifespan, the cannabis industry has learned from its predecessor's mistakes and has left the gate more professionalized and equity-minded than the beer industry can lay claim to even today.

16 | THE FATHERLAND

SISTER DORIS IS SHIMMYING UP another rickety metal ladder. I want to warn her to be careful, or at least offer to spot her habit-covered bum, but I don't speak German and, after all, she's relied on most of this equipment since she started working here as a young woman in 1969.

When she comes down—without a slip—she continues to walk my two companions and me through the chilly space, pointing out dials and gadgets, laughing at their seemingly impossible age (one machine dates to 1972) and telling stories about chastising the welders for their sloppy craftsmanship as we go. Finally, she leads us to her tidy Tudor living quarters, where she serves us a comfortable lunch of pâté, cheese, and homemade bread. But what my companions and I really crave is the beverage she's made almost single-handedly since her predecessor retired more than forty-five years ago: beer.

Franciscan nun Doris Engelhard brews for the Mallersdorf Abbey in Bavaria, where she unspools a thread of German brewing nuns twelve hundred years long. German monasteries and what we now call convents have brewed beer for spiritual and medicinal purposes since, plausibly, the ninth century.

Religious orders in Germany were left to their own invention to support themselves so some, as we see time and again in Belgium, relied on brewing for sustenance (especially during fasts), self-sustainability, and silver. While monks got most of the attention and extraordinarily lavish gifts of cash, rye, wheat, barley, and hops from noblemen, princes, and kings seeking the Lord's favor, nuns brewed right alongside them in their own abbeys across the Continent.

They, too, sold their excess ale, joining the monks in labeling their liquid with the name of their abbey's patron saint.

Nuns received a solid education at their respective abbeys and applied science and methodology to their brewing, unlike eons of homebrewsters who normally relied on intuition, collective memory, nature, the healing arts, and in some cases, mysticism. Nuns were encouraged to refine their techniques with careful observation, trial and error, and documentation. Sometimes the abbess herself would brew. Nuns also contributed to a body of knowledge on yeast that led to the fifteenth-century brewing of lagers, which require yeast that ferments at the bottom of a vessel, as opposed to ales, which rely on top-fermenting yeast. (Note: the word ale here is an umbrella term for styles brewed with top-fermenting yeast, not to be confused with the unhopped beer called ale in early England.)

In the Middle Ages, untold numbers of single women sought shelter in the abbeys. In a society where unmarried women didn't have any rights, couldn't piece together a living, and whose poverty could force them into prostitution, exile, or execution simply for failing to find a husband at a time when such a commodity ran scarce, a convent looked like a pretty good option. When newly minted followers of Martin Luther's early sixteenth-century reforms got caught up in anti-Catholic frenzy, many priests converted to the new Protestant denomination.

Not the nuns. They had no place else to go.

These Protestant reformers expelled nuns from the refuge of their convents, burning some to the ground, and, as Marilyn French writes in volume two of *From Eve to Dawn, A History of Women in the World,* "scoffed at convents as dumping grounds for unwanted daughters and dismissed nuns' reluctance to leave, charging that they wanted to stay for frenzied sexual promiscuity."

Though their ends in no way justified their means, Protestants were lashing back after tolerating many centuries' worth of hypocrisy, sloth, forbidden sexual excesses, corruption, ignorance, and drunkenness from their Roman Catholic priests.

Women were especially turned off by this unsaintly behavior and avoided religion more so than men. Males, at least, had a place in the church. Laymen gathered in confraternities (brotherhoods) to lead rituals such as masses, banquets, and processions.

"To heighten the sense of belonging, most confraternities excluded women, even their wives and daughters," French writes.

It's likely that, intentionally or not, the legendary eighth-century Holy Roman Emperor King Charlemagne and his successor, King Louis the Pious, restricted women as well. Before their time, monasteries lived more or less according to their own, sometimes idiosyncratic, rules. But these royals defined the role of monastic beer, appointing brewers and employing hops for what may be the first time in a secular brewery. Standardization, brewsters have learned, generally bodes poorly for the majority of them, who usually can't afford to meet the requirements.

Under King Louis, Benedict of Aniane traveled the monastery circuit to codify and mandate a set of assorted rules put forth by various saints. One such rule from Ireland ordered the selection of one nun to take charge of each abbey brewhouse, which would set up beer as nuns' standard drink and save wine for special occasions. This holds true at the twelfth-century Mallersdorf, where Sister Doris hopes her nuns won't take too many unlimited bottles at lunchtime because she needs to sell enough to outsiders to keep the brewery self-sufficient.

Other than Sister Doris, Benedictine abbess Hildegard von Bingen lives on as history's most famous brew-nun. Inconsistent facts swirl around her constantly but what we do know is that over the course of her tenth- and eleventh-century life, the herbalist, scientist, physician, and advisor to the emperor receives due credit for writing down the preservative properties of hops in beer before anyone else.

Hops had been growing wild in Germany before anyone there thought to cultivate or put them in beer. German brewers had, in fact, been routinely hopping their beer since at least the ninth century. The first large-scale use of hops seems to have started in the monasteries of King Louis the Pious's era, around the time when Abbot Adalhard of Corbie detailed their preparation and distribution methods for beer.

In her *Physica Sacra* (Sacred World) tome, Hildegard documented her own discoveries with the preservative properties of the plant. By the time the use of hops spread to Northern Europe and then Britain a few centuries later, hops had become the main factor in making long-distance beer sales, hence corporate breweries, possible. Hildegard herself enjoyed the beverage, and whether its preservative properties extended her lifespan is an unanswerable question.

But it bears speculation, considering she lived to an astounding eighty-one years old.

On the secular side, married German women of the Middle Ages home-brewed unhopped, low-alcohol ale for the family and invited friends over to chat and taste one anothers' fresh batches. At varying times in history, the church, feudal manor house, or royal court might contract trained male brewers to run a sizable operation to supply residents, serfs, pilgrims, beggars, and guests. Governing bodies took great interest in beer, as water in some places was deemed unsanitary, and the citizenry—even toddlers—depended on ale for nutrition, quenching thirst, and fostering sociability morning, noon, and night.

For a while, nobles didn't concern themselves with female-brewed ale. But as kings and churches got used to an ever-higher standard of technicality and quality, they started demanding better beer for tithings and taxes. This compelled the lower-ranking nobility to demand better from their brewers, leading them to hire men who'd learned outside the house to brew more scientifically than women and, unencumbered by children and thousands of homemaking tasks, were able to work as paid craftsmen.

To ensure he'd be receiving good ale, Emperor Frederick I wrote Germany's first known nonreligious beer regulation in 1156. It read, "A brewer who makes bad beer or pours an unjust measure shall be punished; his beer shall be destroyed or distributed at no charge among the poor." Note the gendering of the sentence.

As cities started taxing hops, they enacted ever more restrictions.

Brandenberg, for example, in the northeast, prohibited certain types of brewing to protect its economy, which relied on beer taxes and direct revenues from its municipally owned breweries. It also banned the brewing and serving of beer on Sundays and Christian holidays, which further eroded a woman's ability to brew and sell in between her infinite list of other responsibilities.

As a precursor to the famous Reinheitsgebot purity law passed in Bavaria in 1516, Munich enacted a law that banned ingredients other than barley, hops, and water in 1487. The Duke of Bavaria-Landshut issued the same decree two years later.

Duke of Bavaria Wilhelm IV didn't understand the role of yeast in beer making so he didn't include it in the Reinheitsgebot. The same can be said for the nobles in Munich and Bavaria-Landshut. Wilhelm's law, unlike common belief, only applied in the southern German state of Bavaria, where breweries were most concentrated. However, the rest of the country, save the far reaches of the north, have adopted it as well.

Because hops were expensive, taxed, and controlled by governing bodies, women, who received poor pay for their brews and had no rights in society, couldn't compete. They would now be breaking the law to earn a desperately needed bit of money.

Here's a little-known fact: Bavaria's brewing guilds lobbied for the law.

"The modern world was formed in the sixteenth century," writes Marilyn French in volume two of *From Eve to Dawn, A History of Women in the World.* "Politically, primarily feudal systems were gradually abandoned, as European states adopted centralized monarchies. An insurgent bourgeoisie clamored for rights. An economic system based on production for use—a combination of self-sufficiency and barter—gave way to production for profit, a largely capitalist money system. . . . For the first time, a seething mass of destitute homeless people, most of them women, appeared in Europe, and economic, political and social differences between the sexes widened."

After the bubonic plague had taken the last of its victims in 1350, the resurgent population exploded. Europe's new reality expressed itself in unprecedented urban migration and a skewed ratio in these cities of approximately 115 women to every one hundred men. The shift from an agrarian lifestyle to a commercial one built the middle class and rewarded "advanced scientific rationality with messianic zeal, suggesting that the mechanical world view was 'a crusade against the irrational, the mystical, and the feminine.'"

Holistic family production faded and only men could earn a wage outside the home. Women's sanctioned work shrunk to housewifery, servitude, and reproduction. Only poor women could work for a wage, which was never enough to sustain them.

One bright spot comes from early English guilds, whose notes indicate that "sisteren" were welcomed along with "brethren." It seems that generally women and sometimes men were expected to bring ale to furnish monthly guild dinners. Women and men were allotted the same amount to drink, but women were subject to more penalties for violating the rules. The Guild of the Holy Cross in Stratford-upon-Avon, for instance, required only women to bring the ale and fined them a halfpenny for forgetting. And though men faced no corresponding responsibility, both genders could be fined a halfpenny for quarreling.

The tavern keepers guild at Berwick-upon-Tweed only set regulations for women, limiting the amount of oats she could buy at one time and capping what she could charge at certain times of the year.

However, tensions and protectionism rose as vendors split from producers and formed their own guilds. These vendors began cutting out craftspeople and their urban guilds by buying raw materials and taking them to the country to be assembled by rural workers.

This was a time of tremendous poverty, anxiety, and cruelty, and men in the commercial world seemed determined to tear out every stitch of women's economy and independence whenever competition got tough. They picked on the weakest in their ranks—widows carrying on their late husband's trade.

Widows handled up to 15 percent of the shops in any craft. But starting in the 1400s, craft guilds only allowed a widow to finish her husband's existing work or take over the business if she had a son to inherit it when she passed. A century later, most guilds prevented widows from bringing in fresh apprentices or journeymen and sometimes forced them to fire those they already had.

These widows, no longer able to support themselves, begged for mercy and only received it if they pleaded weakness, French says.

Women had no choice but to drop out of the trades and pick up menial work making cheap products in the sewing and fabric business—until male guilds and authorities restricted them from those endeavors too. Arms of the patriarchy, from husbands to employers to church and civil authorities, now controlled women's ability to work, live, and reproduce, and women unprotected from the elements by marriage slipped into prostitution . . . that is, until reformist Protestants, the same ones who shut down the nunneries, closed brothels and prosecuted harlots.

As Sister Doris pours us glasses of her clean and delicate *festbier, helles,* and *zoigl,* she gripes good-naturedly about all the unwanted attention she's gotten since the international press started spotlighting her. Curious travelers show up unannounced to see this strange relic. They come to converse but don't buy anything. They walk into the brewery without an invitation.

One time, she tells us, a couple came by and asked her if she'd seen Sister Doris. She said no then called into the back, "Sister Doris?!"

As she talks, I'm cringingly aware that the celebrity nun who wakes up at 3:30 AM on brew days surely must lump me in with the rest even though I'd flown to Germany, borrowed a car from Weyermann Specialty Malts, and commandeered two of its employees to drive and interpret for me—all to interview her while she's alive and brewing.

Oh well. Duty calls.

Anyway, I'm enthralled, and so are my chaperones: Denise Jones, who worked as master distiller for Weyermann at the time and who planned out the day for us, and chauffeur/interpreter extraordinaire, former Weyermann Craft Beer Ambassador Gregor Fransson. I start the interview by asking Sister Doris how old she is.

She was born January 24, 1949, which put her at pushing seventy when I visited.

"At this age," she tells Gregor in German deadpan, "I should already be retired."

17 | BOOM AND BUST

BETWEEN 1995 AND 1998, the number of US craft breweries shot from approximately 500 to 1,376, doubling in the first twenty-four months. Thanks in part to the go-go Clinton economy and the tech bubble, these were halcyon years for the American stock market. Everybody, brewers included, wanted a piece of the action. Early owners had worked hard for a decade or more; now they wanted to cash in on their sweat equity. Stockholders, corporate investors, and the larger sharks of the brewing world, so different from the bankers of the 1980s, were happy to oblige.

By 1999, the bubble had burst. Two hundred twenty-nine craft breweries closed that year, leaving survivors shaken and trying to figure out how to avoid being next.

"It took us a lot of talking [to one another] to get our confidence back," says Carol Stoudt.

Most observers of today's craft beer industry read the 1990s as a cautionary tale and, perhaps unaware of the closures of the late 1970s and early '80s, refer to this period as the first craft beer bubble, followed by its first shakeout. Certainly, we might call the first wave a micro-bubble, as its death toll rang for radical, undercapitalized adventurers whose numbers can be counted on two hands.

The 1990s bubble blew up, then popped under exact opposite forces. Too much money in the business brought to the surface bottom-feeding opportunists who opened breweries without any passion or know-how. Elsewhere, free-flowing cash churned up the weighty pressures of mergers, acquisitions,

IPOs, and get-rich-quick idealism. It swept some of the original cottage opera-
tors into its undertow and cast a wake that reverberates today.

In a move that would foreshadow the frenzied trades of the mid-2010s,
Washington's original craft brewery, Redhook, went public first, in 1994.
Anheuser-Busch bought a quarter of its shares. Within a year or two, a hand-
ful of other start-ups issued stock offerings, including Jim and Rhonda at
Boston Beer, and the group of Seattle investors who'd bought Hart from Beth
and Tom. The Ponzis sold BridgePort outright to Texas-based beer megalith
Gambrinus in 1995.

While the exhausted former owners of Hart Brewing struggled to keep
their marriage together on a farm in rural Oregon, its new owners took the
brewery through a financial struggle all too common for the era. When they
filed for their IPO on October 7, 1995, under the symbol HOPS, they were
brewing between 160,000 and 170,000 barrels yearly out of three facilities in
Washington. Hart ranked as the fourth biggest brewery in the nation, and
that's not including the barrels brewed under the Thomas Kemper name, which
Hart's investor-owners had acquired in 1992.

In 1996, the investors changed the company's name to Pyramid Breweries,
Inc., and the *Seattle Times* "Stock Talk" reporter Greg Heberlein used the
headline "Hart Brewing Appears to Be a Barrel of Strength" to report that
the company "has strong growth prospects, brand names, and position in the
market at a time when industry stocks are off 33 percent to 45 percent."

"We all became big production breweries, which may or may not have
been what we thought was going to happen," reflects Beth with the hazy irony
of someone who long ago spent fourteen hours a day making beer out of
repurposed dairy tanks with a baby strapped to her back.

But after the *Seattle Times* predicted sunny skies ahead for Pyramid, good
news stopped rolling off the presses. Despite opening a Berkeley, California,
location, Pyramid closed several other sites over the next few years, including
the original Kalama facility, and couldn't revive stagnant and declining sales.

In a history that could have more or less applied to any number of breweries at the time, the *International Directory of Company Histories* writes:

> The craft, or microbrew, market had grown extremely rapidly, with
> small, independent breweries springing into existence at a breathtak-
> ing pace. This proliferation of craft brewers . . . led to greatly height-

ened competition for Pyramid in all of its markets. To make matters worse, the growing consumer interest in microbrews during the early 1990s had enticed virtually all of the major domestic brewers into the fray; such industry giants such as Anheuser-Busch, Miller Brewing, and others had introduced full-flavored, European-style beers to compete with the microbrews. Many had also formed alliances with or made investments in specific craft brewers. Competition from these national brewers was particularly damaging to Pyramid; with their much greater financial resources, influence, and distribution networks, they were able to drive down product prices and reduce distribution options for the smaller breweries.

Carol Stoudt observed many years later, "In the '90s we had the guys with the suits. Well, the liquid got old and it hurt everyone. People wanted consistency."

Though the quality of output varied profoundly, a great many independent 1990s-era breweries did survive the decade by producing superb beer that led the market into the twenty-first century. Two notable examples: the Odells and Janet Egelston at Northampton. Less fortunate were women like Marjorie McGinnis at Maryland's Frederick Brewing Co. who, with her husband, followed the well-tread path to ruin by going public, buying expensive equipment, and producing more beer than the macrodrinking public was ready to imbibe.

Some, like the Ponzis, left on their own terms, only to mourn along with the rest of the historically minded craft community much later when Gambrinus refused to invest in infrastructure for Oregon's oldest craft brewery, ran sales into the ground, and officially buried it in 2019.

Jeff Alworth notes in his *Beervana* column that BridgePort's 1996 launch of IPA had sent Oregon into "the realm of 'juiciness' a decade and a half before that concept would filter into the general public."

Instead of being scared off by the brew, Oregon drank the IPA in never-before-seen quantities, both in and out of what Alworth remembers as BridgePort's "homey, wood-paneled pizza pub [that] was Stumptown's rec room." That beer's release ever so slightly predated the rise of Southern California breweries like Stone and Green Flash, breweries that helped engineer the hoptastic West Coast IPA style.

However, in New Jersey, as with the swaths of America that lay outside the frontiers of the West, adventurous entrepreneurs like Peggy Zwerver and her husband, Tom Baker, learned drinkers most certainly did get scared off by what they were selling. Back east, away from the rapidly climbing hop bitterness scales, beer drinkers had perhaps ventured as far outside their comfort zone as they were willing to go by cozying up with the tame amber-hued stylings delivered by the thousands of brewpubs that cropped up in the 1990s. Though the couple opened as the shakeout was ending and a full four years after Ann and David Hall brought brewpubs and relatively safe English and Irish ales to New Jersey via The Ship Inn, Peggy and Tom soon discovered their obscure and historic styles were simply way, way, way too far ahead of the palates of their market.

Peggy and Tom stopped making beer in New Jersey fourteen years ago. But on commemorative occasions, their old friends and fans might speak in hushed tones as they tiptoe up from the cellar brandishing vintage bottles of Heavyweight Brewing gruits (beers brewed with botanicals instead of hops), Baltic porters, and Belgian-style ales. Back when the lauded couple ran Heavyweight, between 1999 and 2006, and before they gave up on Jersey to open two brewpubs in Philadelphia, the state's infinitesimal cadre of beer appreciators understood that the recipes—designed to fill the esoteric, high-gravity hole that other brewers avoided—were special.

It's just that there weren't enough beer geeks around to keep the brewery solvent. Microbreweries still hadn't hit the mainstream, and New Jersey's taste for epicurean adventure lagged notoriously behind its more cosmopolitan environs.

So Peggy and Tom brought their highly rated beers to festivals in Boston and Pittsburgh and sold them briskly in Philadelphia, New York, and Baltimore. But they had to drive forty-five minutes across the county border to reach any bar that would put them on tap, and they never managed to profit much from their seven-barrel brewery.

"It's very hard when everybody's making more money on your beer than you are," Peggy laments.

Eventually they had to make a decision, the same one that brought down so many of their predecessors: grow up, sell out, or close down. They scrutinized their accounting logs and chose the latter.

18 | WALLFLOWER AT THE ORGY

"The image of the journalist as wallflower at the orgy has been replaced by the journalist as the life of the party."
—Nora Ephron

SINCE THE ADVENT OF THE INTERNET, beer lovers have typically taken to websites, blogs, social media, or online forums to trade homebrewing tips and spread word of new beers and breweries.

Before the Internet, word had to get creative. Though industry publications about beer have existed for centuries, there were few central sources where casual readers could gather information about homebrewing or the emerging craft culture. People who wanted to tap into beer news, learn to brew at home, or—gasp—open their own small brewery had to read newsletters manually typed out by homebrewing hobbyists, pick up tidbits through good old word-of-mouth, or duck into a homebrew shop or club meeting if they happened to live or travel by one.

After spotting a sign in a liquor store window that boasted, "We have FIVE imported beers!" a group of Californians from the publishing business launched *All About Beer* (*AAB*) in 1979 as the first consumer magazine about beer. Former *AAB* editor Julie Johnson recounts that in the fourth issue the magazine broke the news about the construction of Sierra Nevada (though got its location wrong) and published the first public photo of Russian River Brewing cofounder Vinnie Cilurzo.

And though it stopped the practice after readers complained, *AAB* ran a Beer Mate of the Month (a picture of a bikini-clad woman) alongside its reviews of Michelob and Coors. (Before you dismiss this as outdated 1980s playfulness, consider that the Rupert Murdoch–owned British tabloid, the *Sun*, ran daily Page 3 pictures of bare-breasted models *until 2015*.)

What's less obvious and more insidious than the inappropriate insertion of beguiling women into a beer magazine is the absence of women in the first draft of beer's historical record. Archivist Tiah Edmunson-Morton has compiled a tremendous catalog of beer periodicals, to which she's recently added newsletters and small-run publications collected by the late Portland publican Don Younger. With a largely regional focus from the mid-1990s they show things didn't improve much.

"More than anything," Tiah says, "the lack of info on women in these collections is telling."

Even Julie Nickels, who launched *Celebrator Beer News* as the first brewspaper in 1988, admits to not putting women on her pages.

"There were women involved. We just didn't think of it."

It's not from a lack of interest on her part. I believe it's honestly because most any woman supporting a brewery back then toiled behind the scenes while the man—almost always the brewer and the one whose name graced the shingle—stepped out front to claim the glory. It's usually not even a conscious thought. It's social programming.

Even now we journalists have to work hard to go beyond the first source we're offered, though I do see female writers looking for other women to feature, and female and male writers are digging harder than ever to uncover underrepresented voices.

But for the bad, there was also good. Mellie remembers reading an article about women in the brewing scene in a very early issue of *New Brewer*. It was then that she learned there were other female brewers out there besides Beth and herself.

Other than longtime *Brewers Digest Magazine* part-owner and editor Dori Whitney, *Celebrator* cofounder Julie Nickels appears to have been the only female beer publisher out there, not that she had time to notice that either while she and her ex-husband and cofounder, Bret Nickels, worked ceaselessly to keep the shoestring paper alive. Even though Charlie Papazian wrote to congratulate them and Fritz Maytag probably saved their early efforts by buying a full-page ad (credit Mark Carpenter again; he snuck a stack into Anchor's taproom), they had to keep reinvesting to keep it going, and they relied on unpaid labor from friends for help.

But the fact that a woman copublished a beer newspaper in the late 1980s is notable unto itself. Julie wrote about beer styles, what type of beer to drink at Christmas, and, she believes, penned one of the first articles about food and beer pairing. As a close friend and neighbor of Judy Ashworth, whom the Nickels met by happenstance while visiting Sierra Nevada, she had access to practically any beer available in the Bay Area.

But Julie's tenure wouldn't last more than two years. She divorced Bret and sold the paper to Tom Dalldorf, who'd been helping them out for free. Tom kept it alive until 2018 with strong editorial support from the lovely San Franciscan Gail Williams and her equally good-natured husband, Steve Shapiro.

It took about another decade for another woman to top the masthead at a beer publication.

In the late 1990s, Julie Johnson's then-husband, *All About Beer* publisher Daniel Bradford, anointed her as the first female beer magazine editor in memory. Daniel launched a regular department called "Women in Beer" but as Julie recalls, he was always uncomfortable with it and looked forward to the day when a column about women would no longer be necessary. We still haven't gotten there.

I wrote a regular column about women in beer called "Athena's Fermentables" in *Ale Street News* until 2014; Carol Smagalski made beer sound sexy in her Beer Fox column on BellaOnline.com in the 2010s; and to this day local newspapers publish elementary articles informing their readers that "Women not only drink beer, they make it, too!"

When she joined the *AAB* staff, Julie felt a strong need to reassure her mostly male readership that she had no plans to feminize the product. One day not far into her tenure, she received a letter from a male reader. He'd been horrified when he'd learned that a woman had taken over, fearing she'd only write about raspberry beers. When she'd stayed the course, he wrote, she'd won him over.

Mercifully, not everything at *AAB* stayed the same. Eventually, the masthead added more female writers and managers. And ditched the beer mate.

"Once you get the Beer Mate of the Month out of there, it becomes a more welcoming environment," Julie says.

Portland journalist Lisa Morrison started writing about beer around the same time that Julie Johnson became editor. She'd heard of Lucy Saunders and a female contributor to *Northwest Brewing News* in Alaska. But that was it.

She started covering beer as a Citysearch.com editor and as a web content editor for KOIN-TV, part of the first TV news family to develop a formidable web presence. With beer columnist Fred Eckhardt as her close mentor, Lisa made a name for herself as one of the most prolific freelance beer writers in the Pacific Northwest. Reporting under the name Beer Goddess, she hosted the long-running "Beer O'Clock" radio show and wrote *Craft Beers of the Pacific Northwest: A Beer Lover's Guide to Oregon, Washington, and British Columbia.*

At some point between 1994 and 1995, journalists formed the initial iteration of the North American Guild of Beer Writers. Lisa served as founding president when the guild reconstituted after a hiatus a few years ago but even then, she rarely spotted another woman at meetups.

"I'd look around and be like, 'I'm the only girl,' or we're all going to the bathroom and I'd be the one done first because I never had to wait in line," she laughs.

Much progress has been made since. Today, the guild counts around sixty women out of two hundred members.

Because contemporary women have worked in the publishing universe longer than they've been welcomed into beer, it was still more likely in the middle of the 2010s to find a woman working at a beer publication than on the brewhouse floor.

"There are more women writing about beer than making beer," Julie said sometime around 2015. "If you're a woman interested in beer, it's a good jumping-off point."

The story is not so sunny at the beginning of the 2020s. Most print beer magazines have folded, including *Draft*, founded by Erica Rietz and edited by Jessica Daynor. And the Brewers Association, which put women in charge of its Brewers Publications book publishing division (Kristi Switzer); *New Brewer* magazine (Jill Redding); and consumer-facing website, Craftbeer.com (Julia Herz and Jessica Baker); eliminated the position of half of these women in 2020 because of the COVID-19 pandemic.

Fortunately, the web is still giving beer scribes an outlet. Kate Bernot and Beth Demmon are doing some serious cultural analysis at *Good Beer Hunting*; I write about the business of beer for Forbes.com; Cat Wolinski writes beer features for the masses as associate editor of VinePair; and Jess Infante brings breaking beer news to the beer geeks who read Brewbound.

Speaking of the web, shout out to Chris Crabb in Portland and Ashley Routson, formerly in Southern California, who've done a great deal online to get the word out about beer by jumping into social media before most anyone figured out what to do with it.

———

Beer writers can claim untold amounts of credit for spreading the mythology of craft beer to the mainstream, and not just by profiling breweries, explaining styles, or examining the cultural zeitgeist. Many have won widespread recognition for writing books on subjects as varied as history (Maureen Ogle), foraging for ingredients (Marika Josephson), graphical depictions of beer life (Em Sauter), and how to appreciate beer while naked, or something like that (Christina Perozzi and Hallie Beaune). While I don't see women authoring many homebrewing, travel, or business books, they do proliferate between the pages of cooking and pairing guides, where society has historically relegated them.

In the same vein, Lucy Saunders, author of three beer cookbooks, deserves far more credit than she receives for her exemplary work both writing about the crossover between beer and food and directly advocating for it. She wasn't the first beer cookbook writer; that accolade would fall to Annette Ashlock Stover (*Cooking with Beer*, Culinary Arts Institute, 1980) and Carole Fahy (*Cooking with Beer*, Brewers Publications, 1987).

She's not the most prolific, either. But she does without question deserve a more visible seat alongside Garrett Oliver and Michael Jackson in the triumvirate of thought leaders at the table of food and beer.

Michael may have written the first mainstream newspaper article about pairings in a Thanksgiving 1983 edition of the *Washington Post* and later previewed the nation's first commercial sit-down beer meal in the city's Brickskeller bar. However, Lucy's *Cooking with Beer* (1996) shortly followed his *Beer Companion: The World's Great Beer Styles, Gastronomy, and Traditions* (1993) and devoted itself exclusively to pairings, whereas Michael's didn't.

Garrett, considered the world's premier beer/food ambassador, didn't contribute his first essay on the subject to *The Good Beer Book* until a year after Lucy published her own tome. That's not meant to take anything away from the brilliant Garrett or Michael, who passed away from Parkinson's in 2007, but does argue for bringing more visibility to Lucy.

Through the writing of several more books, Lucy has toured the world, educating the cooking and dining public on the harmony between beer and food and on the ways that food can elevate beer as much as wine. She and Garrett have made a powerful pair, hosting dinners, workshops, panels, lectures, and private meetings with groups such as the Association of Food Journalists and the American Culinary Association.

Joining them on the circuit in the 1990s and 2000s were Rogue's Sebbie Buhler, formerly a ranking member of the American Cheese Society, and Fred Eckhardt, who's believed to be the first person to publicly link beer with chocolate. Together, they've been able to define ways for restaurateurs to make beer more dignified and appealing.

Elsewhere, Julia Herz, who worked as a CNN producer in DC before joining the Brewers Association as craft beer program director, surely made her own mark on many a corporate kitchen when she teamed up with sensory goddess Gwen Conley to publish the coffee table guide *Beer Pairing*, which came out not long after Janet Fletcher's hardbound book, *Beer and Cheese*. And Jacquelyn Dodd's *Lush: A Season-by-Season Celebration of Craft Beer and Produce* matches the gorgeously produced aesthetics of the previous two with its own hard cover and lush photography.

As they say, you eat with your eyes.

And who can forget *He Said Beer, She Said Wine*, coauthored by Marnie Old and Sam Calagione, which formed the basis for many a head-to-head pairing dinner in which beer often shocked diners by emerging as the winner.

High-quality cooking with beer requires precision and a technical understanding of flavor compounds. And there may be no one who's read more technical beer books than Kristi Switzer, Brewers Publications publisher since

2008. Although, I'm hoping her stable picks up more female writers in coming years. Though Kristi picks the top experts in the world to write on each brewing subject and she can't help who's out there, the current percentage is paltry. I know she'd love to wrap her arms around more writing about and from women.

19 | ALEWIVES UNFLATTERED

IN 1509, A LITERATE SCOTTISH BREWSTER named Bessy Layng took the law into her own hands. Believing her ale to be worth more than the legally mandated price set that day by the municipal official in charge of such products, she erased the figure he wrote on a placard outside her door and replaced it with her own.

In 1540, Aberdeen, Scotland's town council fined the wife of Gilbert Brabner for charging too much for her ale and ordered her to distribute it for free as punishment. The feisty Mrs. Brabner (whose first name, like most women's, got left out of the criminal record) received a second fine for dumping it out as an act of resistance.

Medieval Scottish and English municipal councils kept a check on home-brewers who sold their extra ale by setting an assize, a writ that standardized prices and measures of quality and quantity. Each brewster was required to let the local ale taster know when she had liquid to sell so he could come mind her pints and quarts and, in some cases, collect fees or taxes.

Vendors constantly rebelled against the ale price, making it one of the countries' most common criminal offenses. Assize trial court records hint that women even acted in concert to violate the ale price at least a few times, collectively agreeing to sell at the higher prices set in nearby towns and simply paying the resulting fines if they got caught.

Penalties for nabbed assize offenders ran high. In Scotland, for instance, a cheating brewster could have her brewing vessels confiscated, the bottom knocked out of her cauldron, and a prohibition enacted against her ability to brew for a year or more.

As in much of Europe, English, Scottish, Welsh, and Irish women in the Middle Ages brewed and sometimes sold ale as part of their household chores to supply the family with safe potables at a time when the average person had nothing else to drink. Sarah Hand Meacham writes in *Every Home a Distillery* that everyone relied on low-alcohol ale because for the most part water wasn't an option.

"Rivers and local water supplies bathed the people and their animals, carried refuse and excrement, and teemed with disease," she writes, commenting that one writer of the period recommended drinking vinegar with fleas to cure the illnesses caused by swallowing the horse leeches that polluted drinking water.

British food historian Marc Meltonville denies the conventional wisdom about drinking water, arguing that even London's water was of perfectly good quality. Whichever holds true, by the 1400s, the consumption of water conveyed a whiff of poverty and thus was abandoned in favor of beer for meals and all other occasions.

But ale soured quickly in the absence of a preservative, so brewsters used almost any ingredient they could find to saccharify, prolong, and flavor their product. They would then sell it fresh within a tiny radius. Thus the trade remained local and small-scale until hops made their way across the English Channel in the fifteenth century. As with other brewing developments, hops took a century or two to migrate from the Continent to the British Isles.

That said, brewing conventions in medieval, Renaissance, and early modern Britain arguably inform later women's experiences making and selling beer in the United States better than any other time or place. As with preceding civilizations as well as the subsequent American experiment, we see here a clear inverse line between modernization and the welfare of women, particularly as pertains to brewsters and alewives.

Judith Bennett writes in *Ale, Beer and Brewsters in England: Women's Work in a Changing World, 1300–1600*, "As brewing became more profitable and more professionalized, it became an attractive occupation . . . in other words, a good trade for men. When this happened, by-industries pursued by wives slowly became occupations pursued by husbands."

She was talking about early modern England. But she could have just as well been describing colonial America or ancient Egypt.

It's incredibly difficult to present a cohesive picture of British brewing in this era, as laws and customs diverged wildly. But it is safe to say that British women of every social strata did participate in this type of cottage commerce at some time in some place, married women more than others. Women's history scholar Elizabeth Ewan notes in 'For Whatever Ales Ye' that married women generally dominate the rolls of registered brewers, with seventy-eight of eighty-eight Aberdeen brewsters listed as wives in 1472, and eighteen of twenty-nine in Dundee in the early 1520s.

Though specific rules for the disenfranchised—servants, widows, and unmarried women—also varied greatly, they too could, at times, eke out a living by making and selling ale; in the likely absence of a space to run an alehouse, they would have sold their wares door-to-door or, later, around the village market instead.

But let's make no mistake: brewing and alewifing, as women's work, never held anything close to an enviable status or made more than a pittance. It did, however, bring women a bit of economic independence or allow them to contribute financially to the family, gaining them a sliver of leverage in a system that gave a married woman no greater rights than a child.

The system didn't usually allow married women to own property, sign contracts, or collect their own debts, meaning a man could determine all aspects of his wife's pursuits and his name would typically replace his wife's on the municipal record-keeping books, even if she conducted all of the business.

As Bennett writes, this made it difficult for married brewsters to "secure credit, form partnerships, or otherwise extend their businesses."

This would prove especially destructive to brewsters plying their trade after the black plague, which British beer historians generally consider the line that heralded the end of England's old feudal and agrarian society and the beginning of the new world order of mercantilism and economic development.

When the black plague decimated what we today call the United Kingdom and Ireland between 1348 and 1350, it and several subsequent outbreaks killed off half the population, upending the previous one thousand years of brewing's economic status quo.

Thanks to less competition, survivors in the working classes could demand higher wages, giving them disposable income for the first time. Demand for alehouses burgeoned, as did the need for off-site taverns and inns. This made a succession of kings and statesmen nervous by distracting men from work, loosening their morals, and taking them away from practicing the skills they needed to form a strong defense in times of conscription.

Whereas the production and sale of ale has always come accompanied by a regulator, a tax collector, and in some cases, a judge, after the black plague rules and restrictions expanded. Though they were sometimes enacted to limit *men's* bad behavior (as in those many times monarchs and municipal administrators put an end to tavern games and entertainment), they almost always subjected women to strict laws and harsh punishments that subjugated them to ever-more marginalized positions.

For starters, the establishment was forever legislating who could legally brew and sell ale. Lawmakers sometimes sanctioned upper-class women at the expense of those beneath them or vice versa depending on whether they wanted to keep poor women off the dole or if they believed a "good" woman might do a better job of keeping the rowdier elements quiet.

Sometimes the authorities limited the brewing of higher-priced ale to wealthier brewers. In 1442 only relatives of guild members could brew in Aberdeen, and in the early 1500s, Edinburgh forbade brewing by women who weren't married to a burgess (who would have either been a local politician or a full town citizen conferred with all of its rights). Generally, says Ewan, the authorities felt more comfortable with wives brewing as one of several diffuse tasks, probably so that she couldn't devote too much attention to mastering any one craft.

Servants could "brew upon your own adventure" for themselves in their off hours by using their mistresses' equipment in exchange for ale. But in 1520, Ewan says in *'For Whatever Ales Ye,'* Edinburgh's council "commented in disgust that it seemed as though every servant woman who could save five or six merks [an old Scottish coin] set up on her own as a brewster or huckster selling ale."

Some places encouraged widows to support themselves with beer, others forbade it. The same can be said for unmarried young women who, as a community's most disenfranchised, could rent equipment for a small cost in place of buying her own.

Because, as Ewan writes, "The idea of independent women was anathema to the officials," England started barring women from setting up their own households in the 1490s. Scottish towns followed.

Edinburgh council ordered in 1546 that brewsters must be married or widowed and at one point limited brewing and selling to freemen (full town citizens), their wives and widows, and the rare brewster who'd obtained a special license. At the same time, lawmakers severely curtailed the professional and personal rights of single women, with Edinburgh going so far as to banish "suspicious" single ladies from the city.

The invention of a central marketplace made it somewhat easier for law enforcement to control women's activities. Kathleen Biddick writes in the *Journal of Economic History* that while historians have an extremely difficult time piecing together the rise of the market economy in England, contemporary archaeologists are concluding that kings likely set up the first public markets in the ninth and tenth centuries. They proliferated by the end of the twelfth.

Once market trading took hold, some alewives' husbands (usually burgesses) managed to secure a permit for them to operate a vending stand alongside the breadwives and the fishwives and the muttonwives. Some towns created exceptions to the burgess requirement by awarding stallanger (someone who runs a stall in a market) licenses to men so their wives could sell other brewsters' beer.

Across the land, the authorities strictly regulated the markets, often allowing hours only on certain days and times so townspeople who could afford to had an equal chance to buy their needed provisions before the processors or resellers.

In some places, licensed brewsters would work with officials to collectively set the price of ale that day. But many outside women, often those who couldn't afford a stallanger's license, resold small quantities of goods to their neighbors who didn't have the money to buy the larger quantities sold at market. Local officials tried to limit this illegal activity by restricting the hours these hucksters could shop until after the burgesses' wives had picked the best produce. But they generally ignored the crime, at least in good times.

However, Ewan writes, "Their activities were among the first to be repressed when famine, plague, or other disasters threatened the town."

Sometimes hucksters circumvented the market's stipulated prices and quality checks altogether by buying cheaper goods out of town and/or vending door-to-door.

In 1521, Dundee huckster Janet Howlk faced accusations of buying barley in bulk before market and selling it out of her house. Officials warned Janet that her second offense would result in her banishment.

Ewan writes in *For What Ales Ye*, "Hucksters were disliked by authorities who saw them profiting from a commodity without adding any value to it."

Hucekstering provided short-term relief for women too disenfranchised to enter the sanctioned market space, and at first they helped brewsters distribute their quick-spoiling ale farther and wider, creating higher profits and filling ever-growing demand.

Meanwhile, as more work moved into the public sphere and grew more specialized, husbands were beginning to take on bigger roles in their wives' brewing activities. Whereas they once lent their wives a hand, they now could be found supervising the work, says Bennett, "that constituted the primary occupation of their households and that sometimes employed more hired than familial labor."

As men put on the public face of their families, Bennett says a husband might have "directed and managed the servants; he might have contracted formal agreements with suppliers and customers; he might have arranged loans and accepted debts," leading him to enlarge his network.

Brewers—both male and female—began wholesaling increasing amounts of their liquid, an endeavor that was aided by the invention of larger storage vessels and more sophisticated means of marketing. But with higher margins practically guaranteed and higher outlays of capital required, brewers started making beer more consistently and pushing out those who only participated sporadically.

A declining number of producers began selling to a rising number of wholesalers. Bennett says approximately one hundred brewers supplied the town of Oxford in the fourteenth century; two centuries later there were a dozen. They invested in more expensive machinery, some of which was heavy enough to be permanently fixed to the floor, and grew their operations.

Demonstrably, any time an industry mechanizes or significantly scales up, women get left in the dirt. The malting business provides a powerful example.

Ewan writes that most surviving receipts show women buying malt or ale but usually not unmalted barley, whose processing required time-consuming labor, floor space, and drying kilns.

By the fifteenth century, maltsters and brewers worked under distinct ordinances, suggesting malting had become its own industry apart from brewing. Edinburgh began leasing its common land to sizable malting operations in 1508, and Perth maltsters organized themselves into a collective independent of brewers.

"Maltmaking fit the patterns of women's work less well than brewing, and it appears that, although there were women maltsters, the industry was dominated by men," Ewan writes.

But it was hops that indelibly altered the gender makeup of beer. Hops first sailed into England on ships in the form of beer imported from the mainland or as plant material destined for London to be used by brewers who emigrated from the Netherlands and Germany. These overwhelmingly male immigrants came from countries whose domestic ale production had given way to unimaginably imposing beer factories by British standards. Both at home and in their new English-speaking cities, these factories were run and staffed almost exclusively by men.

Without the addition of hops, the liquid in question continued to be called ale as it had for hundreds of years. Brewed with hops, it was known as beer. By the end of the seventeenth century, most English women and men drank hopped beer. The impact of this distinction cannot be underestimated.

Meacham writes, "The introduction of hops completed the masculinization of alcohol production in England," hence Western Europe as a whole.

As a natural preservative, hops allow beer to be produced in significantly larger quantities than ale and lend themselves to transporting beer farther from its source. To make more hopped beer, which couldn't be sold while it fermented like the ales of yore, brewers needed more fuel, more labor, more storage space, more capital, more contracts, and more trading partners than most any woman could muster.

Before King Edward VI repealed it, the English passed a law that forbade ale brewers from using hops so that beer brewers could access the imported in-demand crop. Ale brewers made do with old-fashioned ingredients such as bogmyrtle, costmary, yarrow, parsley, sage, hyssop, and tansy, plus an assortment of other edibles, some of which proved poisonous. Eventually, the government put a stop to some of these substitutes as well.

Bennett observes, "If women had once independently brewed hopped beer for profit in towns such as Ghent and Cologne, by 1400 that day was long past. . . . [Foreign] beerbrewers brought to English towns their growing sense that (as Munich brewers would phrase it later), 'brewing is a learned art and given to men alone.'"

———————————

Across Europe in the Middle Ages, guilds began to form among craftspeople as a way to recognize their collective identity and strengthen their political and economic power by highlighting one another's achievements, offering apprenticeships and other training, regulating their own industry, and acting as a unified voice in matters of lobbying and trade. English brewsters, as a dispersed and unaffiliated group who worked part-time at beer making and weren't allowed to attain any real political influence or say over their own affairs, didn't form a guild.

It wasn't until brewing had become a fraternity of men that London brewers received official recognition as the Worshipful Company of Brewers in 1438. At first, unlike most guilds on the continent, it extended membership to women.

But growing competition and urbanization led the guild to tighten its requirements for membership and apprenticeships, and women failed to qualify because as Meacham writes, they were "expected to marry, raise children, and maintain households [and] could not spend three to seven years training with a master as the guild required to become a licensed brewer."

Between the guild in London, the Scottish Society of Brewers, which formed in 1596, and other local brewers' guilds, rules about wifely and general female membership fluctuated but at no time were women allowed to hold leadership roles or wear special livery jackets reserved for the most prominent members.

As Elizabeth Ewan writes in her article "Crime or Culture?" in *Twisted Sisters*, "Within both the rhetoric of social order and the practicalities of male organizational institutions, women were nevertheless seen as subordinate and peripheral." They were also expected to behave like modest, unobtrusive ladies. But as keepers of the household, they had to at times assert their independence in order to procure what they needed for their families, say, in the realm of the marketplace.

"The loud, jostling and competitive atmosphere of the marketplace where sellers called out their wares, and purchasers questioned the quality or disputed the price of the goods, easily gave rise to riotous and rude behaviour. There was a fine line between bargaining and insult. Disputes between buyers and sellers could turn violent either in word or deed or both." Women often found themselves in court defending behaviors as innocent as scolding, leading to the criminalization of their daily activities.

Christopher Mark O'Brien writes in *Fermenting Revolution* that hatred and distrust of women ran rampant at the time. "[These] cultural ideas about women gradually gave brewsters a sleazy reputation." It wasn't entirely undeserved. Bennett writes that ale merchants and "brewers often cheated with impunity, they diluted their ale, altered their measures, and demanded higher prices."

No evidence shows that men in the trade practiced deception any less than women. But contemporary culture turned these women, and women alone, into revolting characters that reinforced the stereotype of alewives as devious and slovenly hags who presided over houses of drunkenness, gluttony, and sinister sexuality.

In poems, plays, pamphlets, and paintings, descriptions of brewsters and alewives started at fat, gaseous, and obnoxious and got worse from there. Pop culture and literature introduced English society to creatures such as Mother Bunch, Mother Louse, Betoun the Brewster, Rose the Regrater, and, most famously, John Skelton's enduring sixteenth-century Elynor Rummyng in terms like these: "Her face bristles with hair; her lips drool like a 'ropy rain': her crooked and hooked nose constantly drips; her skin is loose, her back bent, her eyes bleary, her hair grey, her joints swollen, her skin greasy. She is, of course, old and fat," writes Bennett.

Further, "she adulterates her ale: she drools in it, she sticks her filthy hands in it; she allows her hens to roost over it, using their droppings for added potency." As for her establishment, "Pigs run farting and defecating through the house; fights break out; embarrassed customers—all women, most of them gross women—slink in through the back door."

As if this weren't enough to keep dignified citizens out of an alehouse, Elynor—whose predecessors weren't portrayed this way until hops brought competitive beer men to town—cavorted with Jews (who'd been expelled from England in 1290), conducted what Bennett calls a "blasphemous mock communion," and kept company with the devil.

The Catholic church also participated in the hellish denigration of alewives and brewsters by repeatedly portraying them being sentenced to eternal damnation. A relatively innocent example turns up in the fifteenth-century Christian mystery cycle play *The Harrowing of Hell*, in which Jesus has emptied all of the deserving souls from hell. One person remains: a brewster.

The earliest known anti-alewife iconography comes courtesy of the circa 1325 Holkham Bible Picture Book, in which devils carry an alewife who may have cheated customers into a boiling cauldron. This image repeats itself constantly on church walls across England, with alewives shown more often than any other victualer or trader in Dooms, which are medieval portrayals of the Last Judgment.

Even though, as evidenced by a letter written by Jane Austen and her novel *Emma*, rich and middling women, herself included, did still brew out on the farms at the turn of the nineteenth century, by the end of the Industrial Revolution midcentury, nary a brewster was left in all of Britain.

20 | BEER'S BRIDGE OVER TROUBLED WATER

CRAFT BEER SPENT THE 2000s NURSING A HANGOVER. The public, had it been paying any attention to the brewing industry after the 1990s shakeout, would have noticed that wine was crowning ITSELF king while relegating independent beer to a fiefdom. The number of craft breweries sagged between 2000 and 2005, and a 2009 *Paste* magazine roundup of the country's best breweries included a mere two start-ups from the decade.

Meanwhile, according to the Wine Institute, American per capita wine consumption woke from a thirty-year slumber during the 1970s and 1980s. It slowed down in the 1990s, then more than doubled between 2001 and 2002. Almost without exception, wine consumption climbed every year this century until stabilizing in a record-breaking 2013. Americans may have spent the early part of the aughts greeting one another with a "Wassup" after the 1999 Budweiser ad campaign brought the ubiquitous salutation into our living rooms but what was up over the following five to ten years wasn't barley or hops. It was grapes.

Despite the prevailing lethargy, three young brewsters rose to the top of the field during this time and are respectfully, albeit mistakenly in my opinion, identified as the last members to join the first class of notable beer women.

Laura Ulrich, Megan Parisi, and Whitney Thompson don't fit in the first generation. Spending much of their early full-time brewing careers at well-established, well-funded places like Stone, Cambridge, and Tröegs, respectively, they never had to fabricate tanks from dairy or soda leftovers; they never had to beg friends, family, or bankers for money to fund a business; and they never

123

had to work as hard as their predecessors to convince dumbfounded listeners that drips of American beer could come out of faucets not attached to Bud, Miller, or Coors vessels.

But if Laura, Megan, and Whitney aren't quite like the women who came before them, they're not quite like the women after them, either. Until sometime around 2007, they worked in isolation, believing themselves to be pretty much the only woman in the country, if not the world, brewing at an independent twentieth- or twenty-first-century facility.

Finally discovering one another through mutual friends, coworkers, and the founder of the Pink Boots Society, the three brewsters, at the dawn of 2011, brewed the first all-female beer collaboration in known history. The novelty of the team drew international press coverage (including in my *Ale Street News* column) and inspired three ongoing women's collaboration brews that take place all over the world. The trio christened their Belgian-style *dubbel* Project Venus, a name that alludes to fertility and prosperity in this new era for brewsters, both in America and in the growing craft community abroad.

To repurpose an oft-quoted phrase from Bell's Brewing founder Larry Bell, Laura, Megan, and Whitney serve as bridges between the "end of the beginning of craft beer" and the next steps toward the present.

In February 2011, Boston had a snowstorm. These things happen in Massachusetts, but Laura, flying in from San Diego and a lifetime in warm western states, hadn't packed boots or a proper coat. "Of course we chose the perfect month to make a goddamn beer," she muttered in August 2020, evidently still traumatized by a snowfall the likes of which she'd never imagined until landing at Logan Airport.

Before she went to a welcome dinner hosted by Cambridge Brewing—where owner Phil Bannatyne had decorated the tables with bouquets of flowers for the women of honor—she had Megan, her host, bring her to Macy's. For the next two days Megan and the good folks at Cambridge, where she brewed under her mentor Will Meyers, would be squiring Laura and Whitney, then the quality assurance manager at Victory Brewing northwest of Philly. The women had come together to brew a collaboration beer, an idea that was gaining traction in the craft brewing world.

They brewed the *dubbel* using orange blossom honey and saffron—saffron because Megan had tasted it as an ice cream flavor at an Indian restaurant and wanted to try it in beer. But that wasn't the only reason. No. They'd intentionally selected the most expensive ingredients they could.

Megan, who's as humble and down-to-earth as they come, jokes that like any girls they wanted the most expensive things.

"Hell yeah, we're gonna put saffron in this beer. We're worth it. Everything was, 'We're worth it,'" Laura affirms.

The idea for Project Venus was conceived over a conversation between Laura and Megan at a Pink Boots Society meeting in 2010 where Laura wondered aloud why only male brewers got to have all the fun working on a new Stone collaboration series. Not ones to let boys exclude them from play, they decided to do a collaboration of their own. They invited Whitney as one of the only other brewsters they knew, through her then-husband, brewer Larry Horwitz.

The women's respective employers agreed to split the cost of the project, and the trio showed up ready—well, almost—on that snowy Boston morning. A video crew from the brand-new Brewbound beer news site came over to document, and a few weeks later, the three breweries poured one keg each.

After picking up some Project Venus at Victory, I compared it against Allagash's classic *dubbel* in a blind taste test. Project Venus won.

The women thought they were brewing for fun, trying something new and not much more. But Sara Barton, owner of Brewster's Brewing in England, didn't think so. Immediately after hearing what these brewsters were getting up to across the pond, she established Project Venus UK & Eire by bringing in a few female brewers to brew a version of Project Venus, which they sold out of firkins at the Rake bar in London.

Year two brought five women, plus renowned beer blogger Marverine Cole and a crew from BBC2, to Britain's Oldershaw Brewery for version three. Project Venus UK & Eire carried on through 2017, with brewsters rotating through a different brewery every few months.

Meanwhile, in 2013, brewer Sophie de Ronde, who'd participated in the UK brews, amped the idea up to eleven by taking it worldwide. Boosted by local affirmation, Sophie decided to attach an international women's collaboration brew to International Women's Day on March 8 of every year. She contacted Pink Boots for some US support and found an enthusiastic partner in Denise Ratfield, who ran Pink Boots Society's social media and worked a day job at Stone as "cat herder" ("administrative assistant" in the real world).

With Pink Boots Society founder Teri Fahrendorf's approval, Sophie and Denise set the rules: interested parties should cluster at their nearest participating brewery to follow the same predetermined recipe with the closest ingredients they had available, starting at 8:00 AM local time. New Zealand's Ava Wilson brewed the first one of the day at Pomeroy's Pub, followed by groups of brewsters around the globe successively firing up their own kettles as the sun traveled west to reach their cities and turn their clocks to 8:00.

In 2020 women across the world brewed together in one hundred different locations.

As the project grew, Pink Boots's vision for International Women's Collaboration Brew Day grew apart from the one held by Denise and Sophie. Teri and the Pink Boots board split off to start a new women's global brew day. They changed the rules and the name, and though both continue to uneasily coexist, the two disparate yet overlapping strands confuse many an eager adherent.

Despite the confusion, Pink Boots's Collaboration Brew Day attracts big-name sponsors such as Yakima Chief Hops, and sales of the brew support the organization.

Nine years after the original Project Venus, only Laura works at the same place. She's been promoted to small batch brewer and confesses to having a hard time figuring out how much she should assert herself to move up Stone's career ladder. In the fall of 2020, she joined Stone's communications director, Lizzie Yonkin, and four others to announce the Stone Women's Network, which aims to connect women to opportunities within the company by mingling them with higher-ups and coaching them on what steps to take to reach their professional goals. (At just about the same time, Stone announced a new CEO: Maria Stipp, who crossed over from Lagunitas.)

Whitney—who got her first brewing gig at Starr Hill Brewing in central Virginia by standing up at an all-male Master Brewers Association of America meeting and proclaiming that she'd just returned from apprenticing with a master brewer in Germany, did anyone want to hire her—left Victory to work for Cargill. She's since moved to Ohio, where she works as a procurement manager for a regional malting company, Origin Malt, and is raising her eleven-year-old niece with help from her mom and "life-anchor companion," as she calls him.

Megan's visibility, prowess in brewing sour beers, and genuine kindness have led industry trackers to consider her the country's third female rock star brewer, after Carol Stoudt and Kim Jordan. She left Cambridge after a long stay to open the Bluejacket brewpub in Washington, DC's old converted navy yard, owned by the same restaurant group as ChurchKey, the beer bar most outsiders judge to be the best in the district.

Ahead of Bluejacket's grand opening, Megan traveled extensively to brew her own collaboration brews with the top craft brewers on the planet. She was at the restaurant during its construction phase the day a sniper murdered multiple victims in various buildings around the yard. She, a handyman, and two brewing assistants locked the door and stayed away from the tall first-floor windows until they spotted police escorting people out of another building in the late afternoon and bolted to their cars.

She didn't stay at Bluejacket long, returning to eastern Massachusetts to set up an off-site brewhouse for Wormtown before getting the call she'd always wanted: "Hello, Megan. This is so-and-so from Boston Beer Company. We'd like you to come work for us." At Boston Beer, Megan initially worked under Jennifer Glanville in the Jamaica Plain pilot brewery and visitor center, innovating new beers. When Boston Beer took over the prime space in Faneuil Hall, one of Boston's most-visited tourist attractions, executives tapped Megan to lead brewing operations.

21 | STRANGE BREW: DID RENAISSANCE BREWSTERS PRACTICE FERMENTATION . . . OR WITCHCRAFT?

"The witch was in reality the profoundest thinker, the most advanced scientist of those ages. . . . As knowledge has ever been power, the church feared its use in women's hands, and levelled its deadliest blows at her."

—Matilda Joslyn Gage,
American suffragist, 1893

"The number of witches had everywhere become enormous."

—John Jewel,
English bishop and intellectual, 1522–1571

IMAGINE, IF YOU WILL, a scene of horror. The Renaissance has ushered an age of enlightenment into Europe, yet for the past two hundred years, any woman of any age or socioeconomic status has lived under threat that she might be accused of witchcraft and then slaughtered. Though you live a quiet life as a peasant, your mother, aunt, and sister have been systematically murdered without real evidence or justice. Your father spoke up in their defense, and he was executed too.

The History Channel estimates that European authorities hanged or burned alive up to eighty thousand accused witches between 1500 and 1660 (some sources tabulate up to two hundred thousand for approximately the same time period), with Germany massacring the highest number per capita and Ireland killing the fewest. It formed part of a mass control and terror campaign the Roman Inquisition, the Catholic Counter-Reformation against Protestant reforms, and the fledgling professional class of male doctors and lawyers waged against a formerly feudal and newly liberal population as they sought to consolidate their power and redefine the social structure. Twentieth- and twenty-first-century scholars credit the rise of capitalism to their efforts.

This formed a frightening fragment of the Western narrative, certainly. If you're wondering how it relates to beer, the answer is stark: your mom, aunt, and sister were all brewers.

Fast-forward to today. Every year when Halloween creeps up you undoubtedly greet little witches scratching at your door wearing pointy black hats and clutching broomsticks, with some reference to cats and a miniature cauldron or two. You don't think much of it as you drop gummy worms into their plastic pumpkins. These props comprise the quotidian symbols that live in our collective mythology as the trappings of a witch.

But that little sorceress is sporting a costume that could be scarier than anyone realizes. Some journalists have linked those telltale objects to old-world brewsters' tools of the trade.

"Is it a coincidence that the image of medieval brewsters so closely resembles the popular image of a witch, or was foul play perpetrated by persons who wanted to malign female brewers in an era when witch hunting was rife?" writes Jane Peyton, an alcohol historian and Britain's 2014 Beer Sommelier of the Year, on her website, School of Booze.

As we know, the social structure increasingly stacked up against brewsters and alewives in the early modern era, with literature portraying them as sorceresses and the church preaching against the evils of alcohol and the female purveyors who lured men into sin. "If alehouses were 'the devil's schoolhouse,'" writes Judith Bennett, "Then women were the devil's schoolmistresses."

Let's survey the evidence that suggests brewsters form a basis for our conception of witches.

Cats: Considered a familiar that accompanies a witch, cats made themselves valuable staples in the brewster home by devouring the mice and rats who fed on sacks of stored grain.

The pointy hat: Alewives in some regions donned it when they went on excursions to the market so potential customers could spot them above the crowd.

The broomstick: In some areas, regulations required the alewife to post an ale stick, a long stick adhered to twigs, which might have doubled as a broom, above her door to signal to customers and government regulators that she had beer ready to sell.

The cauldron: This is where the magic happened—literally. Picture a home-brewing operation. A massive cauldron of wort bubbles when it boils over a flame, and this wort froths rabidly as it ferments. It looks like a pot full of spells, and when drinkers partake of the potion within, they might act possessed and speak in strange tongues.

For many thousands of years, a mostly illiterate European populace ascribed fermentation to magic. The English actually called the process, "God is Good."

The Welsh/Irish barley goddess Ceridwen personifies this mysticism. According to beer historian Jay Brooks's blog, *Brookston Beer Bulletin*, "Ceridwen owned the witches' cauldron of inspiration, which presumably she filled with barley to make beer, known as the 'Brew of Inspiration and Knowledge.'" The sixteenth-century *Book of Taliesin* chronicles the iconic Welsh bard Taliesin's birth to Ceridwen. Later reviewers suggest Taliesin could actually be Merlin from the story of King Arthur and some indicate the cauldron could, in fact, be the Holy Grail that King Arthur seeks and Monty Python mocks.

The cauldron, in addition to being seen as an ancient feminine symbol of renewal and plenty, has also been a continuous symbol for enlightenment and wisdom. This pot of female wisdom now shows up as a Halloween caricature.

Similarly, Habonde, the Welsh goddess of abundance and prosperity, is described in original tellings as a goddess and later, in Christian accounts, as a witch, thanks to followers honoring her by dancing around one of her totems—a ritualistic fire. Eight months before the festival of Habonde, held on the first Monday of July, Welsh pagans would light the hearth and use the heat to boil what's interpreted to be ale.

Not only do these beer-based tales teach us the origins and importance of some sacred deities and rituals, they also open a fascinating window onto the ways early Catholic evangelists incorporated stories familiar to each of these cultures into their marketing plans to convert Europeans from polytheists into Christians. In some cases, they deified. In others, they demonized.

Irish Catholics still regard Saint Brigid, Irish patron saint of beer, as among their most cherished, thanks to her compassion and proclivity for brewing and performing miracles. Her story resembles that of the goddess Brigit, the Great Mother Goddess of Ireland. Both share the symbol of the Brigid Cross, a square variation on the traditional cross that hangs in Irish homes to ward off evil.

In these narratives, we witness lines blur between fact and fantasy. Was Saint Brigid a living saint who fictionally morphed into a goddess through willful exaggeration and historical word of mouth? Or was it the other way around? Did first-millennium missionaries turn a pagan goddess into a fake saint? Did Brigid exist at all?

Scribes recorded many perceived miracles over the course of her possible life, with a large percentage describing the inexplicable multiplying of food, namely butter and beer. Most often, she is described as a "dairy woman and brewer." The telling of St. Brigid's biggest and most familiar-sounding miracle—turning water into beer—has inspired people long into today. Two Sisters Brewing in Kildare, the birthplace of St. Brigid, make a Brigid Ale.

It wasn't just brewers, saints, and goddesses practicing the magic of fermentation. Up to and through the Renaissance, Europeans of all stripes used herbs and incantations (prayers) for natural healing and other purposes—it was all they had. They called this common holistic and earthbound practice "low magic."

On the other hand, "high magic" consisted of complex rituals practiced by the skilled and relatively educated: alchemy, botany, and "modern" medicine. As schooling formalized, girls, whose household duties kept them from attending, couldn't access this training. While young men earned degrees in the medical arts, increasingly Christian societies shunned the natural healing arts and the women who plied them.

"'Wise women,' herbalists, and old women have been looked on with suspicion in many cultures throughout millennia, so brewsters joined this group where superstitious, uneducated people considered such people to be 'the other,'" explains Peyton in an e-mail.

It's a devilish tale that these comparisons weave. Unfortunately, we must let the facts get in the way of a splendidly sordid story. Since I wrote some of the above words in the now defunct *New Jersey Brew* magazine in 2014, newly unearthed information has convinced me that brewsters did not get specifically targeted for burning at the stake.

For this bit of myth busting, we turn to Christina Wade, a historian specializing in medieval Irish women. She dispels these alleged connections on her deeply researched blog, Braciatrix.

Cats: In the Middle Ages, people associated cats with heresy and the devil, as hinted at in writings by Hildegard von Bingen and Geoffrey Chaucer, but rarely with witchcraft. The first English witch trial to mention a familiar didn't take place until 1556, when Elizabeth Francis was accused of "keeping company" with her cat, whom she dubiously named Satan.

Erica Fudge, an expert in Renaissance petkeeping, argues that society viewed all pet-owning women with "deeply misogynistic" distrust.

Like Wade, Fudge argues society feared that "without a firm (male) hand the woman would make such a mental descent that she would disregard the differences between the species and show herself to be close to the beast; that she might, perhaps even more subversively, misrecognize the role of the man to such an extent that an animal is felt to be able to fill his place; and that she would reenact Eve's temptation by the Devil and make the animals not merely wild, but satanic."

In other words, Wade says of this suspicion, "Women could easily mistake their pets for their husbands."

Pointy hats: The first pointy-hat-wearing witch seems to have emerged in a children's book from the eighteenth century, long past the end of the witch trials. Wade believes the pointed hat image may have simply borrowed from the floppy conical captain and phrygian-style hats popularized by rich sixteenth- and seventeenth-century Europeans or the dunce's cap worn in royal fifteenth-century courts. While the witch trials rampaged through Europe, witches were often drawn naked and bareheaded or merely wearing the attire of the day, which included a two-pronged headpiece called a devil's snare that drew the church's disdain for its indication of a wearer's potential vanity.

Personally, I resonate with scholar Peter Burke's theory in *Eyewitnessing: The Use of Images as Historical Evidence*. He states that the witch's hat and her stereotypical hooked nose at least partly migrated from anti-Semitic medieval artists' paintings of Jews. Burke ties this to a 1421 Hungarian decree that required anyone arrested for a first offense of witchcraft to wear a tall pointed

"Jew's hat," and mentions that heretics in early modern Spain had to wear similar clothes.

Brooms: The idea of a witch riding on a broomstick predates what Wade calls the "demonization of the alewife in art and literature." She points to one of the earliest references in an anonymous thirteenth-century poem from Tirol, in Italy, that reads, "It would be a wondrous thing to see a woman riding a calf, or a broomstick, or a poker, over mountains and villages." Or its root may be as pedestrian as the fact that women owned brooms, and women bore the brunt of witchcraft charges. Open and shut case.

Cauldron: In *The Silver Bough: Scottish Folk-lore and Folk-Belief,* F. Marian McNeill writes that witch trials rarely mentioned a cauldron.

Moving on beyond the iconography, there's little, if any, historical evidence directly linking real brewsters to witch trials. A project to identify and map women tried as witches in Scotland, home to an intense witch hunt between the late sixteenth and early eighteenth centuries, turned up no direct correlation, and according to Wade, a study of the assize records in Essex, England, between 1560 and 1680 found only one woman with a listed connection to a professional brewer—her husband. Remember, she may or may not have brewed alongside him.

However, it does us little good to depend on legal or municipal records when we attempt to cross-reference alewives with witches, as we must, because as Wade reminds us, they list "only the husbands' occupations, and with the exception of perhaps this woman, we do not know if the other accused women of Essex were also brewing in some capacity."

But that doesn't mean there wouldn't have been a great deal of undocumented overlap. The preponderance of female brewers and accused female witches suggests an almost-certain overindexing traceable to the socioeconomic and gender conditions of the day. By deconstructing the parallels between brewsters and alleged witches, we can glean a great deal about the precarious space women inhabited and how beer genuinely did factor into many a witch hunt.

Alan MacFarlane contends in *Witchcraft in Tudor and Stuart England* that witches tended to be poorer than their accusers and often came from the ranks of single or widowed women, laborers, or those married to a yeoman (a middle-class farmer or servant), the most common occupation listed for accused witches' husbands in Essex. Then as now, poor equaled vulnerable to society's whims. And it wasn't just the church that forced the populace to fit into stiff molds; the shifting economic structure did its damage too.

As Marianne Hester explains in *The Witchcraft Reader*, England's population grew rapidly in the early modern period (Jane Peyton counts four million citizens), with women outnumbering men. Not only did the ruling class try to limit and shut down alehouses for fear they would act as breeding grounds for political dissent, but women faced greater competition for the dwindling jobs available to them in any field.

In an example of feminization of poverty, which describes how social and economic conditions usually relegate the lowest paying and least prestigious jobs to women, lower-class women in this society grew ever more impoverished and dependent. In addition, the growing masculinization of for-profit brewing recalibrated the balance of economic power between spouses to the disadvantage of the wives and further disempowered those who weren't legally attached to a man. More often than not, accusers hurled their accusations at women above forty years old, those potentially wise older "crones" who held institutional knowledge or had whiffs of economic independence that the church and upper classes deemed dangerous.

Bennett writes, "Those women who were still able to compete on some economic level, largely widows, were a threat to this new balance and male dominance in the trade, and thus became targets for witchcraft accusations." Accusations of this type served as an efficient means to silence the outspoken, subversive, competitive, or simply unpopular.

E-mails Elizabeth Ewan, "People accused of witchcraft had often built up a long-term reputation for being assertive or quarrelsome in their community before being accused, and I can certainly think of some brewsters who fit that pattern."

Bennett stipulates that men deliberately spread rumors about alewives to ruin their businesses. She cites two examples, the first in 1413, when a man destroyed brewster Christine Colmere's livelihood by telling her neighbors she had leprosy; and the second in 1641 when the male competitor of an unnamed but reputable widow brewing at the Ludlow castle garrison spread false gossip about her and destroyed her trade.

In Scotland, more common than the brewster-as-bad-girl meme was the notion of ordinary people wielding witchcraft accusations as a weapon of retaliation. Says Scottish witchcraft historian Julian Goodwine, "If two people had a quarrel, and if one of them subsequently suffered a misfortune, then that person could conclude that the misfortune was the result of the other person's witchcraft. This conclusion would be particularly likely if the quarrel had included threats or curses."

"There are a number of cases where the accused had supposedly cursed their neighbors' malt or spoiled their beer," adds Sierra Dye, a Canadian academic who specializes in Scottish history.

In *The Silver Bow*, F. Marian McNeill explains that, according to tradition, when a witch wanted to take away her neighbor's "profit from the malt," she "took her cursing bone and made her way to his croft between sunset and cock-crow," and might have dangled a pot above the brewing liquid. The bone, stained ivory with age, "appears to be that of a deer," and is enclosed in dark bog oak. "This is obviously a phallic symbol," the book continues, "to which the 'witches' were notoriously addicted."

Consider that the accused and the accuser in this case would have likely both been women, who, Ewan writes in *Crimes or Culture*, kept a check on one another's morals, lest they be accused of immorality or heresy first. "Certain women, especially those of the elite, were considered to be 'good women' of whom a higher moral standard of behaviour, especially sexual behaviour, was expected. Reputation was a valuable commodity which could, however, be lost," she writes. "Women, indeed, were among those who policed such ideals most carefully."

Ironically, a woman had to take care in how she called out another's behavior, as many an aggrieved Scottish woman found herself facing criminal charges for scolding someone in public.

When pagan brewster Kathleen Culhane developed her former brewery in Saint Paul, Minnesota, she buried crystals in the corners of the taproom, called it Sidhe to honor a piece of Irish folklore, and designed a logo that visually depicted brewing as a process of nature in five interlinked diamond shapes, as she explained in an article from online beer journal *October*.

"If you think about beer, your grain is earth, your hops are air—because aroma—fire and yeast are equivalent, because they both consume fuel and make something else, and of course, water is water," she told writer Kara Newman. "You combine those four and you get the fifth element, a spirit—which is alcohol! It's glorious."

In her most recent job as a brewmaster in Superior, Wisconsin, she continued a tradition she started as a homebrewer and practiced religiously at Sidhe: performing a sacred earth-inspired ritual to bless every batch she made. Kathleen, who identifies as Wiccan, was back at a brewery where she'd worked in the past—one coincidentally named the Thirsty Pagan.

Kathleen is one of a very few openly identifying pagans to practice professional brewing in America. According to an article in *Good Beer Hunting*, Margaux Moses, owner, brewer, and professed witch at Wave Maiden Ale Works in Los Angeles, is one. She creates a sacred space by burning something—sage, perhaps, or a leaf—around her equipment before every brew and sets an intention, reads a poem or a prayer, and calls in the four directions of the earth. And as research and development brewer at Portland's Breakside Brewery, Natalie Rose Baldwin brings intuition and intention to her beers, sometimes timing them to the seasons or the solstice.

Some pagan brewsters may also call upon Icovellauna, the Ouranian goddess of ale brewing, to watch over their magic making. Writes Jay Brooks, "In occult and magic circles, Ouranian Barbaric is a language and world all its own, and [Icovellauna] is also often thought of a goddess of healing and a spring water deity."

For Kathleen, brewing is how she worships. "I think of this as a meditative exercise to focus my energy and intent to get as much of my spirit into this beer as I can," she tells me. Just as she ties some of her brews to pagan festivals or celebrations to honor the dead, she names some of her beers—such as Dark Moon Rising and Indian Pagan Ale—accordingly. As with many brewsters—pagan, agnostic, Jewish, Christian, or other—she draws not just from her spiritual beliefs but from respect for those women who came before her.

"Like an artisan today, some people who brewed [in the past] focused on a recognition that the materials themselves are alive and that there is a deeper communication involved," e-mails the poet Stephen Harrod Buhner, who wrote *Sacred and Herbal Healing Beers*. "The process was much deeper, more mystical."

22 | THESE BOOTS ARE MADE FOR BREWING

WHEN TERI FAHRENDORF talks about her early years as a brewer, she usually starts by describing herself as a "skinny kid" who didn't pilgrimage to the famous European breweries with her all-male cohort of brewing colleagues because she was too shy to ask to share their hotel room. Instead, she set about to go on her own, doing her best to schedule meetings with key point people via fax at one dollar per page.

To prove to the old masters that she indeed helmed a shiny ten-barrel brewery she dragged pounds of snapshots, swag, and technical brewing magazines along on her trip, an added weight that almost failed to convince Cantillon's legendary Jean-Pierre Van Roy, who, she recalls, first declined to meet with her then came to observe her from his glass-walled office, where he "looked down at me from under his eyebrows."

"They'd never heard of a woman brewer. They didn't believe me," she says.

This was 1994, and the young woman who grew up in a suds-drinking Wisconsin family had already interned and worked at four breweries in Chicago, Northern California, and Oregon. Through that decade and the following, Teri studied brewing technology at the world-renowned Siebel Institute of Technology then went on to train a total of fifty-one subordinates at breweries where she worked. And, as longtime brewmaster at Eugene, Oregon's Steelhead Brewing, she oversaw a team that won twenty-four Great American Beer Festival medals during her tenure.

By 2007, Teri, who had become the nation's first nonowner female craft brewmaster in 1988, was ready for a break from full-time brewing. She quit

Steelhead, and on June 4, the then-forty-seven-year-old packed the new pink rubber brewing boots her mother-in-law had given her as a good-luck parting gift and jumped in the Astro Van and "Fun Finder" Cruise RV camper that, after her cross-country drive, still sits in her Portland driveway covered in beer stickers.

About two weeks into her five-month cross-country road trip, Teri pulled into Stone Brewing outside San Diego for her scheduled day as a guest brewer.

She says, "I'd been invited to several breweries, and when I got to Stone they said, 'You're going to be brewing with Laura Ulrich.' I thought, 'Wow. A woman brewer. Cool!'"

Laura had never thought about making a career as a "woman brewer." She'd previously worked the packaging line with a female colleague at Odell, yet she didn't have any female role models or coworkers on the brewing floor at Stone.

Teri's visit got her thinking, "Oh, there are women who actually brew?"

That night, the two women went to dinner where it became clear to Teri that Laura craved female peers. Laura remembers Teri validating her suspicions that some of her male coworkers might not have necessarily taken her as seriously as they took themselves.

On the spot, Teri came up with a mission: she would collect the names of all the woman brewers she could find. Along the rest of her journey to seventy-one breweries, she asked people she encountered if they knew women in the business. By the time she got to the East Coast, she'd gathered sixty names. And that's when she met Whitney Thompson, then a brewer at Tröegs in central Pennsylvania.

Teri says, "I got to Tröegs and they said, 'You're going to brew with Whitney.' And Whitney said to me, 'You're a female brewer? I thought I was the only one!'"

Again, Teri ate dinner with her younger colleague and again realized how deeply this woman needed to connect. "It was almost this energetic hanging on to my elbow sort of thing," she remembers. She left Whitney with a promise to post her growing list of female beer professionals online as a networking tool. Soon Teri started receiving e-mails from beer bloggers asking if they could repost the list. Shortly after that, e-mails arrived from around the country. The women would write things like, "Hi, I'm the packaging manager at Bell's. May I join?" Teri's reaction: "Holy crap, I didn't know this was something you could join!"

When Teri returned home at the end of her trip, she moved to Portland, Oregon, where her husband had started a new job. She called Laura to suggest a meeting for the women on the list at the 2008 Craft Brewers Conference in San Diego the following April. Laura agreed and organized a meeting for these isolated, eager women, and with help from Jessica Gilman, then an assistant brewer at Gordon Biersch, Laura hosted a beer brunch. Sixteen female brewers and six female beer journalists sipped beer they'd brought from their home breweries and marveled—over linen tablecloths and fresh pink flowers—that they'd found one another.

They also worked out some business. Would they remain a list or become an organization? Organization. Would they include men? No. Would they accept nonbrewing beer professionals? Yes. By the end of the day, the sixteen founding brewer-members of the newly named Pink Boots Society determined that the group stood for three things: women, beer professionals, and free membership for any woman earning at least one dollar of her income from beer.

"We wanted to be inclusive," Teri says. The next meeting took place six months later at the Great American Beer Festival in Denver, where participants decided the group should focus primarily on educating and empowering the industry's women in ways that could help them further their careers and mentor those who follow.

For the next nine years, Pink Boots ran national and then international campaigns that, among other things, encouraged beer lovers to introduce their moms to beer by sharing one on Mother's Day; brought women together at breweries around the world to brew for International Women's Day in March; and twice a year, during CBC and Great American Beer Fest, host a members meeting to pass along organizational information, sample one another's beers, buy Pink Boots Society–branded merchandise, swap job leads and advice, and, more than anything, find some solidarity.

After the October 2010 Great American Beer Festival meeting, then–membership coordinator Anita Lum wrote in her personal notes: "The growth in membership is picking up pace. In March 2010 when I started helping out with the membership we were at about three hundred members. Just a few months later, we have grown to over 470! And, from what I observed at the GABF award announcement ceremony alone, there are plenty more women out there that are automatically eligible members of [Pink Boots Society]—they just haven't officially signed up. At the Denver meeting we had representation from just about all parts of the US and many international locations including Great Britain, Canada and Sweden."

"[Pink Boots] gives you a free place to get some support and advice and not get mansplained to, or to ask about problems that are very specific to women trying to navigate their place in the industry," explains Philadelphia chapter leader Erin Wallace.

Between meetings and an active private Facebook group (now disbanded and incorporated into a members-only forum on the website), members pose questions and give answers on topics from how to deal with sexism in the workplace to where to get the right kind of shoes to do this work and what are the best bras for brewing.

Portland brewer Lee Hedgmon is on record as saying she remembers one meaningful Facebook group conversation about the need to develop institutional changes to create safe workspaces for women. Someone had suggested the unusual and revolutionary idea of helping women manage physically difficult brewery tasks by incorporating an ethos of "Let's carry this together," versus the standard, "Can you carry it?" or "Let me carry it."

Meanwhile, as the group grew past twenty-five hundred international members, Teri, Laura, Anita, and a changing roster of three hundred volunteers scrambled to keep up. Pink Boots needed people to coordinate the two annual meetings, committees, membership, activities, fundraisers, sponsorships, merchandise, web presence, internal and external communications, media outreach, and more. Anyone willing to do something, anything, would be tapped for the job.

Anita started helping out with the website and membership responsibilities in early 2010. With no organizational money, there was no real website or membership roster and instead of a published calendar or list of events, "We had a hodgepodge 'we're going to meet at (fill in the blank),'" she says.

After putting together a database and a rudimentary home page, she relinquished her duties to graphic designer Sibyl Perkins, who could give Pink Boots the website it needed.

Sibyl, who in 2018 won the first Teri Fahrendorf Legacy Award for donating countless hours of her agency's time to the cause, says that taking on the website evolved into "responsibility for the overall brand, graphic design, a new logo, and helping to shape the image."

Then there was the matter of scholarships. To truly fulfill its mission to educate and empower, Teri felt Pink Boots needed to offer scholarships to assorted courses, conferences, and educational trips. But before it could legally raise funds, it had to become a nonprofit.

After floundering with IRS requirements for four years, Teri submitted her ninety-eight-page application to file as a 501(c)(3) charity, with tremendous assistance from her mother-in-law. It took another year of phone tag with the IRS before Pink Boots Society was awarded tax-exempt status in 2012. Teri immediately put together the first six scholarships to launch the Pink Boots scholarship program.

Pink Boots offered its first scholarship to Siebel's web-based Concise Course in Brewing Technology in May 2013. It went to Swedish brewer Jessica Heidrich.

"The goal was always to get a scholarship situation going, and of course now we have. But [at the beginning] it was just a dream," muses Anita, who unofficially ran stateside operations for her son and daughter-in-law's company, Maui Brewing.

For all its merit, scholarship management called for even more womanpower, and Teri knew she was overwhelming her volunteers. Worse, the always energetic Teri, who'd become famous as the voice for women in the industry, was burning out.

In 2014 and 2015, Laura and Denise Jones remember an anguished Teri, who'd had no choice but to let Pink Boots take over most of her nonworking hours, telling them that she couldn't keep it going without significantly more help. If needed, she was ready to close Pink Boots and disperse the collected donations as required by IRS regulations.

Luckily, that step was not needed. Active members mobilized. They set up a new board and contracted executive assistant Emily Engdahl as its first paid employee to take over daily operations. Teri, who by then had transitioned from brewery management into full-time work at Great Western Malting, stepped aside to let the board, helmed by incoming president Laura Ulrich, make future decisions. Teri says, "After that big all-weekend board meeting where I passed the baton to Laura, I cried my eyes out. My girl was grown up and had left for college."

Because Teri had spent nine years building value, the board switched to a dues-paying model of thirty-five dollars per year to generate additional income and simultaneously raised members' minimum beer-income requirement to 25 percent. A formal transition to retire Teri came in May 2016, at the CBC meeting I organized in Philadelphia, where, after a semifrantic all-nighter spent revising and rerevising the schedule and speeches, Teri gracefully and emotionally handed over her baby.

Laura confesses her role overwhelmed her then and overwhelmed her every day until she turned it over to vice president Jen Jordan in 2021. "When Teri was ready to throw the ball, it was on fire, and when I caught it was like, 'Oh shit it's hot,'" she says. Laura worried about everything: figuring out Teri's manual accounting system, following in Teri's "captivating" shoes, fundraising as someone who doesn't like talking to people, disagreeing with Teri on charging dues and whether to set up systems versus lingering in the realm of the grassroots, turning volunteers into overworked de facto staff. In short, Laura was panicking.

The board moved Emily from part- to full-time then eventually eliminated the executive assistant position and in its place hired a professional management company called Scientific Societies, which works with scientific organizations like the Master Brewers Association of the Americas.

Four years into Laura's leadership, a day didn't pass that she doesn't think about how much both she and Teri have conflated Pink Boots with their own identity. She feared from her first day to her last that she'd mess things up so much that she'd lose her job at Stone and ruin the beloved organization.

To ensure the transition to a new president went as smoothly as possible, Laura intended to see Jen through her first few months to pass along what she calls her "tribal knowledge" and set Jen up for success so she doesn't carry the same internalized pressure that her two predecessors have.

"I believe the success and trajectory of Pink Boots never should ever have to feel like that again," Laura says.

Despite the internal growing pains, present-day Pink Boots can boast many indicators of success. On its tenth anniversary, the mayor of San Diego declared an official Pink Boots Day, which the organization marked with a conference and beer festival in the city where it was born. As the lead sponsor, Stone donated $50,000, and Megan Parisi flew in to give the keynote.

The following year, the Brewers Association's Julia Herz gave the keynote, and the two-day conference in Austin covered topics from sour beers to discrimination law. Two members from Texas proposed and planned that one, as if to show the growing strength of the local chapters that started forming a few years ago.

Numerically, the once-centralized nonprofit has seventy-two chapters with paid members living in seven countries from Australia to Peru. A new scholarship structure allows chapters to raise their own money to fund educational events and conferences in their own communities, along with scholarships earmarked for local members.

I helped spearhead the birth of the Philly chapter ahead of the Craft Brewers Conference's arrival to town in 2016, and founding president Erin Wallace, who owns the Devil's Den bar in South Philly, has grown the chapter from twenty-five members in 2018 to around ninety today. With the recent ability to charge local dues and keep 90 percent of the funds the chapter generates from all sources, she's also facilitated an incredible number of educational events.

To name just a few, the chapter has hosted a free off-flavor class, sponsored lectures with the University of the Sciences brewing program, raffled off tickets to the Philly Grain and Malt Symposium, paid to send members to the annual Brewers of Pennsylvania Symposium, and produced the day-long Bold Women and Beer Festival that raised $15,000 for local member scholarships.

That said, not everyone sees Pink Boots as a golden opportunity to equalize the gender playing field. Over the years, men have complained that it excludes and maybe even demonizes them, and women have criticized it for ghettoizing women as "female brewers" rather than plain old brewers.

"Dick Cantwell [cofounder of Seattle's Elysian Brewing] once joked to me, 'Why can't I join? I'll wear pink boots,'" says Carol Stoudt, a supporter with mixed feelings over segregating herself.

Diversity and inclusion specialist Dr. J. Jackson-Beckham, who works in the beer space, says she's happy to make space for those women who don't find it necessary to create their own space but doesn't believe we've quite arrived at a place where we no longer need it.

And Laura, who calls Pink Boots an "absolute necessity," compares it to the gender-segregated Girl Scouts and Boy Scouts, which each ostensibly tailor programs to girls' and boys' specific developmental needs. "People sometimes need someone else to speak for them and stand up for their needs and wants," she says. "We're providing educated professionals to the brewing industry. We're helping the brewers. Why is that a negative?"

As a member since 2010 who's served as both historian and archivist, I can say with 100 percent certainty that Pink Boots in no way demeans men in its objective to educate and empower women. As per Teri's strict orders, it keeps complete political neutrality, welcomes guys to some events, prohibits public negativity of any kind, and doesn't meddle in labor disputes. Ever.

Rose Ann Finkel saw it as a simple net positive for bringing women back into beer. "If we're going to give women the tools to excel in an industry that was theirs to begin with," she said, "they need the support."

23 | COMING TO AMERICA

I HAVE A SHAMEFUL SECRET TO REVEAL.

I've written about Philadelphia's beer history for national publications and the region's official tourism bureau for a decade and a half, nearly as long as I've lived in the area. In an effort to raise my adopted city's underdog reputation, I've spent that time bragging about its long list of firsts.

Notably, as practically any American with an education recognizes, the capital of Colonial America drew the nation's founding fathers (yes, all wealthy White men) from the thirteen original colonies here to write the Declaration of Independence and Constitution in its taverns and—lesser known fact—establish institutions such as the country's original postal service, fire station, public lending library, and zoo. Most local beer people can tell you that John Wagner gets credit—and a state historical marker—for brewing the nation's first lager, in 1840.

But almost no one knows the name of Philadelphia daughter Mary Lisle, the first woman on record to own a commercial brewery in the lower forty-eight. And until well into my research for this book, that "no one" included me. Not surprisingly, not much of Mary's history survives, but we know from legal records that her father, Henry Badcock, bequeathed her the Edinburgh Brewhouse upon his death in 1734. To her sister, Elizabeth, he willed his malthouse. Mary hired a brewer and ran the business until she sold it in 1751.

The property would have likely transferred to their mother, also named Mary, had she not predeceased her husband. Mary Sr. likely passed on the tradition of teaching her daughters to homebrew, as Henry mentions his wife six times in the contract he signed to bring an apprentice into his factory.

"Anthony Morris," he wrote, "Hath put himself an apprentice to Henry Badcock of Philadelphia aforesaid Brewer & Mary his wife. . . . and doth covenant & promise to . . . well & faithfully serve . . . Henry & Mary as his Master & Mistress."

By the time the Pilgrims left the British Isles more than one hundred years before Mary took over her father's brewery, rural English women did still homebrew, though cities had already transitioned into commercial brewing centers governed by men. The Mayflower Pilgrims would have likely drunk both hopped beer and unhopped ale before casting off.

Beer lovers argue over whether the Mayflower actually docked in Plymouth—not their intended destination—because they ran out of beer. The story is basically true, according to Plymouth Plantation governor Wiliam Bradford, who wrote in his account of the Pilgrims that he and around one hundred passengers "were hasted ashore and made to drink water that the seamen might have the more beere" for their return voyage.

Whether or not the Pilgrims mistakenly believed that the pristine waters of the unspoiled land would harm them just like it might have back home (food historian Marc Meltonville contradicts conventional wisdom here again by arguing Renaissance Europe enjoyed perfectly potable water), they immediately set up a common house for brewing. Then they built houses outfitted with kitchen breweries for the women to make beer—as soon as possible, yes, please, and thank you.

Very shortly after coming to America, seventeenth-century European immigrants such as the Pilgrims set up common brewhouses, taverns, and commercial breweries in the population centers of Boston, New Amsterdam (New York), Philadelphia, and others. But as soon as they crossed outside a city border or south of the Mason-Dixon line, old traditions prevailed and women brewed at home while their menfolk generally worked the farms.

When Ellen Wayles Randolph Coolidge got married in Boston, her mother wrote from Virginia to tell her that she hadn't sent beer recipes because they'd prove useless to a town lady such as herself.

"Nor," she wrote, "do I presume you will ever brew your own beer."

That letter notwithstanding, scant documentation survives on colonial brewsters. Even though women ran practically every aspect of their households, colonial law kept women from owning property or suing in court, depriving scholars of records that might have mentioned them.

Even though women commonly ran taverns, also called ordinaries, either out of her house or in a separate facility, men, it seems, usually handled the bookkeeping. In *Every Home a Distillery*, Sarah Hand Meacham says that because most Chesapeake Bay–area women of the day were illiterate and innumerate, historians in the region have yet to uncover a single journal, diary, or letter written in their hand.

Here again we see misogynistic history repeat itself. Many an Old World explorer has landed on our shores in an attempt to discover freedom from the old country's rigid ways. But just as America's promise that "all men are created equal" did not initially include all men or any women, this turning of the page from Europe to the Americas didn't necessarily start a new chapter for women's rights. It simply revealed that the flip side of the paper read almost exactly the same as the first.

In other words, like preceding civilizations seas and centuries apart, colonial America eliminated women from the record while taking advantage of their often unpaid labor. That is, until brewing showed significant financial promise.

"When money got involved, men increasingly started brewing," writes Gregg Smith in his book, *Beer in America, The Early Years: 1587–1840*. "As the industry developed, it went that way even more."

At first, Boston led the colonies in for-profit brewing. Settlers established the first licensed tavern there in 1633, and the first commercial brewery in 1637. New York and Philadelphia followed. The Chesapeake Bay region, consumed with tobacco farming, trailed far behind. Says Meacham, "Chesapeake colonists continued to rely on women to make alcohol for at least one hundred years after Europe, New England, and the Middle Colonies had turned to alcoholic beverages produced by men."

According to Smith, Virginia colonists brewed their first beer in 1584. That's nineteen years after Spanish explorer Pedro Menendez de Aviles named the continent's first permanent European settlement after St. Augustine, the patron saint of brewers, and almost thirty years before the founding of Jamestown as its first permanent English settlement. Virginia, like its more sophisticated northern counterparts, relied heavily on imported British malt for subsequent decades.

Malting barley didn't grow well on the East Coast and Virginians were too preoccupied with their tobacco fields, anyway. Luckily for Virginia, its overwhelmingly British-American population kept strong ties with England, and in the late seventeenth century its ports welcomed approximately one hundred fifty ships from England each year.

In terms of trade, Virginia interacted more with London than with New England or the Middle Colonies of Pennsylvania, New York, New Jersey, and Delaware. Its harbors docked just three or four ships from New England annually and even fewer from New York and Philadelphia. No thanks to nearly nonexistent roads and the fact that colonies that did grow a little barley, oats, or hops jealously guarded their crops for themselves, Meacham says that even in the eighteenth century, production of cider and unhopped ale in the Chesapeake "resembled that of rural England in the sixteenth century."

I write unhopped ale instead of beer because women in the tobacco colonies of Virginia, Maryland, and a bit of North Carolina, like most supply-starved colonists, replaced hops and barley with spruce, birch, molasses, sassafras, pumpkin, parsnip, walnut chips, dried and baked persimmon, Jerusalem artichoke, and a lot of flint corn.

When American schoolchildren learn about the Thanksgiving holiday, their teachers tell them the Pilgrims traded with the Native people for corn. This holds true for Chesapeake colonists, too, though they didn't benefit from Native brewing knowledge like others did because the Indigenous people in their vicinity didn't make alcohol.

According to Tiah Edmunson-Morton, Apache, Maricopa, Pima, and Tohono O'odham women in other parts of the land made a ritualistic beer/wine from the saguaro cactus, called *tiswin*. She says Apache women also produced a corn product similar to Mexican beer called *tulpi* or *tulapa* for the puberty rites ceremonies of girls.

She writes on an Oregon State University library webpage, "This included four days of prayer, fasting, the consumption of ritual food and drink, and runs dedicated to the White Painted Lady, an Apache deity."

But Virginia's Pamunkey and other neighboring tribes did no such thing. For this reason, in addition to the fact that imported shipments of barley, malt, beer, or ale could be sporadic and of poor quality, southern colonists primarily slaked their thirst for alcohol with apple cider and brandy.

When they did want beer, wives of middling-income farmers purchased ingredients from larger farms, and they relied on their husbands, kids, and enslaved women and men for brewing help. Wives of large-scale farmers sometimes hired male servants and almost always employed slave labor.

Enslaved people, for their part, could partake in alcohol but under very strict rules, and an enslaved woman named Anaka Prue got punished once for climbing through her master's cellar window to steal, as the master later described it, "some strong beer and cider and wine."

Beer and cider, says Meacham, were the two beverages colonists literally couldn't live without. She writes, "In a place where the water was unsafe, milk was generally unavailable, tea and coffee were too expensive for all but the very wealthy, and soda and non-alcoholic fruit juice were not yet invented, alcoholic beverages were all that colonists could drink safely."

Some wealthy colonial women took a nip every day for their stamina, and women who couldn't afford spirits considered low-alcohol beer and cider healthy daily drinks for the whole family. They and their enslaved people used them to treat everything from a runny nose to hysteria, and breastfeeding women drank hoppy beer to help their milk run.

Beer was so critical to the functioning of the family that Meacham reports an Englishman named John Hammond severely castigated the brewsters of Maryland and Virginia in 1656 for failing to make enough corn-based ale to meet the colonies' needs. Calling these multitasking wives and mothers negligent, idle, careless, and slothful, he admonished, "They will be judged by their drinks, what kind of housewives they are."

No one could dispute what kind of wife Elizabeth Haddon was. She proved herself one of New Jersey's most resourceful colonial women starting at twenty-one years old when her ill father sent her over from England to claim a five-hundred-acre parcel of land he'd bought in the colony of West Jersey. Not long after she made safe landing in 1701, she named the land Haddon's Field (now Haddonfield), then allegedly scandalized her family and friends by proposing marriage to Quaker minister John Estaugh in a courtship that Henry Wadsworth Longfellow immortalized in the poem "Elizabeth."

The president of the Historical Society of Haddonfield calls the unusual proposal a compelling myth. Nevertheless, Elizabeth and John did marry, and in 1715, the couple built a three-story brick mansion on the property with a brewhouse and distillery that still stands in back.

Elizabeth kept herself very busy brewing, distilling, and serving as clerk of the local Quaker women's meeting for almost fifty years after her father directed her to build a meetinghouse and cemetery. She learned the properties of medicinal plants from the surrounding Native Lenape tribe and applied her knowledge to mixing up medicines and serving as doctor to many a sick associate.

Elizabeth controlled her own affairs and even managed other people's estates until she died at the very old age of eighty-two. Thanks to Elizabeth's influence, Haddonfield emerged as the commercial center of South Jersey and, to the delight of many a visitor and homeowner, still retains its leafy and historic charm.

Though it's not clear if Elizabeth Haddon sold any beer, many colonial brewsters made a side hustle out of their excess ale by fashioning a tavern on their property. Frequently, a woman would own the tavern with her husband, with the deed in the man's name. Marc Meltonville says in these cases the matron usually ran the front of the house while the husband brewed in back.

In another kind of common setup, the woman handled all of the business and brewing responsibilities while performing multiple additional household and moneymaking tasks. Her husband likely did some other type of work entirely.

Meacham says that in addition to contributing to family incomes and socializing with neighbors and visitors, "Women could run taverns out their homes while they raised children, oversaw servants and slaves, grew herbs and vegetables, dipped candles, sewed clothes, washed laundry, made cider, and cooked dinner."

In the second half of the seventeenth century these brewsters would, as in the past, advertise beer to passersby and tax collectors by erecting an ale stake—often a pole with a bush or hop bines tied to one end—outside their doors. In the eighteenth century, middling Chesapeake wives and wealthy widows most frequently filled the role of official tavern keeper because lawmakers believed they'd serve as a civilizing influence on unruly patrons.

The stakes for maintaining order were high, as taverns held enormous influence in their communities. These gathering spots doubled as hotels, meeting rooms, game parlors, exhibition sites for exotic animals, retail boutiques, trading depots, and unofficial lending banks.

As the daughter of Thomas Jefferson, Martha Jefferson didn't operate a tavern. But she developed a reputation for brewing excellent wheat beer at her family's Monticello estate in Charlottesville, Virginia, where she moved to care for her father after her mother, also named Martha and also a prolific brewer, died. As brewmaster, she worked with the enslaved Peter Hemings (brother of Sally and esteemed gourmet chef, James) to brew all-grain beer with quality hops that gave beer-curious dignitaries an extra reason to pay her father a visit.

Martha prided herself on bargaining for ingredients, once writing that she'd "bought 7 lbs of hops with an old shirt." Eventually a hop garden was planted at Monticello and her enslaved staff did the malting on-site as well.

While it seems that Mr. Jefferson, as they call him in Charlottesville, did write his own recipes and did some of his own brewing, his daughter and Peter were the true stars. Though men around the world asked the statesman for brewing advice and sent their servants to Monticello to learn for themselves, he never attained Martha's level of skill. Not only did she brew enough beer to fill eighteen hundred glasses her first year home, her father bragged about her prowess in a letter inviting James Madison to spend a day brewing with the best.

Between 1797 and 1801, Thomas served as second-in-command to second president John Adams (cousin of Sam). Unlike his peers of the day, President Adams completely trusted his cherished wife, Abigail, to manage not just their homestead but their farming, too. In many letters home, he asked her about the condition of the barley fields and apple orchards.

Though he called her "so valorous and noble a farmer," he may have engaged in a bit of presidential mansplaining when, according to Gregg Smith, "he couldn't help offering advice about how to manure the barley field."

Local ordinances determined who could run taverns, with seventeenth-century Massachusetts Bay Colony Puritans, for example, limiting licenses to well-off men whom they believed would best keep order. After 1720, the Anglicans who took over the colony favored poor women for tavern ownership to keep them off the dole. Widows, especially those of tavern owners, could support themselves with this type of income just about everywhere.

For instance, Dorchester, Massachusetts, authorities twice allowed Dorothy "Goody" Upsall to officially take over the inn her husband owned: first when he went to jail and again after he died.

In the buildup to revolution, two female-owned ordinaries in New England found particular renown with the rebel crowd. In Portland, Maine, the widow Alice Greele hosted three decades of pre- and postwar planning beginning in the 1750s. And after the death of the war hero Israel Putnam, who had led the Yankees in the Battle of Bunker Hill, his widow, Avery Gardiner Putnam, carried on his legacy as a tavern owner in Connecticut.

Back in Boston, a Harvard student, a woman called Sister Bradish, earned her place in the annals of the university at the turn of the eighteenth century for selling good off-campus beer. Students must have raised some glasses to their university president, as well, when he defended her against parents who complained that their children were spending their money on her beer instead of books.

Despite claiming the title of America's first non-Indigenous brewing hot spot, brewing didn't continue to catch on in Boston as it did in New York then later in Philadelphia. In 1810, the nation's first brewing census enumerated 132 licensed brewhouses: 48 in Pennsylvania, 42 in New York, and 13 in Ohio.

Smith writes, "Vigorous economic growth encouraged [town and city dwellers] to indulge in the luxury of buying commercially brewed beer. Greater turnover of currency placed more luxuries, including relief from household work, within reach of the growing populace."

Producers and ingredient suppliers couldn't keep up as drinkers insistently demanded more ale, more beer, more cider, more wine, and more whiskey, rum, and brandy. Some taverns could sell all of the above while others could only sell beer and cider.

As more currency started circulating around the colonies and merchants began making sales calls farther away, ordinaries grew in number and began to occupy an even greater share of daily life. Finally, demand for barley and hops forced certain states, such as New York, to launch their industries in earnest. As these agricultural pursuits expanded, they required a structure and labor force that homebrewing women couldn't afford or access.

But that didn't stop the nation from clamoring for ever greater quantities of alcohol, with intoxicating beverages showing up everywhere, even at church services, in court proceedings, as part of political procedures, and on the job.

By 1770, says Meacham, Americans drank a "startling" amount of alcohol: the equivalent of seven daily shots of rum for the average White man and almost two pints of hard cider per day for the average White woman.

It didn't take much time at all for municipal leaders to worry about overconsumption and other ill effects. From the earliest days of the colonies, they regulated alcohol as they did back home in England and still do today. According to Lauren Clark, Concord, Massachusetts's town fathers decreed as early as 1635 that no one could run a tavern without a license, and in 1651 they limited brewing to those they deemed to have "sufficient skill and knowledge in the art or mastery of a brewer." In 1637 Puritans in the Bay Colony restricted the number of tavern licenses for fear of allowing too many to operate. The same year they ordered tavern keepers to stop brewing their own beer and buy exclusively from a licensed brewer. There was just one problem in that last law: the colony had only licensed one brewer and he clearly couldn't supply everyone. This edict bore little consequence. Most people ignored most of those laws anyway, to the indirect benefit of women who earned income from brewing. More often than not, women, who have historically lacked access to political and economic capital, lose when the authorities get involved in sanctioning the production or sale of ale.

The same can be said of the times when brewing grows beyond its origins as a localized mercantile endeavor. Before revolutionary zeal swept the colonies, each one acted as an independent agent in matters of trade with the others and sometimes enacted protectionist policies that pushed colonists to import goods they couldn't make within their own borders. This pushed them to either import alcohol from abroad or rely on local suppliers. This worked out well for brewsters who earned money from their craft, particularly after shipping costs became increasingly prohibitive and tensions rose with the motherland.

However, it backfired for brewsters when mounting tariffs on British goods and the anger that ensued brought activists from up and down the Eastern Seaboard into so much solidarity against England that they began boycotting British products and even collectively refused a shipment of malt. While this new nationalism may have boosted brewsters' sales a bit, the high earning potential ended up pushing more patriots into brewing beer for commercial use.

Though the fervor started building before the war, it primarily played out afterward. Philadelphia's beer and porter production doubled in 1788, and the commonwealth shipped more beer than the rest of the United States combined to ports as far away as China.

With these expanded networks came the scientific progress needed to support it.

Rich Wagner writes that by the end of the eighteenth century, breweries had mechanized grinding malt and pumping liquid. Brewers reduced the time it took to cool wort by directing fans at the hot tanks then ran insulated cold water pipes to further accelerate the drop in heat. Philadelphia brewery owner Francis Perot installed one of the first stationary steam engines to power most of his brewing processes. Not only did the steam engine replace the need for some industrial labor, these mechanical advancements chipped away at the need for at-home labor too.

"The advent of technological advances," writes Meacham, contributed to "the masculinization of alcohol production in the second half of the eighteenth century."

This technological pressure wasn't just cooking in America. An era of scientific discovery was sweeping England, and Meacham argues its advocates were consciously turning cookery into chemistry by telling men that "a man who had mastered alcoholic beverage production did not need to feel ashamed of performing women's work."

Evidence of this was everywhere, most notably in the pages of published instructional guides. Whereas beer recipes used to readily show up in women's cookbooks that assumed readers already knew how to perform the basics, a new generation of husbandry texts geared to men detailed every step of the process using intentionally serious-sounding words such as specimen, alkali, and narcotic. As drink recipes started disappearing from the pages of cookbooks or referring to "his" malt and "his" apples, these scientific manuals seemed intent on turning brewing into a job for men by lecturing them to transform the feminine art and mystery of producing alcohol into a masculine skill that required certainty and mastery.

The Complete Distiller, written in 1757, tells men that "distillation, tho[ugh] long practiced [by women] has not been carried out to the degree of perfection that might reasonably be expected" because female distillers were of the "idle opinion" that their process was difficult to understand thus didn't need improvement. The author assured his readership he would teach men how to "proceed on rational principles."

To those men who might doubt or disagree, authors warned that women used too much intuition in their process to brew or distill properly. They went so far as to accuse women of not being able to decipher bio-available malt from spent grain and cautioned men that letting a servant girl assist them in their own efforts would lead to inevitable mistakes that would discredit them undeservedly.

Meacham says hundreds of these books proliferated in the colonies alone. The impact became obvious when parents eventually stopped passing their production equipment down to their daughters and started willing it directly to their sons.

Despite these almost innumerable threats to women's alchemic artistry, the most sinister was yet to come. England packaged and shipped its first Industrial Revolution to our shores at the end of the 1700s, and German immigrants began populating the new nation in the early 1800s, bringing a new style of beer with them. Why, as Smith asks, drink the old "crude and unattractive" handhewn English-style ales when Germans' "new, bright, sparkling clear" lager could be had? Transparent glassware that showed off its brilliance gradually supplanted the impenetrable leather tankards and pewter, wood, and clay cups of yore.

Sporadic part-time homebrewsters couldn't possibly compete with lager, whose yeast ferments in cold temperatures, and therefore had to be brewed over the winter or in chilly caverns or tunnels.

Though lager wouldn't really begin to fundamentally change American beer making until several decades later, Smith writes, in a way that sounds foreboding to anyone chronicling the downfall of woman-brewed beer, "Everything was coming together to make beer big business."

24 | FROM THE BACK OFFICE TO THE BOARDROOM

THE YEAR 2013 WAS PIVOTAL FOR THE INDUSTRY. The Brewers Association says craft brewery output shot from fifteen million annual barrels to around twenty-five million barrels, and it's when a lot of people (myself included) started to notice the numbers of women—both those working and those playing—really ballooning at beer fests, beer bars, and beer events. The following year a pair of female Stanford researchers surveyed more than twenty-five hundred breweries and found that one-fifth had a woman as CEO, executive, top manager, brewmaster, or head brewer. Shockingly, that was a significantly higher percentage than the number of Fortune 500 companies, finance, healthcare, or IT companies with women in leadership positions.

A lot of states finally updated Prohibition-era restrictions that stymied the ability of small breweries to make money around that time, and Pink Boots, then six years old, also deserves credit for the influx. Whatever the reason, the change is proof that diversity has a multiplier effect. Festival organizer Jon Henderson noticed the change, and he says first he saw more women representing breweries at his events. Female consumers followed.

Do you remember that Heather Locklear commercial for Faberge from the 1980s? Here's the edited script: "I told two friends about Faberge. And they told two friends, and so on, and so on, and so on."

Before that pivot point, I used to complain that the vast majority of industry women I encountered worked in brewery sales, human resources, or the lab. But then something happened. I met female brewers. And more female brewers. And so on and so on and so on.

Mary Pellettieri, who brewed briefly at Goose Island in the 1990s before moving into top sensory positions, thinks, "Early women were in it for the science and the flavor."

Former beer journalist and craft beer bartender Julie Nickels says that in her beer travels she spots equal numbers of women and men at work. Not as many in production, she observes, but a lot.

Jen Jordan is one woman who got into production at that time. Anchor hired her as its first female brewer in 2014. Though she toiled alone on the floor she did work closely with Andrea Devries, who runs the lab, and less closely with Kenda Scott, who's been the head distiller since Fritz launched a very early craft distillery. Both women have been there more than twenty years.

Jen, a former teacher and serious homebrewer, was originally hired for a packaging position. Within three months, the brewing department hired her to fill a vacancy. Because she didn't meet a few of the requirements, she almost didn't apply. She thought it might be disrespectful. Her romantic part- ner reminded her that men "apply for jobs that they are underqualified for all the time without thinking twice about it. She said that I should apply, and that was great advice."

Lest you think that's a biased generality, the Center for Women in Politics at Rutgers University, along with other reputable organizations, states unequiv- ocally that overall, men run for office regardless of whether they have the qualifications. Overqualified women, on the other hand, wait to be asked.

Jen must make for a very quick study because after less than two years at Anchor, a panel of esteemed brewers and beer writers awarded her with the very selective Glen Hay Falconer Foundation scholarship to the American Brewers Guild. She took the twenty-two-week Intensive Brewing Science and Engineering course, stayed on at Anchor another few years, and now reports to the brewmaster at San Francisco's Laughing Monk Brewing.

Obviously, not every beer-minded woman wants to brew. The hours are long, the pay is low, and the physical demands are intense. Many women enter the industry through established channels such as the supply chain or guild management. Barley grower and maltster Hillary Baker Barile, who practices the traditional floor-malting technique at her family's Rabbit Hill Farms in South Jersey, is one; Jaki Brophy, communications manager for the Hop Growers Association of America, another; Garden State Brewers Association executive director Alexis Degan, another still.

Others draw new routes onto old, established maps. As creator of the world's first archive dedicated to hops and craft brewing, Tiah's contribution to preservation of related stories, along with the history of women in beer, is unrivaled. Theresa McCulla is steering the Smithsonian's first foray into modern beer scholarship.

The Chicago Brewseum's founder and executive director, Liz Garibay, spent years as a mainstream curator pushing on her supervisors to let her study and incorporate beer history before she drew up plans for the brewseum, which hosts an annual beer history and culture conference that lures the likes of luminaries such as Garrett Oliver and *Tasting Beer* author Randy Mosher.

And others yet, to quote Rhonda Kallman, see there is no bridge to cross so they build one. These women carve their own spaces and fill them. Their entrepreneurial vision can make the beer industry, very literally, richer.

I still very fondly remember spending many hundreds of dollars on the most exciting packaged beer selection I'd ever seen, at the Craft Beer Cellar bottle shop franchise in Waterbury, Vermont, part of a foundational Boston-based chain opened by wives Suzanne Schalow and Kate Baker in 2010.

In 2009, Melani Gordon and her husband released the TapHunter app and website as the original searchable platform to list beers on tap, steering drinkers and dollars to bars serving local and out-of-town beers. This gave those curious about craft beer a novel way to interact with the breweries starting to make names for themselves.

"When we started doing tours in Florida in 2009, 2010, something like that, we were the first people to bring somebody to Cigar City," says Ruth Berman, who brings beercationers on immersive and very exclusive river boat and land tours around the United States and Europe through the Bon Beer Voyage agency she owns with her husband. "It brought dollars not only into the breweries but also into the communities they're in."

When Cigar City applied for a zoning permit to expand its taproom, the brewery's neighbors in Tampa fought it. Beer tourism was an unfamiliar concept, and they wrongly suspected the taproom would usher in cars full of drunks. The case went all the way to court, and in testifying on behalf of the brewery, Saint Somewhere Brewing founder Bob Sylvester—one of Ruth's clients and friends—stated that she brought many visitors and money to Cigar City and mentioned Ruth by name. The brewery got the permit.

Today, they have three locations in Tampa and are the fastest growing brewery in the United States.

Had she been practicing in Florida and not California, Candace Moon, who advertises herself as the Craft Beer Attorney, could have probably represented Cigar City in court.

"I've never done anything but beer law," she says. She started specializing in craft beer law before almost anyone else thought to.

She's worked for a firm and on her own. These days she works for herself. She contracts with around thirty California breweries and is constantly upgrading her services by creating a network of beer attorneys around the country who work together and share resources. She calls herself the anti-attorney attorney because she says most attorneys don't like to share.

She puts her gender on the stand to develop her clients' trust by taking a let-me-help-you approach with them while gaining credibility in the men's eyes with her law degree. "I've got more work than I know what to do with," she says.

Julie Rhodes didn't know what to do with her marketing degree and vast beer knowledge gleaned from bartending until an import company gave her the sales break she needed. She moved on to a larger importer where she worked her way up to sales manager, in part by taking on marketing duties. But last year she knew it was time to leave. This year she's selling herself—teaching marketing, sales, and management strategies to small- to medium-sized breweries.

Though she markets her services by making herself known on the beer-speaking circuit and engaging deeply on social media, the baby-faced forty-one-year-old says she feels that instead of taking her seriously, prospective clients metaphorically pat her on the head and think that's so cute that you own a business.

She struggles to convince condescending strangers that despite or because of being a "girl" in the industry, she possesses a lot of self-education and expertise.

"I get the same question all the time and that is, 'So who do you work for?' No. I'm the owner."

Janet Johanson says she was able to stop the older male production guys at Minnesota Brewing from condescending to her as a young employee by asking incessant—but apparently not annoying—questions about brewing and sitting in a dingy little office listening to the pedagogical head brewer and quality assurance manager joyfully talk about beer.

They would even give her optional homework—just to see if she would do it, she suspects.

Her endless pursuit of information seems to have paid off. She earned $50,000 in revenue the year she founded the BevSource contract brewing facility in the Twin Cities in 2003.

"Now," she says, "we're at $50 million."

One thing former Boston Beer creative director Meagen Anderson learned in her last job is you can't get successful without getting humble. "I've made so many mistakes but I've learned from everyone," she says.

As a business development manager for hops engineering firm Kalsec, in Kalamazoo, those mistakes have given her insight that inform her current role as North American business development manager for the New Zealand Hops co-op and will inform her if she starts her own business, which she's considered several times since leaving Boston.

"I came in not knowing anything and I've already filled five notebooks," she says six months into her job at Kalsec. "Every day I get to come into work and talk about something I know nothing about. I'm really proud of that but I'm not going to let that scare me."

Today, as opposed to in the beginning and middle of craft beer's history, endless opportunities exist for women ambitious enough to seize them. Rachel Greider sells brewery and distillery insurance for Malena Farrell, whose family agency in New Jersey had the foresight to add craft beverages to its repertoire.

"The doors are open for women who're willing to work," says Carol Stoudt.

"People who have insurance companies or the people who run the farms or take the spent grain or who puree or sell the fruit or run a bar or make or design labels or design flavor profiles—the amount of people who touch a beer can without touching a drop of beer are huge," says Alexis. "If you don't know how to get into beer, call me."

25 | RIVERS OF LAGER FLOW TOWARD TEMPERANCE

THE FIRST INDUSTRIAL REVOLUTION in the United States began not with beer but with Englishman Samuel Slater's construction of the country's first textile mill, in Pawtucket, Rhode Island, in 1793. But considering how profoundly industrial beer brewing influenced the next two centuries of American life, it has proven nearly as monumental as textile technology.

As the United States grew more mechanized, urban, crowded, ethnically diverse, squalid, and harsh for the laboring classes over the 1800s, breweries both benefited from and contributed to the idea of modernity. Taking advantage of the two hundred thousand miles of railroad track laid between 1840 and 1893, US breweries began sending their beers farther and wider across the land.

Anheuser-Busch, in St. Louis, pioneered the refrigerated railcar in the mid-1870s to keep its fresh lager from spoiling in the heat, and the company hired its first wholesaler around the same time. The Boston-based distributor repackaged beer that arrived barreled into newfangled mass-produced bottles and marketed them to families for picnics and other wholesome activities.

Within the breweries themselves, the nineteenth century buzzed with shiny new automation. Ice houses for preservation; pressurized carbon injection for a foamy head; and discoveries in yeast and bacteria, that, like Louis Pasteur's famous isolation of lager yeast at Carlsberg Brewery in the 1870s, brought consistency and reproducibility to previously less stable beer.

Women, who for the most part didn't take part in factory work, were especially unwelcome in brewhouses. Though a small number of women continued to homebrew on far-flung points on the map up to and during Prohibition, by this point, the obliteration of cottage and village brewsters in the Western world was complete.

These brewery inventions occurred thanks primarily to German immigrants, who fled Europe by the hundreds of thousands in the nineteenth century, their arrivals surging in the 1850s and 1880s and adding to the robust existing German populations concentrated in the mid-Atlantic, Midwest, and Upper Midwest.

First-generation immigrant Frederick Lauer opened one of the first German-owned breweries in 1823 near Reading, Pennsylvania, where he brewed "ale and porter," according to *Beer: Its History and Its Economic Value as a National Beverage*, commissioned by the United States Brewers Association in 1880. Mr. Lauer added lager to his repertoire after John Wagner brewed the nation's first, in 1842.

The following decades saw the rise of thousands of breweries established or assumed by men with last names like Krug, Schlitz, Kruger, Uihlein, and Weinhard. Some of their wives, such as Oregon's first-generation Frederika Wetterer, who owned and ran her late husband's brewery until she remarried, seem to have taken on roles, though documentation about them, once again, doesn't really exist.

Tiah notes in a blog post about Frederika that even her newspaper obituary laid her to rest in history as "Mrs. William Heely."

One exception was the Miller family, whose late patriarch, Frederick Miller Sr. had established his namesake brewery in Milwaukee in 1855. According to Maureen Ogle in her 2006 book *Ambitious Brew: The Story of American Beer*, three of Frederick's children—Elise, Clara, and Fred—turned Miller into a national brand in the 1930s by spending $500,000 to advertise Miller High Life on radio stations and in newspapers in new sales markets far beyond their Upper Midwest territory. After Clara's retirement as vice president, Elise, as president, bought full-color magazine ads, bringing her brewery to all forty-eight existing states and catapulting it into the top twenty American breweries. They also numbered among the first to take advantage of a modern distribution system that relied on third-party vendors.

Rivers of lager kept flowing through the nineteenth century as waves of German immigration continued and domestic drinkers developed a thirst for lager's clean, crisp taste. By 1859, Rich Wagner reports, thirty lager brewers had invested a total of $1.2 million in Philadelphia, and sales of lager surpassed ale for the first time, by $60,000.

Germans, who found the idea of a dark and dingy saloon depressing, set up spacious halls and gardens where they could congregate over beers and entertainment with their landsmen, wives, and children. "It was part of the rise of working-class leisure activities," said Christine Sismondo, author of *America Walks into a Bar: A Spirited History of Taverns and Saloons, Speakeasies and Grog Shops.* "Some beer gardens would have had bowling alleys, sketch artists, classical music, opera, folk dancing, and singing."

While this probably sounds inviting to contemporary beer drinkers like you and me, it horrified the members of polite society who took for granted that public drinking places had become dives of iniquity where no decent woman would dare enter.

Ogle writes, "Beer gardens became playgrounds of unrivaled comfort and modernity while saloons served as havens for the era's masculinity, poverty, and corruption."

Despite their disdain for beer halls, gardens, and the unacculturated immigrants who favored them, the rekindled popularity of relatively low-alcohol beer came as a temporary relief to American women, whose husbands (plus not an insignificant number of sisters, aunts, and girlfriends) had spent the first half of the nineteenth century sucking down more alcohol than at any other time in the history of humanity.

Reports Daniel Okrent in his groundbreaking historical biopic, *Last Call*, the number of US distilleries quintupled starting in 1790, reaching an unimaginable fourteen thousand in 1820.

He writes, "In cities it was widely understood that common workers would fail to come to work on Mondays."

In 1830, Americans drank a mind-numbing seven gallons of ethanol per capita every week, which equals 1.7 bottles of a standard 80-proof liquor per person, per week, or, as Okrent writes, "Nearly 90 bottles a year for every adult in the nation, even with abstainers (and there were millions of them) factored in."

This sort of drunken nonsense sat poorly with reform-minded activists, many of them female, who by 1820 were crusading for moral rectitude; blaming alcohol for a host of social ills, including penury and domestic violence; and fighting to raise awareness of wellness for those who could afford it and the basic standard of living for those who couldn't.

Writes Ogle, "There were campaigns against spitting, bad architecture, masturbation, and for exercise, well-chewed food, cold baths and better ventilation. This is also the time of the crusades for abolition, female suffrage, free education, and temperance," which Ogle calls the "jewel in reform's thorny crown."

The reform era lost momentum as the Civil War ripped apart the nation. But immediately after war's end, protemperance fighters picked up further along than where they'd left off, augmenting their capabilities and forging political power by braiding themselves inextricably into women's fight for the right to vote—for themselves and, in some cases, Black men.

The first women to effectively renew the operation to limit or ban alcohol got their inspiration from a man, Dr. Diocletian "Dio" Lewis. The Harvard medical school dropout had spent thirty years traveling the country preaching the benefits of better living through exercise and clean living. But it wasn't until he spoke in Hillsboro, Ohio, on December 22, 1873, that his message compelled protemperance women to take unprecedented collective action.

With the support of sixty to seventy men, approximately fifty women in his audience agreed to gather the following morning to elicit pledges from the town's druggists, grocers, and doctors to stop selling and prescribing alcohol. After that, they would try the same tactics on the local hoteliers and saloonkeepers.

The children of Hillsboro's prominent Eliza Jane "Mother" Thompson ran home from the talk to tell her the ladies would be expecting her to lead them the following morning. She agreed, reluctantly, and dutifully met her teetotaling fellow townspeople at church to pray and ready themselves for their mission. After prayers, the men in attendance wished their ladies well and left "this work with God and the women."

God and the women met with quick success. Like dominoes, three of the town's four druggists fell for the pledge. Then the women, flush with victory, stormed the saloons. At first proprietors viewed the odd procession with curiosity and a little amusement.

But as Hillsboro's respectable, God-fearing matrons went on to hold their vigil for days, bar patrons stopped showing up so regularly, and, says Mark Lawrence Schrad, author of *Smashing the Liquor Machine: A Global History of Prohibition*, "The sight of the community's most respectable ladies kneeling in the filth of the worst dives in town shamed some saloonkeepers to capitulate.

As one contemporary noted, when 'The wives and mothers of the best citizens came, with tender words and earnest prayer, it was an enemy he hardly knew how to fight.'"

On Christmas Day, the ladies of Washington Court House, Ohio, began their own identical battle. This time, the parade wasn't so peaceful.

Schrad quotes one observer as saying, "'Axes were placed in the hands of the women who had suffered most,'—presumably the wives of drunkards—as the barrels were rolled out. 'Swinging through the air, they came down with ringing blows, bursting the heads of the casks, and flooding the gutters of the street. One good woman, putting her soul into every blow, struck but once for a barrel, splashing Holland gin and old Bourbon high into the air amid the shouts of the people. Four barrels and one cask were forced open, the proprietors giving a hearty consent.'"

By day eight, the city's eleven saloons and three druggists had, to use Schrad's words, "surrendered." Across Ohio, more women followed, working in shifts from early morning until late night to pray steadily against the moral scourge of liquor. The success of these protests quickly propelled them across state borders.

Within three months of the Hillsboro action, a majority of liquor peddlers in 250 Ohio, Michigan, Indiana, Pennsylvania, and New Jersey municipalities signed the pledge; by the end of 1874, women, most with no prior activism experience, organized these "Women's Crusades" in 912 communities spread over thirty-one states.

"The sight of these women kneeling on the snow and ice and offering up their songs and supplications has melted many a stout heart," wrote abolitionist Henry Ward Beecher in the *Christian Union* newspaper over the Christmas holiday in 1873.

Of course, not *everyone's* heart melted.

Many a saloonkeeper filed injunctions against the protesters, who responded by writing down every possible sales transaction and taking owners to court over each illegal infraction. Schrad reports that a saloonkeeper in Michigan locked his town's demonstrators into his establishment, and a mob in Cleveland doused five hundred peaceful protesters with sour beer, kicked the women praying on their knees, beat others with brickbats, and unleashed dogs on the crowd. This particular blowback, like others, was funded by beer brewers.

That didn't stop them. They continued to march and they continued to organize. Over the coming years, their peaceful protests turned political as they flexed their newfound muscle. They couldn't vote but they could pamphleteer and they could politick.

Schrad posits that the temperance movement finally took off with the vengeance that it did when it did because public drunkenness ran rampant again in the 1870s, a time that coincided with the paradox of an economic depression and a rise in affluence and leisure time that gave middle-class women an opportunity to get involved in advocacy.

Threatened that the female-fueled temperance mobilization would detract from the fight for women's right to vote while simultaneously motivating beer and liquor interests to target them too, some high-profile suffragists scorned the activists. Susan B. Anthony muttered that until they secured the vote, women "will quickly learn the impossibility of accomplishing any substantial end," and Elizabeth Cady Stanton compared the "whiskey war" to mob law that would fail to achieve either movement's goals.

Suffragist and temperance activist Anna Gordon wrote, "With ribaldry and sneers the liquor men had written and talked of the Woman's Crusade. . . . To them it was merely an absurd, ephemeral movement that would be quickly crushed by the age-long appetite and avarice of men. What could ballot-less and money-less women do against a business entrenched in politics and in partnership with the government of the United States?"

They were wrong about ballot-less women's ability to win, though they were right that the temperance movement pressured the liquor industry to train its hoses full-force against both, eventually interlinked, causes.

When I did my graduate studies at Northwestern University in the northern Chicago suburb of Evanston, I found it odd that the town didn't allow liquor stores. It's only now, twenty years later, that I know why: a world-renowned nineteenth-century temperance crusader and feminist named Frances Willard had lived there, and her house remains the headquarters of the infamous Woman's Christian Temperance Union (WCTU), which she led for two decades.

Her committed activism began gradually, first when she followed news of the Ohio crusades, then when she began tracking and joining political suffrage and temperance actions in Illinois. During the 1870s, the lifelong teetotaler and iconoclast accepted invitations to speak to audiences about temperance, and she called off her engagement to Northwestern's dean along with quitting her job as dean of the university's women's college once she determined her fiancé would never allow the school the self-government she requested.

Unemployed and unattached, Frances threw herself into the budding temperance movement, joining Annie Wittenmyer in 1874 to cofound the WCTU. For what might have been the first time in history, the union's membership blocked men from voting or holding an official position. What it did encourage was autonomy among state and local chapters to translate the national group's goals into workable solutions to local issues, which comforted women around the world that they wouldn't have to back initiatives such as suffrage or civil rights if they so chose.

That said, it turns out that WCTU women did want the vote, even though the bold notion scared them at first. Frances took over as president after she declared the WCTU should support women's right to cast ballots on matters that pertain to them. As wives and daughters, they believed alcohol pertained to them very much indeed.

The marriage of the women's temperance and women's suffrage movements was consecrated once Susan B. Anthony, a longtime active opponent of alcohol, reached out to the WCTU to ask it to support suffrage. Writes Okrent, "The merging of Anthony's campaign and Willard's brought a critical realignment among the era's feminist activists: the WCTU had acquired a very specific goal, and the suffrage movement had acquired an army."

He continues, "Not only had the suffrage movement found its most effective generals among women who had first developed their political skills in the temperance ranks; in addition, thousands of women in the WCTU had come to realize that no antialcohol weapon could be as potent as the franchise. . . . Comfortable affinity [between the prohibitionists and the suffragists] had been transformed into absolute interdependence."

Among other signs of solidarity, Frances gave Susan an audience at WCTU conventions and Susan once rebelliously introduced Frances to a congressional committee as "the commander in chief of an army of 250,000 women."

Women, Susan signaled, were now an irrefutable force to reckon with.

(As if to prove this point, Marie C. Brehm, the first female to legally run for vice president, did so as a member of the Prohibition Party.)

If Frances Willard served as the army's commander in chief, Mary Hanchett Hunt served as its general in charge of the next generation, earning a salute from Woodrow Wilson's secretary of state, William Jennings Bryan, for waging a campaign of lobbying and educational indoctrination that did, as Bryan described it, "more than any one thing" to bring about Prohibition.

First Mary took it upon herself to strong-arm local school boards into requiring "Scientific Temperance Education" in their curricula and deputized WCTU members to ambush classrooms to enforce the edict. Then, with the blessing of the WCTU, the nicknamed Queen of the Lobby went above the heads of school board members to persuade state and federal lawmakers to mandate the teaching of temperance.

But Mary wasn't done. Next she convinced Congress to pass mandatory "Scientific Temperance Instruction" for all military academies and schools located on federal land. By 1901, twenty-two million American students took a temperance class three times a week.

Critiquing the lessons as "propaganda" and "intimidation," Okrent describes them this way: "Students were force-fed a stew of mythology ('the majority of beer drinkers die of dropsy'), remonstration ('persons should not take a stimulant before bathing'), and terror ('when alcohol passes down the throat it burns off the skin, leaving it hard and burning')."

Even though the misinformation campaign embarrassed WCTU leadership, Mary had long passed the point of concern, having independently manipulated textbook publishers into submissively seeking her approval before publishing any scientific pedagogy and eventually demanding personal royalties for her endorsements.

Half of the nation's public school students used these texts.

Though the WCTU may have exhaled in relief when Mary finally died twenty-seven years into her crusade, they would have had to acknowledge the political doors she opened for them. In the 1870s and 1880s six states approved a prohibition measure, and thousands of government entities denied license renewals to alcohol vendors and cracked down on Sunday closing laws, which had tended to get overlooked. The so-called high-license movement raised saloon licensing fees manyfold and caused many of them to close.

———

It may be fortunate for Frances Willard that the WCTU's most extremist and reviled associate didn't launch her own saloon-closing campaign until after Frances's death. But, like Mary Hunt before her, Carry Nation did more for the movement than almost any other single person, so much so that her name personifies prohibition.

Carry, who had founded a WCTU chapter in Kansas, found out that mere prayers and petitions couldn't accomplish what a single act of property damage could. With a maddening inability to electorally effect change, Carry turned to aggressive hatchet-wielding action in midwestern saloons to bring global attention to her antialcohol cause.

But poor Carry. Arguably the most vilified American woman of the twentieth century, the devout Christian teetotaler lost her first husband to alcoholism in her early twenties, which left her broke, without legal rights, and caring for an infant and a malcontent mother-in-law. Much later in life, after she'd built up enough money to buy a hotel, whose facilities and profits she used to succor and shelter society's most downtrodden—both Black and White—she was thrown out of the church, arrested thirty-two times, and beaten bloody by prostitutes paid off by an angry saloon owner.

Her second husband divorced her after decades in a loveless marriage, and that's before multiple lynch mobs tried to hang her; a proprietor threw a chair at her head and another held a pistol to her temple; and revelers in Coney Island, New York, pelted her with hot dogs. (After one incident, she calmly went to a nearby butcher, bought some frozen meat, came out holding it up to her badly bruised face, and kept right on going.)

History has treated her just as poorly, with male biographers and others denigrating her appearance, grotesquely exaggerating her size, calling her all sorts of synonyms for crazy, and blaming her actions on menopause and a lack of sex. Not much has changed since then.

But the truth is, Carry Nation wasn't any of those things. She was a fiercely progressive ally to all races and religions, a dedicated protector and advocate for women, and a caring grandma with a self-aware sense of humor. To wit: she sold hatchet pins to help fund her activities; she named her charity-driven home for poor old people and abused women and children Hatchet Hall; and she once downed so many bottles of Schlitz Malt that she intentionally gave herself alcohol poisoning, just to prove to her shocked and helpless doctor that beer was not, in fact, "healthful."

Conducting her notorious affairs from 1900 until her death in 1911, Carry's methods were eccentric but not unique, and she only started taking a hatchet to bars and bottles after finding her disenfranchised, powerless pleas to politicians to enforce dry laws ignored and her protestations to tavern keepers to stop breaking those dry laws—which she at first reinforced with rocks instead of an axe—went unheeded.

She didn't want to hurt anyone. Just the opposite. She simply had a passion for saving the souls of those she believed had become victims of the devil's drink.

"She did not view drinking as a sin, or the drinker as a sinner. Instead, like the prostitute, the prisoner and the slave, the drinker was the victim, to be loved and cared for. The true sinner was the enslaver of men: the drink seller. And she would use all means at her disposal—from prayer and persuasion to hatchetation—to get the man who sells to change his ways," writes Schrad.

Like Carry, the WCTU packaged its message into one that turned men who spent their money on hooch into victims; the producers and sellers, villians. Blanketed with images and stories of beaten wives, starving children, and bankers banging on doors with repossession notices, the group's Home Protection defense-posture slogan tugged at public sympathies.

Parlaying female and family issues into larger societal ones, Frances Willard expanded the campaign for prohibition into one of broad social justice. Though many within her ranks didn't feel comfortable taking their eyes off the dual prizes of temperance and suffrage, it wasn't long before the WCTU was charging ahead on matters of workplace safety; prison reform; free kindergarten; government ownership of infrastructure, business, and culture; and even vegetarianism and loose-fitting clothes. Frances called this her Do Everything campaign.

By 1889, the WCTU was running two nurseries and Sunday schools, an industrial school, a domestic violence shelter, a free medical clinic, and a restaurant and shelter for itinerant men—all in Chicago alone. That year's national convention passed resolutions opposing cigarettes and animal testing and entreating Tsar Alexander III of Russia for humane treatment of Siberian exiles.

Believing in the power of numbers, Frances forged strong links with the Knights of Labor and other trade unions to promote better working conditions and equal pay for equal work. She and her adherents befriended Catholic and Jewish organizations and helped Native Americans by pressuring the federal government to enforce laws written to protect Indigenous tribes from what Schrad describes as "the predatory white man's liquor trade."

When an Okrent-curated exhibition on Prohibition came to Philadelphia's National Constitution Center for the second time, I took a quiz to determine whether I'd have been a "wet" or a "dry," as opponents and supporters of temperance laws came to be called. After answering questions about my higher education, upper-middle-class upbringing, and progressive values, I learned a nineteenth-century version of myself would probably have supported prohibition, too.

The march toward temperance took hold in dozens of different countries. With the assistance of the Independent Order of Good Templars, WCTU global ambassador Mary Clement Leavitt traveled one hundred thousand miles over six years to organize 130 temperance societies in forty-three nations around Europe, imperial Russia, Turkey, India, China, Japan, Australia, and New Zealand. Back at home, international WCTU ambassadors defied the anti-immigrant sentiment of the day to greet passenger ships arriving at Ellis Island with armfuls of temperance materials written in sixteen different languages.

But in forming alliances with issue-based organizations, the struggle got messy between forces myopically devoted to one cause and those open to supporting multiple matters in the service of practical politics. The WCTU worked side by side in uneasy partnership with the fleeting Temperance Party and the powerful Anti-Saloon League (ASL), which refused to allow female leadership. And even though Susan Anthony had sprung from temperance into suffrage activism, she refused to directly endorse temperance until she had won the right to vote.

In the early twentieth century, the raging topic of immigration found progressive, mostly Protestant and White, temperance and franchise workers uncomfortably contorting themselves to side with all sorts of very strange bedfellows. For example, the Ku Klux Klan, out of hatred for the Jews who got rich off the hard liquor economy and the German, Irish, and Roman Catholic immigrants who sustained their beer-selling coconspirators, supported prohibition and as a result, women's suffrage.

Writes Okrent, "In the two decades leading up to Prohibition's enactment [in 1920], five distinct, if occasionally overlapping, components made up this unspoken coalition of racists, progressives, suffragists, populists . . . and nativists."

The interconnectedness of the movements cost each some allies, particularly among the very immigrant communities that temperance activists were trying to court and liberal reformers were trying to "civilize." But beyond the common condescension and occasional outright racism with which these Christian crusaders viewed unassimilated newcomers, immigrants presented a serious problem: most of them were very wet and a lot of their votes could be bought for the price of a drink.

Motivated by ethnic and economic allegiance to brewers, distillers, saloonkeepers, and politicians on the alcohol industry's underground payroll, foreign-born drinkers came out strong against temperance and suffrage.

The Nebraska chapter of the German-American Alliance, basically comprised of foot soldiers for the United States Brewers Association (USBA), proclaimed, "Our German women do not want the right to vote. . . . And since our opponents desire the right of suffrage mainly for the purpose of saddling the yoke of prohibition on our necks, we should oppose it with all our might."

The USBA subversively threw its money to whomever showed willingness to catch it: newspaper publishers, politicians, and Black and Mexican people who needed help paying their poll taxes and encouragement as to which way to vote. The association funded many a wet's political campaign and used what one employee of the iconic Anheuser-Busch leader, Adolphus Busch, called "forces best not written about" to reverse the outcome of a Texas dry's electoral victory.

Knowing that a vote for suffrage basically equated to a vote for prohibition, brewers and their suppliers showed up to intimidate participants in marches, protests, and actions. They funded widespread misinformation campaigns through fake news sources that quoted make-believe farmers asking such guilt-inducing rhetorical questions as, "Is it not sufficient political achievement for women that future rulers nurse at her breast, laugh in her arms and kneel at her feet?" They even bought off famous former suffragette Phoebe Couzins in exchange for her disavowal and public disapproval of the cause.

Their stop-at-nothing campaign backfired. Women who may not have cared much either way about alcohol turned out to help sweep prohibition and pro-prohibition candidates into office in states where, beginning in 1890, they'd earned the vote. Even Jeannette Rankin, the first female member of Congress, endorsed prohibition in her home state of Montana because of "political exigency."

In the years following the Civil War, the Thirteenth Amendment had abolished slavery but the Constitution still considered Black men inferior to White people, and Jim Crow laws were on the rise across the South to codify unequal and confining treatment. Without federal suffrage or equal rights for Black males, Black women were speaking out. They understood that the disenfranchised Black population mostly wouldn't have the capital to buy into any part of the liquor industry and would risk becoming enslaved by it instead.

Sure enough, both wets and drys tried hard to curry Black favor. Wets courted the Black man's vote and dollar, with one particularly straightforward attempt coming bottled as Black Cock Vigor Gin. Drys played to the sympathies of religious African Americans who heard the word of their pastors who preached moral rectitude every Sunday.

Throughout Reconstruction and its aftermath, racist dry Southerners spun a false narrative about drunk Black men being uncontrollable, dangerous, and inclined toward raping White women, even though Black people of the era drank statistically less than White people.

But Black women knew. They knew White men had reversed the story to suit them.

Drunken White mobs would sometimes terrorize Black neighborhoods and lynch men they accused of raping White women. Equal rights journalist Ida B. Wells found her Memphis newsroom burned to the ground when she editorialized that her investigative reporting had shown no sexual relations in more than two-thirds of these lynchings. But that's not what got White Memphians mad enough to run her out of town. What she went on to say was that her research found many of the encounters between Black men and White women had been consensual.

She wrote, "If Southern [White] men are not careful, a conclusion might be reached which will be very damaging to the moral reputation of their women."

Ida's friend and noted African American poet and author Frances Ellen Watkins Harper embodied what we in contemporary times might liken to a classic intersectionality in her avid commitment to the triad of temperance, women's suffrage, and equal rights for Black men.

Harper often spoke her mind through her literary characters, denouncing sexism, racism, and drink with a forthrightness that seems surprising for her time. In her 1876 serialized fictional story "Sowing and Reaping," the friend of an African American who plans to open a tavern warns him against it in a refrain often repeated in the language of temperance activists: "Husbands and fathers will waste their time and money, and confirm themselves in habits which will bring misery, crime, and degradation; and the fearful outcome of your business will be broken hearted wives, neglected children, outcast men, blighted characters and worse than wasted lives."

Another character, Belle Gordon, refuses her significant other's hand in marriage because he refuses to renounce the tipple. She pushes back on a cousin who criticizes her decision by insisting, "A young man has no more right to sow his wild oats than a young woman. God never made one code of ethics for a man and another for a woman. And it is the duty of all true women to demand of men the same standard of morality that they do of women."

The story concludes with Belle rebutting claims that women didn't need to vote because they could simply influence their husbands at home by proclaiming, "On this liquor question there is room for woman's conscience not merely as a persuasive influence but as an enlightened and aggressive power."

Frances Harper brought her ballsy proclamations to the stage when she spoke at feminist gatherings, even though she usually stared down at crowds of predominantly White faces. At the first Women's Rights Convention, in 1866, Harper attacked the gathered White women for being as racist as their male counterparts because they declined to put temperance and women's voting rights on the back burner long enough to temporarily prioritize the urgent postwar cause of universal Black male suffrage.

Echoing some of her pro-Black-suffrage contemporaries, she told the audience, "I do not believe that giving the woman the ballot is immediately going to cure all the ills of life. I do not believe that white women are dew drops just exhaled from the skies. I think that like men they may be divided into three classes, the good, the bad, and the indifferent."

She continued, "I tell you that if there is any class of people who need to be lifted out of their airy nothings and selfishness, it is the white women of America."

Then she strode off stage.

"The next day," the National Women's History Museum writes, "the Convention held a meeting . . . to work for suffrage for both African Americans and women."

After being recruited to the WCTU, Frances Harper took on a position as emissary to the African American community. It took her little time to rise to the position of national superintendent of the Department of Colored Work in the North, which, ironically, had the Philadelphian spending tireless hours traveling through the South. She also traversed the country to lecture; build Black unions and youth groups; and collect, compile, and present data that informed the WCTU writings she then distributed along her sojourns.

As Reconstruction waned and White supremacy rose, Frances Harper continued to believe her social justice work on behalf of Black women would be best served by joining forces with White women, who had access, influence, and resources that those who shared her skin color didn't have.

But she had gone on record saying that if forced to choose between supporting women or Black people, she'd choose race over gender. This led to her break ranks with former allies Susan Anthony and Elizabeth Stanton when the organization they ran used racist language to dismiss Black male suffrage until White women first won their own right to vote.

In 1868, a majority of states ratified the Fourteenth Amendment, granting equal protection under the law to all citizens. Two years later, the Fifteenth Amendment gave Black men in every state the right to vote.

Try as she might, Frances Harper never fully succeeded in racially integrating the WCTU. Despite becoming American history's most powerful women's organization up to that point, its leadership claimed it couldn't force integration on its chapters.

Feeling underappreciated and underfunded, Harper grew increasingly frustrated. Then, after she clashed with the WCTU president Frances Willard, who'd decided to pull back from doing everything to refocus on the group's primary mission, Willard demoted Harper's department to one with far less autonomy. Though she stayed on as a WCTU member, Frances Harper started working more with groups of political Black women, helping to form the National Association of Colored Women (NACW)—with its own temperance unit—in 1896.

In spite of her successive rebuffs, Frances Harper kept touring and speaking for social reform. She continued to urge White women to not only welcome their Black compatriots as full equals in their efforts but to do so by viewing Black Americans as contributing partners working to fully express their own agency rather than charity cases who needed saving. Though she remained well known and respected into her old age, her views failed to generate much traction among women coming of age as the nineteenth century begat the twentieth.

"Harper's leadership as the most prominent African American female reformer was eclipsed by the rise of a new leadership, which was mostly younger, well-educated, articulate, attractive, and extremely impatient with their white counterparts," writes Bettye Collier-Thomas and Ann D. Gordon in *African American Women and the Vote, 1837–1965*.

In a biography written in July 2020, the Frances Willard House Museum and Archives apologized, "The failures of white WCTU members to answer Harper's call for 'co-operation and active sympathy' represented a lost opportunity for interracial collaboration and serves as a lesson for present and future reform movements."

The Mother of Black Journalism, the poet, the teacher, the author, the activist Frances Harper died in 1911 and was buried with her only child, a daughter, in Philadelphia.

Frances Willard died before her, in 1898, and was buried at her Rest Cottage in Evanston. Schrad feels the women of the WCTU subsequently wasted their energy canonizing Frances instead of keeping up the fight, and the male-dominated Anti-Saloon League's (ASL) flower blossomed as the WCTU's wilted.

The year after Frances Willard's death, Susan Anthony asked the ASL to help her by endorsing suffrage. More than a decade later, its superintendent offered his personal support, calling women's franchise the antidote to the beer and liquor lobby. Five years after that—in 1916—the ASL finally acquiesced.

Though the Anti-Saloon League may receive more recognition as the primary organization to finally succeed in pouring out America's wine, beer, and spirits glasses, no one can deny it was women who prepped the country for Prohibition and set the table for its passage.

"Even a group as powerful, wealthy, and self-interested as the United States Brewers Association met its match in the foe who would engage it for nearly half a century: women," writes Okrent.

In 1919, approximately one hundred years after the beginning of the temperance movement, the United States ratified the Eighteenth Amendment, which banned the production, transportation, and sale of recreational alcohol. The year after that, the Nineteenth Amendment gave women across America the right to vote.

26 | THE CUSTOMER IS SOMETIMES RIGHT

IN WHAT I CALL A CYCLE, a symbiotic relationship, or maybe a question of chicken versus egg, it's nearly inevitable that three things would follow so many women entering the beer industry: they would raise awareness for women's issues; they would join together in various ways to highlight their contributions; they would attract the notice of nonindustry women. The more consumers explored, tried, and talked about beer, the more they joined the professional ranks and perpetuated another round. And so on.

Cinzia Wallace hosted the first known beer event exclusively for female customers, in 2007, at Left Hand Brewing, the Colorado brewery she owns with her husband. They served relatively few females in their taproom when they opened as one of Longmont's first craft breweries in 1993. But as the number of women served grew, she noticed they'd taken a few enduring stereotypes to heart. One: beer is for men. Two: beer gives you a gut. Three: women don't work in beer.

Having grown up in Italy, Cinzia had made beer and wine drinking a part of her daily habits and, according to her, hasn't busted a paunch from doing it. What these women were missing, she came to realize, was education. She launched Ales4Females on a Monday night with a light meal, beer pairings, and a speaker. It sold out.

She hosted another one. It sold out, too. So she started hosting monthly, then twice monthly meetings that generally followed the same format: dinner, pairings, speaker, an audience of women.

Soon, women began hosting similar get-togethers around the country. Each had its own structure, or lack thereof, but each pursued the same goal: to expose women to beer in a nonthreatening, nonjudgmental, nonmansplaining environment. Brewery sales rep Suzanne Woods hosted some of the earliest such meetings in Philadelphia, and I followed her by launching Beer for Babes on the New Jersey side of the river in 2010.

Homebrewer Lisa Howard-Fusco drove nearly two hours to come to one of my first events. Though we'd never met, she hugged me when she got there.

"This is the group I never knew I needed," she gushed.

Lisa's story was a common one. She loved good beer but didn't know any woman who did as well. The other refrain I heard all the time was, "I don't like/drink beer but my boyfriend/husband wants me to."

So I made the group as accessible as possible, promising that every attendee would be able to learn *something* about beer, no matter how much or little she already knew. Our events, planned by me and so many unbelievably enthusiastic volunteers, spanned the basic—a guided tour of Asbury Park's breweries, for example—to full-on commercial brew days, formal beer-cocktail classes, a private pizza making and beer pairing with the chef at an Uno's restaurant, virtual meet and greets with female beer cognoscenti, and an overnight to Dogfish Head's Delaware headquarters, where microbiologist Aimee Richards gave us a multihour behind-the-scenes tour and took us to dinner at the Dogfish Head brewpub in Rehoboth.

Most of all, I loved staffing festivals, where we'd command a table to auction off swag, sell logoed Babes T-shirts, shoot video interviews for social media, and sometimes pour a VIP beer, or serve as the official info booth.

Gradually, these groups sprung up in every state and a sizable number of countries. Barley's Angels emerged as an umbrella organization spun off from Pink Boots that requires chapters to follow certain guidelines, including a mandatory educational component.

"Our purpose is to grow the women's consumer base in craft beer," says Christine Jump, who took Barley's Angels over from Pink Boots. "When we started we felt that was really the next demographic for craft beer. I think for every one of those [women] who've 'graduated out' so to speak, there are one hundred who are still in the dark."

Founded around the same time as Barley's Angels, Girls Pint Out has become a popular, albeit more social, collective.

I speak from personal experience when I say that countless lifelong friendships have formed among Beer for Babes members deeply grateful to find like-minded women in a landscape that until recently remained relatively devoid of other enthusiasts. I'm so proud of how we helped women discover beer and one another and made businesses across New Jersey aware of women's interest in this "man's drink." And I'm particularly proud of the fact Beer for Babes probably propelled half a dozen women into careers in brewing and beer sales.

Regrettably, I charged little to nothing for Babes events and burned myself out. Without a volunteer able to take on the commitment of leading, I dissolved Babes in 2018. Sometimes I console myself by saying groups like ours did what they set out to do by bringing more women into beer. Then I remind myself that our past successes should inform future growth, not give us permission to stagnate.

At least Ales4Females is still going strong, and Cinzia can quantify the overall impact of groups like hers and mine.

Any time she walks into any bar, any brewery, she says, she sees 50 percent female attendance.

Obviously no one's arguing consumer groups should take all the credit. Festival organizers have done a lot of this work, too.

Jon Henderson, who puts on the mammoth two-day AC Beer and Music fest along with others, says his events have increased ticket sales to women by 40 percent in five years. Andy Calimano, who produces multiple large-scale mid-Atlantic beer and cider fests per year with his wife, Lynda, and a team of paid staffers, says the unofficial accounting system in his gut tallies 15 percent female attendance in 2005 and 45 percent in 2019.

Anyone can witness the shift by looking at beer fest bathroom lines. Women used to joke that for once they could get in and out of the bathroom faster than men. Fortunately or unfortunately, depending on your perspective, that no longer holds true.

In step with women's increasing penetration into beer events and jobs—which many disparate people I interviewed say they first noticed in 2013, right before the number of US craft breweries started to spike—planners are staging events to highlight and target this population. Competitions and collaborations, festivals for women by women; and conferences, fundraisers, and panels—it's all here.

I judged my first all-woman homebrew competition, in 2013, with an all-female judging panel and fifty-nine female entrants from up to four states away. The idea for Queen of Hops arose when NewJerseyCraftBeer.com regional manager Heather Berz took offense to an oh-so-typically wine-centric Mother's Day promotion at a liquor store and decided to do something empowering for women who like beer.

At the time, I counted four such competitions.

In 2020 a Google search also turned up four: two in New York, the fourth annual SheBrew competition in Portland, and the first online version of the nation's biggest and oldest female homebrew competition, Queen of Beer. Placerville, California's QOB has reigned as the only one sanctioned by the AHA since H.A.Z.E. homebrew club president Beth Sangeri developed it twenty-five years ago in response to male homebrewers who answered her questions by saying, "What your husband should do is . . ."

As Sangeri has told *Brewing Techniques* magazine, she aimed to create a nonintimidating environment to encourage a "silent group of women brewers" to enter competitions that wouldn't be "male dominated and sometimes fraternity-like." Instead of embracing her efforts, critics accused her of being sexist, self-defeating, and patronizing.

Nevertheless, they persisted, as did a New Zealand homebrewer in 2012 when organizers of a local competition wouldn't let her enter because, as the would-be entrant said, she "didn't have balls." The fracas made international news and compelled a spokesperson for the country's Human Rights Commission to weigh in that the exclusion may have violated New Zealand's Human Rights Act.

In New Jersey, Queen of Hops got criticized as sexist, too, by certain members of my own homebrew club who cheaply wondered aloud whether it showed bias against *women* by presuming they can't fairly compete against men. The club, despite my casual attempt at a complaint after it formed in 2009, is still called Barley Legal so feel free to question my fellow members' motivation and genuine concern for gender parity as you see fit.

As far as I can tell, women's beer festivals, as opposed to competitions, don't generate critique, maybe because while they only invite women to exhibit, they do invite everyone to attend. The first such fest took place in Florida but didn't get the same amount of attention as the second, perhaps because that one was organized under the banner of Pink Boots by Jordan Boinest, who sells yeast products and services for White Labs.

Bière de Femme took place in Asheville and exclusively showcased beers brewed by brewsters. All of the proceeds went to Pink Boots, and because local chapters can keep most of the money they raise, they used it to send Highland Brewing brewer Katie Smith on a Pink Boots beer-themed bus tour of Germany. Over the course of three festivals, they've raised a total of $33,000.

Jordan, who won a national Pink Boots scholarship of her own, has since stepped back from the festival. She says, "What's been really cool is the torch has been passed to other women. They're getting experience marketing and doing things they might not have gotten to do before."

Variations on the festival model abound. The annual Beers without Beards Festival in Brooklyn, produced by Grace Weitz of the Hop Culture website, includes a standard festival that limits itself to female brewers only, plus a panel of female speakers talking about, say, women in beer history or best practices in advertising beer on social media.

Many of these fests are also shaping up as vehicles for women's charities. As I mentioned in chapter twenty-two, my local Pink Boots chapter staged the really successful Bold Women and Beer fest in 2019. Pike Brewing puts on a women's craft and beer fest every year for Planned Parenthood, and though they're not female-focused, two San Diego breweries host nationally known beer fests for boobies.

Bagby Beer Co. holds the annual Brewbies fest for a local breast cancer charity, and Green Flash, whose cofounder Lisa Hinkley survived breast cancer herself, famously puts on its annual Breast Fest and Treasure Chest that's raised $130,000 for the Susan G. Komen Foundation over eight years. Jordan's boss, White Lab co-owner Lisa White, established Beer for Boobs in 2008, which has raised up to $450,000 for breast cancer research and the American Cancer Society.

In addition to festivals, collaboration brew projects sometimes raise money for charity, too. Though women certainly have philanthropic interests beyond breast cancer, it does make for a convenient beneficiary of women's collaborative efforts in this space.

Suburban Philadelphia's male-owned Free Will Brewing ran a five-year campaign that brought me together with Erin Wallace, wine consultant and author Marnie Old, and beer journalist Carol Smagalski to brew Saison de Rosé, a hibiscus *saison* to benefit research and community initiatives sponsored by the University of Pennsylvania's breast cancer center.

Finally, if women get together to do something, and no one talks about it, did it really happen? Women's panels emerged as a regular activity around the start of the decade.

A one-time Washington, DC, beer columnist named Tammy Tuck organized several women's speaker events at the woman-owned Black Squirrel beer bar to coincide with the Brewers Association's annual SAVOR pairing event, which brings a few hundred beer cognoscenti to the district every spring. The bar's owners filled the downstairs taps with beer brewed by women.

In Philly, University of the Sciences hosts an annual women's symposium through its brewing sciences program. The symposium is co-organized by the local Pink Boots chapter. I moderated year one, which brought Megan Parisi, Whitney Thompson, Aimee Richards, Fifth Hammer Brewing co-owner Mary Izett, and Colleen Rakowski, at the time a brewer at Free Will, in front of a ticket-buying audience to talk about the state of women in the industry.

And my personal favorite: I traveled to the Twin Cities twice and got to know lots of the region's dynamic beer ladies when I moderated and helped plan a women's forum at the Herkimer brewpub in Minneapolis. My client (the Herk's public relations agent) and I brought eight of Minnesota's most prominent female brewery owners and beer educators onto the stage to talk about the status of beer women and sample one another's beers.

We had a very minifest outside afterward to socialize and encourage attendees to visit promotional tables for Barley's Angels, Girls Pint Out, and the nascent Pink Boots chapter. Kelsi Moffitt, former director of operations for the Better Beer Society academy, set up fun sensory games. As the first event of its kind in the state, we also had a representative from the governor's office come and got a fair bit of press.

I feel as if every state hosted some kind of women's panel before they mostly trickled off, maybe because women brewing beer has thankfully become old news. Or maybe it's because the industry is actually evolving and ideologically following a call to action issued by Maine beer writer Carla Jean Lauter, who proclaims, "Let's have fewer panels about women and more women on panels."

27 | PROHIBITED FROM THE HALLS OF POWER NO MORE

HISTORY, AS WE KNOW, has not been kind to Prohibition, considered one of the most abysmal policy failures in the life of the republic. The Twenty-First Amendment ended the thirteen-year noble experiment on December 5, 1933, with lawmakers and voters concluding that the obscenely unenforced ban on the manufacture, transport, and sale of alcohol had actually created more trouble than it had averted.

But Prohibition, for all of its flaws, actually proved a boon for women, and not just because they'd ushered in its passage and not just because it had, in fact, accomplished one of the things it had set out to do by drastically reducing the amount Americans consumed.

Prohibition completely reshaped society in a way that put women on much more equal footing in terms of inhabiting men's spaces; creating work opportunities, hence, independence, for themselves; defying narrow definitions of how women should look and act; and placing even greater political power in their hands.

Until Prohibition, tippling women were to remain unseen and unheard. Saloons were playgrounds for men, quietly equipped with back doors to sell women and their children growlers, buckets of beer smeared with lard and designed to take home for women's social gatherings and other occasions. With the exception of German beer halls and gardens and inconspicuous ladies-only drinking rooms or wine rooms that were set off from a main tavern barroom by partitions and a separate entrance, women drank in private, alone, or with other women, inside someone's house.

"In essence, it became the woman's job to provide a counterbalance to the moral taint of the public sphere, and with it, the taint of liquor," Nicola Nice, a sociologist and founder of the Pomp & Whimsy gin liqueur brand, tells *Wine Spectator* in a 2020 article.

In 1907, Montana went so far as to ban women from entering saloons and ordered proprietors to do away with all vestiges of wine rooms, which lawmakers assumed, sometimes correctly, incubated or covered for prostitution. Ironically enough, critics today might deride this as an early example of the nanny state, as the law emerged as part of a progressive package to promote wellness.

But wellness didn't occupy much share of mind for many young women in the 1920s. Caught up in the excitement of the underground economy that encouraged them to break social mores while patronizing businesses that broke the law, they plunged right into the tantalizing glitz and glamour promised by the better speakeasies and, later, nightclubs.

True, a number of speakeasy clip joints sold "cheap booze and suggestive women serving as shills to make men spend more," according to the Mob Museum in Las Vegas. But women owned or managed some of the nice and not-so-nice ones. The museum lists three women who ran "stylish nightclub-type speakeasies for the affluent crowd—Texas Guinan, Helen Morgan, and Belle Livingstone—[who] dominated New York's nightlife from the mid-1920s to the early 1930s."

Speakeasies appealed to both sexes because they were generally less intimidating and sleazy than the old saloons. With their food menus, booths, table service, jazz music, and glitzy female performers, rather than dark, dingy, open spaces, women didn't have to worry so much about getting jostled or groped by drunk strangers. And thanks to the fact that relatively complicated cocktails gained traction to hide the often poor quality of the alcohol, the potency of women's drinks got diluted by the concentration of the mixers.

They catered to single-gendered groups as well as couples. Because the second industrial revolution and the First World War had pushed working-class women into factory jobs and single urban life, they had grown accustomed to taking part in the public sphere and would no longer be shamed for sharing the all-male drinking space.

And let's not forget, patrons weren't the ones violating the law at these illegal establishments. Therefore the safety, ambience, and illicit intrigue attracted young women from "good" families to partake without taking hits to their reputations. The freedom to flagrantly drink, dance, and gamble—and, yes, vote—got heady, and jubilant women started smoking cigarettes in earnest, cutting their hair, and raising their skirt hems.

"Young women who ventured into these new institutions knew they were crossing a divide between an old set of assumptions about behavior and morality and a new code they were creating," writes Mary Murphy in an *American Quarterly* article entitled "Bootlegging Mothers and Drinking Daughters: Gender and Prohibition in Butte, Montana."

However, she continues, "Men shared an uneasy feeling that more was at stake than a woman having a drink. Indeed, male writers' caustic remarks about ladies lunching in speakeasies were a defensive response to women's invasion of traditional male territory. As one scholar of drinking habits noted, men defined the use and abuse of alcohol as a male privilege, a symbol of power and prestige. What bothered men was not that women drank but that they drank in public commercial institutions."

If this behavior bothered men then they were probably horrified that women went back into the kitchen, not to cook, necessarily, but to make and sell wine, beer, and whiskey, just like in the old days. The Volstead Act that officially created Prohibition allowed for home production of up to two hundred annual gallons of wine and cider but not beer or spirits; despite this, stores sold so many ingredients to homebrew that Michigan eventually taxed them.

Home stills and beer- and wine-making equipment typically found their way to working-class women, who augmented their incomes and independence by engaging in the illegal alcohol market. Court personnel had no idea what to make of the women hauled in for bootlegging. In the past, they'd tried most of the women in the legal system on prostitution or public drunkenness charges.

But now! Now married women and widows in their eighties—mothers, daughters, granddaughters—they were all making and distributing hooch.

In Montana, eighty-year-old Lavinia Gilman had her three-hundred-gallon still confiscated. Maud Vogen's mother was helping her distill whiskey when police raided her house. Mrs. Michael Murray's husband and friend marketed the liquor she made. And the widow Nora Gallagher told police she had a makeshift still on her stove so she could afford to buy Easter clothes for her kids.

The illicit activity ran so rampant that the local Montana papers constantly ran stories about police arresting women "selling liquor and beer in grocery stores and boarding houses and others attempting to destroy incriminating evidence by dumping liquor and mash into cellars," writes Murphy.

In North Carolina, a Greensboro paper reported that the mayor and two police officers had busted one of the area's biggest blind tigers (another word for speakeasy), operated by African American mother-and-daughter team Alice King and Jessie Hairston.

"The joint has been doing a flourishing business," wrote the paper, "being regarded as a sort of base of supply for many people in the mill villages north of the city."

Judges got so rattled by so many women challenging what Murphy calls "male notions of women's place," that they sometimes refused to believe the women who insisted they owned the operations. In Montana, Livinia Gilman's judge told her to send her son in to confess himself as the real distiller, and when Susie Gallagher Kerr admitted to owning the still that police had seized, officers argued that it must belong to the two men they'd arrested along with her.

Likewise, in 1933, the *Greensboro Record* reported that "women assistants in the rum-running profession are the latest methods of state bootleggers." That intro led into a brief about the arrest of one teenaged Mackalina Rebecca Johnston for giving police chase while carrying fifty gallons of whiskey in a roadster. Two men had jumped out of the car and presumably hadn't been found. But here's the catch: the clip never says whether Mackalina owned or was driving the car, choosing instead to assume that she merely assisted the men, who they believed certainly carried the real burden of blame.

Sometimes the police were correct in assuming that law-breaking women must have been working with a man. In a revival of the traditional alehouse, married couples such as Montana's Mike Erick and his unnamed wife, plus the African American Mr. and Mrs. Charles Martin ran "home speaks" from their houses.

Almost anyone could operate a home speak so almost anyone did. A 1929 police blotter printed in a Greensboro newspaper reports that the courts charged a "negro" woman named Cora Cotton with possession of alcohol and sentenced her with a fine of twenty-five dollars, a suspended ninety-day jail sentence, and a warning to stay away from liquor for two years after police heard her arguing with three White men inside her house over the price of some fifty-cent drinks.

Less common were the middle- and upper-class women who made booze for fun; more common were the middle- and upper-class women who entertained with alcohol . . . all the time. Cocktails didn't just hide out in speakeasies, they permeated high-class homes so pervasively that in 1930 social scientists coined the term "feminization of drinking."

A man came home from work. His wife waited with his martini or highball and her gin fizz, bees knees cocktails in hand. A society matron hosted a ladies' luncheon. A 1928 edition of *Lucy Allen's Table Service* invited women to prepare a "light cocktail accompanied by sandwiches or small wafers" for her guests. A housewife read a magazine or a book about etiquette or entertaining. Advertisements bombarded her with appeals to buy hipflasks, glassware, bar tools, and even free-standing portable bars for her living room.

"There are not many ladies in well-to-do houses now—certainly in the Eastern States—who are not experts at making cocktails," observed an article in a 1923 edition of *Nineteenth Century and After: A Monthly Review*.

"Women in the 1910s had drunk quietly," writes Catherine Gilbert Murdock in *Domesticating Drink*. "By the late 1920s, they were doing so flagrantly."

No one embodied this lifestyle more than the extraordinarily well-connected Long Island socialite Pauline Sabin. Born into a political and financial dynasty and married to a prominent banker, Pauline's luxurious trappings and social affairs were the stuff of *Great Gatsby* legend.

Pauline, founder of the Women's National Republican Club and the first female to join the Republican National Committee, had initially supported Prohibition. But instead of fostering a safer, more stable world for her two sons as she'd hoped, she'd watched in disgust as it caved in on itself, promoting excess drinking and hypocrisy and crime and revulsion.

She wasn't alone in her change of heart. The Republican Party, blamed for its stewardship of the 1929 stock market crash and Great Depression, was in the process of some serious soul-searching. Dry Republican candidate after candidate lost his election in 1930, swept out by wet Democrats. These politicians, nothing if not shrewd, were rethinking their positions on Prohibition and everything else.

Meanwhile, Pauline Sabin was growing increasingly emboldened. She made international news by quitting the Republican Committee in 1929 and the cover of *Time* magazine for endorsing Democrat Franklin Roosevelt in 1932. In the intervening years, she founded the Women's Organization for National

Prohibition Reform (WONPR) and stacked it with women with unimpeachable pedigrees (read: money and influence).

McCall's covered the inaugural meeting.

Sabin, the magazine published, was "fond of sports suits, wears purple and blue well, and usually affects pearl lobe earrings. . . . Her color sense is unfaltering." Her office walls, "pale green, harmonizing with salmon pink curtains."

The same reporter might have covered Hillary Clinton's presidential campaign.

By the end of 1933 Pauline's group, which started with eleven disenchanted colleagues from the women's Republican club, boasted 1.5 million members, plus chapters around the country. She and her associates conquered the halls of power, giving countless speeches, testimonies, and interviews.

Pauline and her bejeweled acolytes commanded attention, not just because they defied (and encouraged) the out-of-touch, fuddy-duddy stereotypes used to describe the politically active women of the temperance era, and not just because these crusaders for Prohibition's repeal emphatically contradicted the WCTU's assertion that all women spoke with one unilateral voice. Rather, they grabbed the world's gaze because they empowered women of all classes to speak up for the matters that mattered to them.

In the authorized history of the WONPR, author Grace Root explains the phenomenon by mimicking an imaginary American husband, who might ask, "What have you done to my wife, Mrs. Sabin? She now insists upon reading the editorial page before she will pour my breakfast coffee!"

Sabin's real-life critics didn't handle her or her ilk with such bemusement. Dry women such as Lucy Peabody, who founded the Women's National Committee for Law Enforcement, had insulted their wet counterparts before, failing to understand why any "normal" woman would drink or favor repeal.

Calling them "abnormal" and "subnormal," Lucy wrote, "They are not fit to guide automobiles, children, or society."

But Pauline had given anonymous wet females a face, one her opponents could personally attack with characteristic misogynistic ugliness. The dry press called Pauline's emissaries "scum of the earth" and accused them of "probably late at night flirting with other women's husbands at drunken and fashionable resorts." But these offenses slid off the WONPR's back like oil on Teflon. They were doing some incredibly heavy partisan lifting and they were closing in on victory.

Okrent writes, "While Pauline Sabin made the repeal cause respectable, even fashionable; while the government's enforcement efforts remained pointless and its diplomatic efforts turned futile; while there was more drinking, and talking about drinking, writing about drinking, winking about drinking, more everything about drinking . . . as all this moved the possibility of Repeal from the realm of the unimaginable toward the province of the conceivable . . . the ASL and the other components of the dry coalition, already strapped for leadership . . . began to run out of money, influence and will."

Pauline dissolved her organization immediately upon repeal. She disassociated herself from alcohol policy but remained active in politics—spending the World War II era heading the massive volunteer effort of the American Red Cross.

Alas, for all the strides taken for and by women during the 1920s, society still blacks out their accomplishments like a penniless drunk tossed out of a saloon.

A short biography of Pauline—inarguably the punk rock star of the Repeal movement—posted on the Public Broadcasting Service (PBS) webpage for Ken Burns's landmark documentary *Prohibition* (based on Okrent's *Last Call*) indecently begins, "Pauline Sabin was the wife of Charles Sabin, chairman of the board of the Guaranty Trust Company."

I guess we should be grateful that the venerable PBS at least, unlike earlier women such as Frederika Wetterer, published Pauline's own first name.

28 | BIG BOSS LADIES AND THE FAMILY TIES THAT BIND

I HAVE GOOD NEWS AND BAD NEWS to report about female brewery ownership in the 2010s. The good news is women own breweries in the 2010s.

The bad news is according to a Brewers Association member survey, women-owned breweries comprise a miniscule 2 percent of the total. That's 160 out of 8,000.

(Actually, the very fact that I can report this is good news considering stats about women in the industry only started coming out seven years ago. Trust me, it felt like an eternity.)

The Brewers Association goes on to say that men alone own more than half of member breweries, leaving less than half with mixed-gender ownership.

———

I'm counting Gretchen Schmidhausler at Little Dog on the Jersey Shore in that 2 percent, even though she does have silent male investors. She swears none of her business challenges have ever come as a result of her gender. But her challenges owning and operating a tiny brewery, she says, wrap in just about everything else.

"I wear a lot of hats," she says. "I'm the bookkeeper, tasting room manager, sales person, brewer. I miss working for someone else. I miss having someone else pay the bills. The robust number of breweries reduces the number of people that come to see you. Professionally it has been very rewarding. Financially it has not."

That's not to mention that with the proliferation of breweries, craft beer novices who come in for a pint during an afternoon spent brewery hopping don't realize how desperately she needs their support. "I really love this beer," they tell her. "I've just got so much beer in the fridge."

Gretchen is far from alone in her frustrations. The beer game can prove a crazy-making slog for anyone trying to make money on it. That explains one reason most brewery owners pair up with someone else—to shoulder some of the burden. One-third of BA members split ownership fifty-fifty between a woman and a man, and, by my unscientific account, the vast majority of those are wife and husband or, to a lesser degree, girlfriend and boyfriend.

————————

Lauri Spitz, who opened Moustache Brewing on the east end of Long Island in 2013 with her husband, Matt, offers one such example.

The first time they homebrewed, back in 2004, they had so much fun they declared in jest they should open a brewery. For the next seven years, they said that every time they brewed, which they did a lot for entertainment, given neither could settle on a career that didn't make them miserable.

They got serious about the professional brewing idea, agreeing they'd rather try and fail then fail to try at all. With less than zero idea how to fund or operate a brewery, they did what so many wannabe brewery owners do: they launched a Kickstarter campaign.

They raised $130,000. At that point, Lauri jokes, they looked at each other and said, "Oh fuck. I guess we have to start a brewery."

Like so many stories of misfortune that seem to befall start-up business owners and can only be laughed about after the passage of plenty of time and alcohol, the lead-up to opening their one-barrel brewhouse didn't, as an understatement, go well. It started when Matt broke his leg then was diagnosed with multiple sclerosis just as they were readying to open.

Then came the bad news.

As Lauri waited for Matt to finish a neurology appointment, she got a text telling her a sheriff was at the brewery putting a lock on the door because the landlord had neglected to pay the mortgage.

Typical.

Luckily, Matt manages his disease well and doesn't have to take much time off from brewing on what's now a seven-barrel system. This is good because Lauri, who calls herself too artistic and fun-loving to enjoy the precision demanded of brewing, mostly manages the taproom and business end of the business.

In all of the breweries owned by hetero couples, I don't think I've ever seen these roles reversed. Though I'd like to watch traditional divisions of labor collapse, I do appreciate a woman's touch on a taproom. Lauri, who told me half-ironically not long after she opened that she bases some of her beer recipes on scented candles, said in the same interview that she decorated Moustache's tasting room by "nesting the shit out of it."

Nice.

In a fairy tale, Moustache would live happily ever after. But in real life, Lauri and Matt spend a lot of their time stressed out and exhausted. Lauri says with all seriousness she had a nervous breakdown in the summer of 2020, and that was before a three-month COVID-19 shutdown, following their tourist town's dead winter season, pushed them into bankruptcy.

Bankruptcy notwithstanding, unsurprisingly the question Lauri hears most often is, "How do you and Matt work together without killing each other?"

Though I don't have an insider's view, it looks like my friends Lauri and Matt have an intensely resilient relationship, probably aided by the fact that everyone I know who knows Mr. Spitz thinks he's just about the nicest guy in New York.

Lauri attributes much of their success to the fact that they communicate the way a skillful corporate human relations specialist would train personnel. They listen without ego or judgment and say things to each other like, "Do you have five minutes for some feedback?"

Sometimes the answer is no, I want to go cry this out in a corner. Can we talk about it later?

Describing a relationship that reminds me of what celebrities often say about their equally famous significant others, Lauri actually prefers working with Matt because if only one of them worked at the brewery, the other couldn't possibly understand the crazy ups and downs of running one.

Lauri, who's teaching herself to take time for self-care, marvels, "When we originally decided to open, we said to each other, 'You know, best case scenario is we make it and we look back in seven years and say we did it.' Well, it's been seven years. And we're doing it."

Natalie and Vinnie Cilurzo have been doing it together since 2003, when they took over Russian River Brewing from Korbel Champagne Cellars in Sonoma County, California. With Natalie running the business and Vinnie manning brewing operations, Russian River has won more accolades and developed more of a cult following than most. Though Natalie oversees a sprawling destination brewery and a separate brewpub, invented the idea of a global charity beer, chaired the board of the California Craft Brewers Association, travels to big festivals and conferences and conducts the majority of the team's media interviews, she is still surprised when someone requests a picture with her instead of Vinnie.

Even though she says he makes a point to publicly call her "the backbone of the brewery," it bugs her how often people say things like, "Your husband's brewery," "What do you do here?" and "You don't LOOK like you own a brewery."

She notices that these assumptions can also shift into reverse, as when a female customer bluntly expressed disappointment that Natalie doesn't brew Russian River's beer.

"I thought she would be even more impressed that I own the brewery, run the business, and sign everyone's paychecks," she e-mails. "But she threw up her hands and walked away! It was an odd reaction."

Unlike Natalie, Mariah Calagione, co-owner of Dogfish Head, has chosen to labor—and labor, and labor—behind the scenes in relative anonymity as her photogenic and endlessly charming husband, Sam, has modeled himself into what many call the face of craft beer.

Mariah says it works for her. She doesn't like putting herself in the spotlight and she's thrilled that Sam's ubiquity in the media and public eye brings them positive attention.

However, as she says, not being the face of the company doesn't equal having no voice. She poses the tough questions, especially those that people who aren't married to Sam may be afraid to ask him.

"Of course," she says, "I don't want to be 'bad cop' all of the time, so I try to keep my tough questions to the important issues."

She is claiming a bit more of the limelight these days, as she and her coworkers whom she's quick to credit develop the Beer and Benevolence community programs that she oversees. She'll surely get even more face time as she takes on the role of Social Impact Leader in charge of diversity, equity, and inclusion (DEI), community engagement, and related issues for Boston Beer, which absorbed Dogfish in 2019.

Mariah says the couple's college-enrolled daughter and son have benefited enormously from the opportunities the brewery has given them to travel, meet other entrepreneurial families, and obtain summer jobs. They were born a few years after the brewery, so while they spent a lot of time there as babies, they didn't get the chance to do any homebrewing until very recently with their busy dad, who got his start making his own kitchen beer in grad school.

I love the idea of brewers teaching their young kids, especially daughters, to brew when time allows. Not only does it give children a respect for alcohol and responsible consumption, it gives them hands-on ways to learn and apply math and science.

The most prominent example of daddy/daughter(s) brewing comes out of Pottstown, Pennsylvania, where the four Yuengling sisters have taken over the largest and oldest American-owned brewery from their dad, Dick. As the first female stewards of the D.G. Yuengling & *Son* Brewing Company in its six generations, they're using their gender as a novel selling point and nurturing other beer women by, among other initiatives, already donating $75,000 to Pink Boots scholarships.

Vice president of operations Jennifer Yuengling told me for a *Forbes* article, "We recognize we have the opportunity to lead by example and influence future generations of women in the industry."

While the Yuenglings stand atop a mighty platform, many other women have entered the business because of their dads. Founders Brewing sales rep Natalie DeChico first learned about beer from her father, by helping him homebrew when she was a teenager, as did Lisa Allen, whose father founded Heater-Allen Brewing in Portland in 2007. Laura Bell, daughter of Larry Bell, has said she was the only four-year-old on her Kalamazoo block who knew what water, malt, hops, and yeast made.

Some of these father-daughter brewing relationships develop into business relationships. And I do know of one mother-son team, at Lower Forge Brewing in Medford, New Jersey. But Jacqui Town is the only woman I know to actually open a brewery with her father.

She wouldn't do it again.

In the ten years I've known Jacqui and Chip Town, neither has seemed any less than deeply warm, personable, and emotionally grounded. And Chip and Jacqui have always enjoyed a close relationship.

Yet . . .

"My dad always said it best," Jacqui says. "Working with my daughter is the best and worst thing I could ask for."

Jacqui started helping her dad homebrew as a teen. It got more fun after she graduated from college and moved back to near where she grew up on the Jersey Shore because she could actually sample the product. Chip had long daydreamed about opening a brewery, and good fortune struck, paradoxically, when both he and Jacqui got laid off from their office jobs within two weeks of one another following the recession of 2008.

It took them a year to write a business plan, secure funding, and sign a lease, and in 2014 they cut the ribbon on Rinn Duin Brewing, named after an Irish castle with distant ties to the family.

Chip oversaw brewing, accounting, and finance and Jacqui managed the taproom, sales, and marketing. Because Chip had invested more money, he got final say on big decisions.

When they were deciding on packaging, for example, Jacqui wanted to try cans and Chip insisted his demographic would feel more comfortable sticking with bottles. And though Jacqui would prove to have good instincts by the time can-craving craft brewers sent bottles to near obsolescence, she simultaneously chuckles and grimaces as she asks rhetorically what may have happened to the business—whose traditional English and Irish beer styles catered to a slightly older crowd and ran counter to the craft tastes du jour—if they'd unveiled cans to their conservative Jersey clientele back in 2014.

Ken Grossman, who finds it fun working with his daughter Sierra and son Brian, tells me he and his wife have tried not to push any of their three kids into the business.

Rick Allen's daughter, Lisa, who didn't think of brewing as an occupation for women, first went into wine.

And Larry Bell's daughter, Laura, who couldn't find a job after college, accepted her dad's invitation to try out the company until she figured out what to do with her life. After Larry got prostate cancer in 2008 and the family started taking a hard look at succession planning, she took herself on a three-week road trip to think about what she really wanted. She returned with a decision: she would devote her professional life to the brewery.

Larry made her a partner and she set about setting up and directing a marketing department before taking on his job as CEO in 2018.

Over beers in the brewery's Eccentric Cafe one afternoon in 2016, Laura tells me she somewhat resented the practically penniless start-up growing up because she had to fold T-shirts and label bottles. Plus, her mom and dad had split amicably when she was ten, and the brewery, which they opened two months after she was born, stole most of Larry's time.

Though she says her dad "loved the crap" out of her and her younger brother, she didn't necessarily appreciate what the sixth-largest brewery in the country provided her and the greater Kalamazoo community until she worked there and not only heard positive stories about the notoriously opinionated Larry from longtime employees but also for the first time had a chance to significantly deepen their relationship.

Jacqui says she and her father loved spending time together over their passion project, and Chip could usually help her calm down or figure out a solution to a problem because he could predict her reactions. That said, Jacqui both admits and quotes her mom, Ann, in saying that her personality shares a lot of traits with her dad's, which they agree ranks high on the stubbornness scale.

In addition, Jacqui says she wasn't immune from taking things personally or getting triggered by the usual unresolved childhood issues. She laments that their relationship turned pretty tense around three years ago when she took two maternity leaves, and she spent the time feeling guilty about leaving Chip to run the business with just two employees.

Laura, who learned unequivocally from Larry that neither she nor her brother was to flaunt their last name while working for his company, also learned that her father leads with a supportive yet hands-off approach that requires his employees to develop their own leadership style.

In retrospect she appreciated that her lack of a micromanaging boss had prepared her to be a strong leader, but she'd been expecting something different.

"I was looking for this magical experience where my dad would take me by the hand and guide me," she says. "Instead I got the, 'Figure it out.'"

One thing Laura hadn't quite figured out when we met was how to find social fulfillment living as a single, childless thirtysomething who worked as an executive for a mature company in a small Michigan town where people think of her as little more than Larry Bell's daughter. She was lonely, trying to date and relate to other millennials. She and her dad would "freak out" pondering the future of the brewery once she and her brother, who had no kids at that point, got too old to carry it forward.

Sometimes, she told me, she wonders what would have happened if she'd opened a plain old noodle shop in downtown Kalamazoo instead.

By the time Jacqui took her maternity leaves, Rinn Duin was in economic turmoil. The Towns had taken on an investor-partner whose vision didn't align with theirs and whose financing couldn't bail them out. Jacqui says she and Chip were exhausted, stressed, and, when she wasn't on maternity leave, working with no days off. In 2018, Jacqui stepped out of the arrangement, and Chip followed by selling his remaining stake a few months later.

Now, Jacqui says the family dynamic has mostly returned to a relaxed normal, unencumbered by what she saw as the elephant in the room. Pop-pop and Nanny come over a few times a month to drink a few beers on the deck with their daughter and son-in-law and play with their two toddler grandsons, TJ and Evan, at the pool or beach.

Jacqui, who's launched a clothing line in her spare time as a stay-at-home mom, concludes, "It taught me so much but I don't think the strain it put on my family was worth it in the end."

In April 2018 Laura left her job at Bell's, telling the City Tap blog it was time to discover passions outside of beer.

"If I don't leave now, I might never do it," she said.

Working jobs from TV news production to sales, Renee DeLuca didn't know she had a famous beer father until she hit her thirties. It's not that her father never told her he was famous; it's that as an adoptee, she didn't know who he was.

When she was in her twenties, Renee met her birth mother. The elder woman passed along her father's name: Jack McAuliffe.

"I always knew I had beer in my blood!" Renee is famous for saying.

But Jack, who'd had a fling with Renee's mother in high school, hadn't known about her, and it took him years after Renee contacted his relatives to connect. He'd never married and had made his intentions regarding children clear at age twenty-one by getting a vasectomy. When Renee found him through an ancestry website, he was living on disability in a trailer on his sister's land in Northwest Arkansas.

Once they did meet, he was delighted to get to know the daughter he hadn't had to raise.

"We had lived separate lives. It's been this incredible journey," Renee gushes twenty years after the fact. "It's created this whole identity for me."

The identity it created is that of *The Brewer's Daughter*, the name Renee uses for her blog about her experiences with beer and family. Wearing the label proudly, Renee has introduced the initially reluctant Jack back into the beer world, where brewing celebrities treat him like a star, and he gets to feel the glow of adoration from those who inherited what he created.

After Jack gave the nod to Jim Koch and Ken Grossman to brew beers in his honor, Renee commissioned Platform Beer Co. in Cleveland and Raleigh Brewing in North Carolina to recreate New Albion's recipes.

Jack, frail and confined to a wheelchair in his mid-seventies, enjoys that Renee dotes on him and visits frequently from Ohio. In late 2019, he took what Renee says would be his last trip, to accept honors from the Smithsonian's National Museum of American History in DC in a ceremony to christen its craft beer collection, on permanent display in the newly remodeled Julia Child's kitchen exhibition on food.

After hearing from an esteemed panel of craft beer pioneers, curator Theresa McCulla brought the microphone to Jack, seated in the audience. Waiting more than a moment for him to speak, Theresa moved the handheld mic to Renee, who said, "I'm here because of Jack."

Jack, who has trouble speaking above a stilted whisper, startled and amused those of us in the audience by replying very clearly, "I think we all are."

29 | DON'T WORRY, DARLING, YOU DIDN'T BURN THE BEER

WHEN I TELL NON-BEER-GEEKS that I write about women in beer, they invariably exclaim, "Oh, like Laverne and Shirley!" Though I've never seen the episode of the 1970s sitcom where the two friends work a stint at a brewery, I do recognize the bottling line scene from the opening credits.

I bring this up for two reasons on opposite sides of the coin. Until about ten years ago, I had no idea that women worked at macrobreweries in the twentieth century. Any woman. Anywhere. And around ten years ago I learned that women did work in macrobreweries in the twentieth century. A few women. In a few places.

But that doesn't mean life was easy for them.

"There was a belief among many of the brewers that our hormones would affect the yeast," says eighty-year-old Gerri Kustelski, who's still working in chemical and sensory analysis toward the end of an illustrious career in the Minneapolis–Saint Paul brewing world.

This notion didn't just sound ridiculous to Gerri, who went to work in the lab at Theodore Hamm Brewing Company after she graduated college with a chemistry degree in 1962, twenty-five hundred years after Iron Age Northern Europeans believed similarly. It thoroughly pissed her off because it meant the all-male operations team wouldn't let her or her female lab colleagues, who wore crisp white uniforms like nurses, fetch their own samples from the production floor. "We started being allowed out into the plant probably with Olympia [Brewing]," which bought Hamm's in 1975 and in Gerri's mind fostered a less antiquated environment.

202

Kristi McGuire says her supervisors and most of her underlings at Anheuser-Busch from 2000 to 2009 treated her with the dignity her senior roles in operations and marketing deserved. At least one of those bosses, the legendary Anheuser-Busch veteran Jane Killebrew-Galeski, was female. But middle managers in other departments didn't always do the same.

"Later in my career, after I'd spent six years in Juneau [at Alaskan Brewing] and worked at five facilities at Anheuser-Busch, I'm at taste panel and still get called kiddo," she recalls.

In her *Road Brewer* blog from 2007, Teri Fahrendorf writes about sitting in on a sensory panel with Jane and Kristi during a visit to their workplace and getting the opposite impression from the men in the room.

"I was a bit wary, having had the experience in 2001 and 2002 of judging the Australian International Beer Awards with a lot of large brewery bigwigs who just didn't know what to make of a young(ish) female brewer/judge," she wrote. "The atmosphere in the Anheuser-Busch sensory room was decidedly different."

Mary Pellettieri, known as one of the top quality-management minds in the world, says the minute she started working as quality manager for MillerCoors (now Molson Coors) in 2009, she knew she wasn't alone. Right away she noticed a strong number of women leading other quality programs within the company and met some "unicorns"—female engineers who led operations, particularly packaging, overseeing "a complex array of tradesmen and brewing staff and other engineers." She says she'd walked into the end of a cultural overhaul that had started ten to fifteen years earlier.

Kristi found it refreshing to learn that her managers at Anheuser-Busch's Ft. Collins brewery had been watching her hide in a broom closet to pump breast milk after she had her first kid. It sounds creepy but it wasn't. Within a year, the factory had installed lactation stations.

In 2020, AB InBev (ABI) offers its pregnant workers what Whitney Burnside, head brewer at the corporation's 10 Barrel brewpub in Portland, calls a very generous maternity leave and full benefits. Though most small breweries have no formal policies in place, potentially scaring would-be moms away from getting pregnant, ABI extends sixteen weeks of paid leave to new mothers and two weeks to fathers. Molson Coors gives fathers four weeks.

Despite the fact that 10 Barrel simply brought over a brewer from the mother ship in Bend to cover for her, Whitney admits to feeling worried and almost guilty for taking leave because in the cobwebby corners of her mind, "That's not what brewers do."

Luckily, her manager and coworkers assured her they certainly do, and her husband lovingly scolded her for fearing her conscience would make her quit before asking for time off to have another one.

Now, a reassured Whitney hopes other motherhood-minded women at ABI will feel more confident taking maternity leave after seeing how smoothly it went for her.

———————————

Patricia Henry already had kids when she went to work at MillerCoors and climbed the corporate ladder to become the first woman to run a major brewing plant. Pat had walked into the Eden, North Carolina, facility, still under construction, in 1977, to submit her résumé. She confessed to zero experience with beer, even as a drinker, but was ready to leave her career as a corporate chemist and systems engineer. She got hired on immediately as a brewing supervisor, charged with training brewers despite having never brewed herself.

"I tried to get them to look at this as a big kitchen. You've got the big kettles, and you put the different materials and water in it. It's like making oatmeal," she told *Business North Carolina* magazine in 2002.

Twenty-five years after she held that role, the magazine says employees still called the brewhouse Pat's Kitchen.

The woman who'd turned down a full ride to Harvard med school (family problems, career indecision) worked her way up through jobs normally reserved for professional brewers with much more experience.

In 1991, the brewery sent Pat to study at the world-class Siebel Institute of Technology for three months. When she returned to Eden, MillerCoors named her brewmaster, making her the first female to hold this position at a major brewery in America. Four years after that, she took over the plant.

"Honestly, in my wildest dreams, I never dreamed I'd be plant manager. This is a male-dominated business," she told *Business North Carolina*.

Before retiring, Pat, who is African American, moved up once more to become director of strategic projects for Miller, shattering the industry's ceilings one last time, not just for her gender but for her race, as well.

Perhaps reading the tea leaves, both Anne Sprecher of Sprecher Brewing and Jodi Marti of August Schell retired from the breweries they owned in 2020. For decades, the two women have contributed richly to their families' nineteenth-century companies.

Considering almost no legacy brewery in the United States has managed to survive this long, Anne and Jodi number among a precious few old-time matriarchs in the business. However, in Europe, where family breweries are a bit more plentiful (not having suffered through Prohibition), a slightly larger share of women have steered and supported these private endeavors.

Rosa Merckx's parents called her a rebel without a cause, and not just because she was the first woman in her town to drive a car. In 1946, she started work as a secretary for the manager of the three-hundred-year-old, family-owned Liefmans Oudenaarde in Belgium, and it didn't take long for her boss to reward her intelligence and interest by teaching her about malt, hops, the brewing process, and quality control. It turns out he had an ulterior motive.

As soon as he deemed her educated enough, he informed her, "Good, you know how to brew. Now my wife and I can go on holiday."

When he died in 1972, his family asked her to take over. Upon saying yes, she became the first female master brewer, operations director, and—in her words—"brewhouse mother" in modern Belgium. She held the position until she retired in 1990. Over that period, she had a huge hand in spreading the *kriek* (cherry) ale style throughout Europe and the United States.

At ninety-six, she still walks regularly to the brewery to socialize, greet international dignitaries, and taste beer to ensure its quality and consistency. She insists no one has ever underestimated her.

"All the brewers in Belgium were very nice to me because they had respect for the way I was carrying on in the brewery," says the trilingual "Madame Rose" in fluent English. "It was hard work. I had a husband and two sons. But a day has twenty-four hours so you need to know how to arrange them."

Today, one of those sons, Olav Blancquaert, has earned his own fame in the brewing world. The former Liefmans brewmaster now holds the same title at Duvel, owned by Duvel Moortgat, which bought Liefmans in 2008. His mother retains her role as one of the most beloved beer people in Europe, while Anne-Françoise Pypaert, Orval's brewmaster since 2013, carries on her legacy as the first female to hold that position at a Trappist brewery. The few monastic Trappist breweries are considered among the very best in the world.

Sabine Weyermann, of Bamberg, Germany, also lights up beer lovers' smiles when she greets them. A highly respected figure in the international world of beer, Sabine represents the fourth generation of Weyermann Specialty Malts, which she took over when her father passed in 1985. Her cousins called her crazy.

But she and her husband, Thomas Kraus-Weyermann, sensed the coming craft beer revolution and turned what had been a primarily pale and pilsner malthouse into one that can sell small quantities of many different types of malts that meet fanatically rigorous standards.

"I'd love to meet my great-grandparents for half an hour. I think they shared a vision," she tells me in the conference room of the corporate campus, whose buildings take up several blocks. The fragrant smell of roasting malt hangs redolent in the air.

"I think everybody is proud of me," she muses. "Whenever I face a situation, I think all my ancestors are behind me. The whole Weyermann world is protecting me."

Franziska, her only child, sits in on some of our interview but doesn't say much. Replaying the situation between a young Sabine and her parents, she hasn't committed to providing the family business with generation number five.

"I think Franny would die if I said you have to take over the company. But I think this is one hundred percent of the goal," Sabine says. "It's nice to see the work of your life being carried on. Wouldn't you be happy if you had a daughter who could add another chapter to the family tradition?"

One hundred sixty miles south in the Bavarian village of Aying, that wish has come true for Angela Inselkammer. The partial owner of the Ayinger brewery has run its four-star inn for decades and has been awarded Bavarian Order of Merit for her outstanding contributions to Bavaria as the first woman elected president of the Bavarian Hotel and Restaurant Association. Her daughter, Ursula, has worked with her.

Though Angela has been called the soul of the company, another woman's presence is never far off. Before Edith Haberland Wagner died, she owned 51 percent of the company. As the fourth generation of the Wagner family that bought the brewery from the state in the nineteenth century, Edith inherited Ayinger's controlling shares yet had no fifth generation to bequeath them to. She left its care to a close friend with a request for him to start a foundation to keep it perpetually in private hands. He did so in 2013, and a seventh-generation Wagner heiress, Catherine Demeter, now directs the foundation and chairs the brewery's board.

In this capacity, Catherine also oversees the Oktoberfest museum, steps off Munich's picture-perfect historic main square, where I ate dinner one dreamy snowy night. Between the soft snow, low ceiling, German dollhouse decor, and older gentlemen out of central casting drinking from steins in the museum's cozy underground bar and dining room, I honestly imagined I'd been transported to a quintessential German winter wonderland. I'll never forget it.

Across the Channel, in England, renowned author Roger Protz has brought British brewery women to life in his 2020 release, *The Family Brewers of Britain: A Celebration of British Brewing Heritage*. In the twentieth century alone, many of the United Kingdom's most aristocratic old breweries have had women in charge. Happily, there are too many to report but it's worth noting that Catherine Maxwell Stuart, the twenty-first Lady of Traquair, is the first to own and direct brewing operations at the oldest continuously inhabited house in Scotland. Female family members at three other British breweries took over before 1917 and in two instances remained in control for more than fifty years.

"It's clear that women have played a significant role in family brewing over the last few centuries, although it is rarely talked about. Beer is often portrayed as a male domain, even though many of these iconic breweries would not be what they are today if they did not have strong women at the helm," writes Roger.

He points out one woman in particular, early 1900s St. Austell Brewery chairwoman Hester Parnell, who frightened her employees so much that when her chauffeur would pull her car into the brewery, Roger says, "Workers would rap out warnings on pipes."

A former employee called her, "A proper dragon."

While the perception of Hester may not have paved a golden path for women who followed in her footsteps, gender expectations for British beer life have loosened up significantly since then.

Roger recalls going to a pub with a female friend in the 1960s; he says everyone stopped talking until they left.

Belinda Sutton, who runs Elgood's Brewery with her sister, Jennifer Everall, can appreciate that. She tells a British newspaper that she was the only woman at her first meeting of the British Beer and Pub Association in 1984.

"Two of the men asked me to fetch them a drink, and another asked me where the loos were," she's quoted as saying. "Now I deal with more women in the industry than men. There's been a huge cultural change."

That's true for the women who represent the American industry, too. The National Beer Wholesalers Association's (NBWA) senior vice president and COO and its vice president of operations tell *The Hill* political publication that when they entered the industry, thirty and nineteen years ago, respectively, they'd be the lone female in a conference room or in line for the loo. The 2019 article reports that, "The NBWA has twelve women in its fifteen senior-most positions, the Beer Institute has six women on its eleven-person staff and the Brewers Association's only DC staffer is a woman."

The Beer Institute is the new name for the old US Brewers Association of pre-Prohibition infamy. The stats and the status of the women in these organizations represents true progress. But the big-beer industry still has decades worth of amends to make, and not just for siccing dogs on a crowd of righteous women praying peacefully in the street.

Brewers staggered out of Prohibition horrifically scarred. Those that managed to survive by surreptitiously brewing beer or pivoting to production of something innocent, such as malt ice cream, met with a dystopian streetscape clouded by the Depression and preparation for a second world war. Beer's popularity would take repeated blows over the next century, and a Darwinian feast of consolidation and closures left former brewing beacons such as Philadelphia without a functioning brewery in 1987 for the first time in three hundred years.

At the conclusion of World War II, a dozen years after Prohibition, brewers could discern one sunny spot on the horizon: their former nemeses—women. Looking to capitalize on the shift toward suburban society, they conducted market research and followed consultants' advice to appeal to this untapped demographic, who weren't just buying beer for the household but drinking some, too.

Beer sales had exploded after 1940, thanks in no small part to the fact that US breweries, as "essential" businesses, didn't have to give up materials to the war effort like distilleries did. That said, they hadn't necessarily gained women as new wartime customers as UK and Irish breweries had. British and Irish women entered the low end of the brewery and pub workforce while their men were off fighting.

While a scattered few American breweries did hire women to temporarily (or in some cases, permanently) fill vacant jobs in almost every department during the war, the industry didn't lose too much of its regular workforce of generally older, established career men. Those breweries that did employ female personnel found them to be such competent workers that Gulf Brewing in Houston hired women over available men for a time.

Gulf's personnel and safety director wrote in *American Brewer* that after vehemently opposing the idea of bringing in women, men in production described themselves as relieved to learn their three hundred new coworkers didn't need help performing physical tasks and didn't expect a lighter workload.

Other magazines advised bosses to pay their new female employees as much as the men they replaced, warning them that women notice and complain about conditions at much higher rates than their male counterparts. Despite viewing women in the brewing workforce with earned respect, the men offering opinions in these articles retained a surprised, bemused, distant, and patronizing attitude toward them.

A photo caption from May 1945 read, "Now that the war in Europe has ended and we are moving into the reconversion period, women are becoming restless in away-from-the-home employment."

No matter, US breweries could use women in the capacity of consumers after the war and quickly seized on the idea of a light beer for the little ladies.

Although Miller claims it invented "lite"—which it introduced in the mid-1970s—it seems light beer actually launched full force in the 1940s and '50s, and that's if you don't count Acme Breweries' 1930s-era cartoon spokesmodel calling the brand "dietetically non-fattening" or the lighter styles for sale all the way back in ancient Sumer.

Regional breweries such as George J. Renner Brewing in Akron, Ohio; Fort Pitt Brewing in Pittsburgh; Red Top Brewing in Cincinnati; and Jacob Ruppert Brewery in New York followed the promise of money and advertised modern low-calorie lagers that wouldn't fill you up.

What seems strange about Miller's spurious claim about Miller Lite, whose recipe it actually acquired when it bought Meister Brau and its failed light lager in the early 1970s, is that Fred Miller himself already had a light beer recipe in his pocket all the way back in 1903, brewed by his grandfather. He didn't brand Miller High Life as a light beer but he did market the Champagne of Beers to women.

He ran full-page color Miller Lite ads in women's magazines such as *McCall's* and *Vogue*. He hired one of the nation's top industrial designers to conceptualize feminine in-store displays. And he packaged it in six-ounce splits, sold as "a dainty package aimed at women's appetites." In five years, the brewery's sales shot up 275 percent at a time when 2 percent growth was pretty good.

No one knows who really invented the six-pack holder, either, though one prevailing yet probably invalid theory holds that Pabst Brewing commissioned research that convinced its marketing team to calculate how many beer bottles a woman could comfortably carry home to her man. Better data exists to prop up an alternate explanation that Florida's Jax Brewery couldn't afford the aluminum cans that replaced the steel ones during the war effort.

According to VinePair of Jax, "Their solution? Sacks. One hundred thousand of them, labeled 'Jax Beer' and filled with six bottles. The six sack."

Wherever the truth lies, the reality is that it likely did relate to the fact that women had become the primary purchasers of take-out beer, a pretty novel concept in the 1940s and '50s.

After more than a century of viciously antagonizing women, breweries now wanted to use advertising in addition to packaging innovations to enlist them as allies. Taking advantage of the postwar moment of radical cultural restructuring to bolster previously frowned-upon home consumption as well as the role of beer in everyday life, the US Brewers Foundation (formed from the USBA and the United Breweries Industrial Foundation) launched the spectacularly successful Beer Belongs campaign. Coupled with the same tired tropes about beer as wholesome and nourishing, the industry aimed its messaging at women in an attempt to ward off any potential threat of a Prohibition 2.0 and make friends with its new audience. Say hello to glossy appeals like "Home Life in America" in mass-market magazines.

Rockwellian scenes of Americana littered the pages, reinforced by milquetoast text that played on the heartstrings, promoted moderation, and, as a bonus, fired up jingoistic sentiment. Part of the tagline would read something like, "The right to enjoy this beverage of moderation . . . this, too, is part of our American heritage of personal freedom. . . . Beer belongs . . . enjoy it."

"Whether being served while friends picnic on the beach or being the celebratory drink of choice after a marriage proposal, the images from this campaign made these and many other occasions synonymous with beer," says Jim McGreevy, president and CEO of the Beer Institute, successor to the Brewers Foundation.

It was not surprising that the ads exclusively depicted White families of means. On the surface, these and other ads from the era appear to empower women but underneath subliminally work to undermine them. More often than not they sized women smaller than men, with at least a few suburbia types down on their knees.

The title for this chapter comes from a 1952 print ad for Schlitz and perfectly demonstrates this point, down to the relative size of the illustrated couple, their placement in a kitchen, and the business suit and long skirt worn by the husband and wife.

The apron-wearing woman is distraught. She holds a frying pan with smoke pouring from it. Her smiling husband comforts her. The caption: "Don't Worry Darling, You Didn't Burn the Beer."

In retrospect, it's possible to feel almost wistful for this patronizing portrayal. That's because we know what came next.

Light-hearted iconic commercial characters like Carling's bartender, Mabel, morphed into the Saint Pauli Girl, whose buxom bosom was always on display, who morphed into the Swedish bikini team who morphed into countless life-size cardboard cutouts of models endorsing some brand in some way or another.

Even the more offensive ads of the 1950s—think Natural Light's 1957 "Wet, Cold and Delicious" female swimmer gazing at a bottle of light lager— spoke in soft sexual overtones. By the time Colt 45 revealed its "Bottom's Up" ad prominently featuring a bikini-covered woman's bottom (playing a board game, of all the silly things), all bets were off. For the next half-century, women primarily appeared in beer commercials to attract the male gaze and stimulate the male libido.

Ad after ad after ad brought bathing-suit clad girls into men's and women's living rooms, billboards, sport sponsorships, and anywhere else you can slap a sexy image. And let's not forget the wet T-shirt contests and the live beer babes.

I have personal experience with that last one. I moonlighted as a "brand ambassador" in bars throughout my twenties and thirties. My Heineken Light costume consisted of a skin-tight see-through white spandex halter dress that hardly covered my assets. I managed to snag two so I could wear them on top of each other and not display my nipples. Most of my colleagues were not so lucky.

In 2007 ad critic Bob Garfield asked if a contemporary Heineken TV spot was the most sexist beer commercial ever produced. It converted a female robot's uterus into an animated beer keg. That particular advert contained no speech—thank god. But god help you when the photos of come-hither females came accompanied by narration, such as in 1999, Miller Lite: "Pilsner is a type of beer. Kind of like Rebecca is a type of woman." In 2003, Coors Light: "Here's to going for two. Or one." And in 2015, Bud Light: "The perfect beer for removing 'no' from your vocabulary for the night."

More recently, the big boys of beer have tried to change their image, engaging in media outreach campaigns to promote their women in leadership roles and female-friendly recruitment and promotion campaigns. I remember nodding with approval when MillerCoors appointed Michelle Nettles as head of human relations and announced initiatives to recruit women in 2014. (Looking back, I'm wondering what took so damn long.)

I do have to hand it to AB InBev: almost half of their US breweries have brewsters in charge, with a decent bit of racial diversity on the list. In March 2020 ABI named Natalie Johnson as its first African American female brewmaster at its St. Louis headquarters. However, of eighteen senior executives pictured on ABI's website, only one, the general counsel, is female. Every one of them is White.

In 2016 MillerCoors announced it would no longer partake in sexist advertising. In 2019 Budweiser made a splash by modernizing and reimagining three of its most misogynistic vintage ads.

But macro-beer marketers are nothing if not savvy. And sneaky. They made unimaginable amounts of money from all those unfortunate ads the first time around. Then they got to capture goodwill and share of mind when they circled back to repent.

Well done, guys. This Bud's for you. Please allow me to throw it in your face.

30 | BEYOND BEARDS, BEYOND BREASTS

WHEN DEB LOCH AND JILL PAVLAK tried to open Minnesota's first women-owned brewery, they couldn't get a loan. They found this suspicious.

Minnesota already had its share of craft breweries by 2014, and they planned to open Urban Growler in the metropolitan state capital of Saint Paul. No one could argue they didn't deserve to qualify, either.

Deb, a homebrewer since the 1990s, had completed the Master Brewers program at UC Davis and had brewed at Summit Brewing. Jill had owned two businesses.

But even as recently as 2014, Deb and Jill had two strikes that they believe made loan officers squirm: they were women and they were married . . . to each other. Eventually it worked out. The couple raised the money privately and still anchor their little corner of the Twin Cities' beer landscape.

Fast-forward four or five years. Situated next to the biggest military base in the country, Army combat veteran Torie Fisher's been providing handcrafted beer and hospitality to members of the military, law enforcement, first responders, and their families since 2015. As a publicly out lesbian, Torie invited the well-known transgender vet Sgt. Maj. Jennifer Long to speak at the brewery.

Straight men with buzz cuts and upright postures packed the taproom. During Jennifer's presentation, Torie fretted about how her conservative clientele would react. She needn't have worried. When Jennifer finished talking, the crowd gave her a standing ovation.

Based on years of careful observations and intimate conversations, I've concluded that lesbians working in craft beer far overrepresent their percentage of the population. I'd argue that they drastically outnumber every other group that falls outside the White straight beer paradigm.

That said, the beer industry severely *under*represents every non-cis-White-male grouping that exists. According to brewers and bloggers who've crunched the numbers, Black people own a mere 1 percent of US breweries. The BA reports non-White production staff makes up less than a quarter of the overall production workforce while just 11 percent of brewers identify as non-White, according to a member benchmarking survey given in 2019.

Brewer Celeste Beatty got a fair bit of attention but inhabited a lonely space as the only Black woman to own a US brewery when she opened Harlem Brewing in 2000. No one's done an official count but I'd bet we could use one or two hands to enumerate any others who've set up shop since.

Working out of a second brewery, this one in Rocky Mount, North Carolina, Celeste is working toward incubating Black talent to open breweries in typically Black spaces. She says, "My vision for the company is to open breweries in beer deserts. There's no craft beer culture in many of our communities, but there's an interest."

As the industry matures and the number of people populating it balloons, its face soothingly gets a little darker, a little queerer, a little more feminine, and a little more outside the norm.

How is the industry reacting? Many would argue not well.

Founders Brewing permanently lost a lot of its customers when it profoundly botched its response to a lawsuit filed by its Black events and promotions manager for what the staff member alleged was an ongoing climate of prejudice against Black employees.

While that measures as the most recognizable racist beer incident, instances of bias occur every day. A Kalamazoo bottle shop owner repeatedly posted anti-Semitic and racist "jokes" and memes on his Facebook page. Black blogger Chalonda White, who goes by Afro.Beer.Chick on Twitter, feels a cold vibe and a lack of service in a lot of the taprooms she visits. DEI specialist J. Jackson-Beckham reports that the very few gay men and transgender women in the industry are feeling very, very isolated these days.

There are pockets of optimism, however, even for the most marginalized among us.

Kathleen Culhane wanted to open the first female-owned brewery in Minnesota and confesses to feeling slightly jealous that the ladies at Urban Growler beat her to it. She was fortunate enough to get a loan from a female officer with strong emotional ties to Kathleen's Saint Paul neighborhood but not fortunate enough to keep her brewery open more than a few years.

Her primary business regret? She didn't do enough to advertise the brewery ownership team as the bisexual, trans, genderqueer romantic quad that it was.

"I didn't want to be the gay or trans brewery," says Kathleen, a trans woman who identifies as queer. "I also didn't want to be pushy about it."

Despite the failure to successfully launch in the long term, she says she never attributed any of Sidhe (pronounced "she") Brewing's problems to a lack of acceptance. Inside the brewery she literally let flags fly to represent pride, bisexuality, and transgender identity next to flags of Saint Paul and her ancestral homeland of Ireland. When she schmoozed with the tasting room crowd she never picked up on any discomfort with her long hair and "obvious boobs" that intermingled with her deep voice and hulking frame.

This type of mellow reaction doesn't much surprise Annie Johnson, whose perspective as a queer Black woman means she tends to notice who's around and what kind of vibe they're putting out.

She says "no one gives a shit" that her Seattle homebrew club is home to trans members. She states that in her liberal city, at least, the twenty- and thirtysomething professionals who're entering the hobby have a more progressive mindset than the homebrewers who came before them.

"They don't subscribe to that older 'bro' White male typical homebrewer makeup," she says.

Despite Kathleen's patrons' presumed desire to see the veteran homebrewer and her partners succeed, she couldn't prevent the business and romantic relationships from turning ugly. She closed Sidhe and went back to where her professional brewing career started—near Duluth, at Thirsty Pagan Brewing.

Charlotte, North Carolina, beertender Eugenia Brown confesses to being afraid to homebrew. She doesn't know anyone who does it. So as a Black woman whose life experience has trained her to stay watchful for unforeseen racist reproach, the idea of walking into a meeting where she's been invited but doesn't know who or what to expect intimidates her.

Herein lies the crux of the conflict raging within many businesses and communities as the world grapples with how to realign its relationship with race. There's a difference between *Sure, c'mon in* and *Let me do my best to ensure your comfort.*

As diversity and inclusion specialist Dr. J. explains, diversity means *You are welcome here.* Inclusion means *I made this space for you.*

Ever since the 2020 protests for racial equity, conscientious brewery owners have been auditing their business models to eliminate any unconscious bias that threatens to lock diverse patrons and employees out while seeking to incorporate strategies and relationships that invite all segments of their geographic community in.

DEI experts like Dr. J., Patrice Palmer, and Graci Harkema are working to get brewery personnel rosters to at least index with their communities' demographic makeup in addition to building systems to ensure all groups are receiving invitations to engage and feel safe once they do—women and White guys included.

Tiesha Cook is one who doesn't want to wait around for institutional change to bring more Black people into craft beer. She and her husband, Dom, have created the Beer Kulture nonprofit to umbrella their efforts to bring beer to Black people. Apart from programming a website, hosting craft beer events in Black communities, and running a charitable foundation, Tiesha and Dom have taken donations to buy beer, set up on street corners in St. Petersburg, Florida, and hand cans out to the people.

Eugenia, who's trademarked the name Black Beer Chick, strives to give Black women, specifically, the confidence to enter racially mixed beer spaces where they may have to knock on the door. She raised money to send fifty Black women to an online course to study for the international Cicerone Beer Server exam (similar to an entry-level sommelier exam), which she expects will give them a credential to add to their résumés when they apply for beer jobs. When the people behind the Cicerone program heard about her campaign, they matched her money and paid for fifty more students to enroll in the class.

Even though she's long since met her goal, Eugenia is keeping her fundraising going.

She's also working to connect Black women with Pink Boots and Pink Boots with Black women. Some of her Black sisters give her the side eye for it, as she says, feeling like they don't belong in a dominantly White organization and distrusting the members, no thanks to more than a century's worth of rejection from far too many feminist movements. But Eugenia says she's bought into the sincerity of the sisterhood ever since Pink Boots Society national invited her to take over its Instagram page for a day and her local chapter asked her to be a coleader.

This time, she accepted.

While she does believe in the power of all-Black spaces, she doesn't feel the need to create a "Black Boots" answer to the original.

"We already have these systems in place," she says, "and why shouldn't it be inclusive anyway?"

After the protests, Pink Boots took what I perceive as a strong stand. On its blog and in an e-mail to members, the board promised, "We are dedicated to taking concrete action toward social justice and to continue to support change within our industry."

It announced three initiatives:

1. Hire a consultant and/or speakers to inform Pink Boots Society on its long-term strategic DEI plans.
2. Constitute a diversity task force.
3. Develop a budget for DEI efforts.

The e-mail went on to say that the board hopes the fact it has opened up to women across all alcohol industries will give the group a greater opportunity to grow diversity within its membership.

"It all comes full circle," Eugenia says. "By making Pink Boots more diverse you make the industry more diverse."

But what happens when your own community tries to shut you down for opening up a brewery? Members of the Cherokee Nation in North Carolina petitioned to keep Morgan Owle-Crisp from using Indigenous names for the beers she produces at her 7 Clans brewery, located just outside tribal lands on the outskirts of Asheville.

She says she's honoring and promoting her culture. Her critics ferociously accuse her of insulting her people by associating them with alcohol.

Ultimately, she renamed her inaugural flagship MotherTown Blonde Ale, which refers to a sacred Cherokee site, but refused to replace the name 7 Clans Brewing Co. because, she tells me, "It's been going on forever that products have been attributed to Native people, including at unaffiliated breweries here on the Qualla Boundary [her local Cherokee territory]. It's a matter of, 'What do tribal nations have access to and what do they have the energy for?' I was easy. But this really is my heritage."

Located in the hippie stronghold of Boulder, Colorado, the Brewers Association presents pretty White, and a lot of its stakeholders angrily accuse it of doing nothing to make the industry more diverse. Over the mid-2010s I could predict the first question that any public audience with the BA would ask: why aren't you doing more about diversity?

On one hand, the expectation that it should do something puts it in an awkward spot. Its primary mission is to lobby for its trade members in Congress. At the time, staffers were saying in so many words that its member breweries had more pressing concerns. Their main priorities had them spread thin enough. On the other hand, evolve or die, and the White male wall of brewing was blinding.

Finally, the BA made a move. Around 2016 it announced the formation of a diversity and inclusion committee and the hiring of Dr. J. as its first diversity ambassador. However, because the BA doesn't have a women's subcommittee, its efforts on gender diversity would live with everybody else in the sprawling house that is diversity.

As Julia Herz, who was the BA's craft beer program director at the time, told me, the initial work would be "very, very broad."

At least we could hope to see more forward motion from the state guilds, which Alexis Degan of the NJ Brewers Association assures me we have, at least indirectly.

First of all, Alexis commands attention by standing out when she stands in hearing rooms full of White men at the state capitol. Her large lavender hairstyle doesn't hurt. Second, she says the younger generation of men who lobby Trenton, New Jersey, like she does prove extremely supportive to the increasing number of women who're trickling into the capital.

Most important, she concludes optimistically, "It's a lot of White men saying the current system works for the people currently in the system; then you have me being the only woman testifying in multiple hearings saying the current system doesn't work, while across the world we have women standing up to systems that don't work."

31 | IT'S A WOMAN'S WORLD AFTER ALL

IT STARTED, in my mind, with Anne-Catherine Dilewyns in Belgium. Then the Meinel sisters in Bavaria along with the Friedmanns. I should have known about An de Ryck in Belgium but I didn't.

Then, poof, poof, poof went the United Kingdom.

And just like the dots on the digital map that marked the breweries participating in the first International Women's Brew Day, craft brewsters popped up in my consciousness and everywhere else. Australia, New Zealand, Mexico, Argentina, Israel, the Palestinian Authority, China, Vietnam, and a few spots in Africa.

February 2015*, Dendermonde, Belgium

Twenty-seven-year-old Anne-Catherine Dilewyns is looking at her great-great-great-great-great-grandmother's passport. In the space for profession, someone has written, in Flemish, "brewmaster." Anne-Catherine's maternal ancestor founded a brewery in 1875, and her family ran it until the Germans seized the kettles for munitions in World War II. As the brewer and production manager for Brouwerij Dilewyns, which her father built in the same town for her and her sister, she's felt nothing but support from the community around her.

---

*In the interceding years, Anne-Catherine has decided to take leave and pursue a master's degree in supply chain management, but her sister, Claire, still runs the brewery with their father.

"Everybody was surprised and curious how I would do," she e-mails. "I had the feeling they were willing to help me out when I needed."

In return, the brewster with the slight build wants to show the strength of women in beer. When she travels to the half-dozen countries, including the United States, that sell her beer, fans marvel at the fact that she's the youngest female brewer in Belgium. She answers their questions patiently and has learned that, "Sometimes there's an advantage being a woman in a male world," she says. "With a smile you can achieve a lot."

Meanwhile, Gisi and Moni Meinel are going strong in the 332-year-old brewery they inherited in the sleepy town of Hof, in Bavaria's Franconia region. When I met them they were busy hosting a multicourse private lunch for about a dozen friends (plus, graciously, me and my tour guides, Denise and Gregor), yet the twentysomething sisters had a cheerful, warm, quiet, and busy air to them spiked with a dose of nervousness considering they could hardly communicate with the non-German-speaking journalist from America dropping in on their party.

As they've settled into their visible roles as the twelfth generation—and first females—to tend to the family's brew kettle, they've gotten more expressive about brewing bright, full-flavored beers designed to appeal to women.

They have to have some strong nerves as young women taking over a landmark brewery in an old-fashioned part of a country where beer tradition is deeply entrenched and most of the population still doesn't necessarily accept deviation from the brewing norms that were codified into law five hundred years ago.

But the sisters have definitely earned their cred. Moni, who earned her master brewer title in 2009, was the youngest female brewer in Germany for a time and manages production, while Gisi, also a brewmaster in her own right, oversees marketing and sales for the brewery, a courtyard distillery, and a line of soda.

Their gender has never disadvantaged them, they tell me through our interpreter, Gregor, during a break in lunch courses. "Ladies can be emotional, we can cry, we can give love to the business, to beer lovers. Men aren't permitted to do that."

I didn't get to meet the mother/daughter duo that manages the 135-year-old Friedmann brewery but when mom, Sigi, tells the story of taking over from her father, who had no sons, in 1982, she admits she was "met with skepticism on all sides." She quickly showed the proverbial "them." The fourth-generation owner scored higher on her master brewer's test than most of her male colleagues.

Today, she works with her daughter, Barbara, by her side.

The UK's old-school breweries are just about as deeply rooted in tradition as Germany's are, so it was a Really Big Deal when, in 2008, Ffion Jones started brewing at Brains Brewery, the oldest family-owned brewery in Wales. Though it was her first brewing job, she had a certificate from the venerated Institute of Brewing and Distilling in London.

Her arrival signaled brewery modernization in more ways than one. Before leaving for New Zealand, where she worked under the Mother of NZ Brewing, Tracy Banner, she formed a key member of the team who established the ten-barrel Brains Craft Brewery pilot system. Jones's position at Brains brings so much pride to the native Welsh woman who calls the brewery "an iconic name in Wales" with a longstanding heritage known for quality and synonymous with the national pastime of rugby (as a long-time shirt sponsor).

It's hard to keep up with how many breweries, companies, schools, conferences, and competitions some of the world's top beer women have started.

Silvia De Tomás Ayllón, who began homebrewing with her dad as a kid in Peru, cofounded (with her brother) 2Broders brewery, whose IPA won gold in the country's national beer competition. She co-owns Cebichela, the first brewery in Lima; established the Chilean Academy of Sensory Analysis for Beer; and founded and organizes the Latin American Beer Cup, the Peruvian Cup of Beers, and Homebrewers Cup of Peru competitions. She's only twenty-six.

After brewing and working in management at SABMiller, Apiwe Nxusani-Mawela cofounded Brewhogs Microbrewery, where she worked as brewmaster, then founded the highly acclaimed Brewsters Craft in Johannesburg as the first Black female majority-owned brewery in South Africa. With mostly female employees, Brewsters Craft offers accredited training in brewing, quality testing, and contract brewing.

In 2019 Apiwe launched a Brewsters Craft beer and cider brand named Tolokazi, which is what women from her clan are called. In addition, she earned a master brewer diploma through the Institute of Brewing and Distilling, became the first Black African woman to become certified there as a trainer, and she chairs and sits on about a million boards, representing her country and continent to the rest of the brewing world.

"Our struggles today are paving a path for the next generation of women in our workspace," she says, noting that South African women commonly brewed beer until the eighteenth century.

Peace Onwuchekwa says when it comes to her country's acceptance of women in beer, the public is curious but hasn't quite gotten there yet. "They always want to hear me say it a second time that I brew beer," she says of Nigeria, where she brews and supervises quality control at Bature Brewery. "The men in my country say I drink a lot of beer. We have ladies show up at the taproom who prefer a glass of gin and tonic or wine. Some think it's not ladylike to drink beer."

That's part of why Apiwe considers the mission to educate African women about beer critical.

"The biggest stereotype is that brewing and beer are only for men," she says. "Like in any other industry, we need equal representation of women."

That sentiment steers Silvia, Argentine sensory expert Carolina Perez, and Mexican multi-award-winning brewer and educator Jessica Martínez Ignorosa. While these women's CVs go on for pages, it's marginally possible to simplify their ambitions into one cohesive whole: to elevate the collective knowledge of Latin America's female beer professionals.

"Women in the beer scene of our country began to be visible and to have great prominence," says Carolina, who joined the industry in 1996 as a sensory analyst and now co-owns a malt shop, brewpub, and training center. She brought the first BJCP exam to South America and teaches classes to one hundred mostly Argentinian women at a time.

"It arose from the desire of a group of women who wanted to know how to evaluate beers to improve their products," she says of her courses. "I do it on a nonprofit basis with the aim of empowering women in the beer market."

Mexico's craft beer industry started early on, in the mid-1990s. Jessica, a brewery owner, contract brewer, consultant, conference organizer, and winner of the Mexican craft brewers association's 2019 Ninkasi award for female brewer of the year, cofounded the Adelitas Cerveceras Mexicanas as the first group of female brewers in Mexico. It started with 160 members and grew 25 percent in year one.

"I am a promoter of beer culture," Jessica says.

Silvia describes herself the same way. Working at one of fifteen Peruvian craft breweries, she commits herself also to training others through organizations and academies. Notably, she has served as director and a brewing and sensory analysis teacher at the Brewmart Peru school and specialty shop since 2006.

"I love being able to inspire, spread, and create more lovers of craft beer," she says, mentioning her participation in Pink Boots Peru as well as pan-American partnerships between brewsters. "I have created different projects that not only make me grow in the brewing world but also the people and breweries of my country, Peru, and Latin America."

I hear a recurring theme from these jaw-droppingly educated and accomplished women: a motivation to inform and empower not women in general but specifically women in their own national markets, all in various stages of development.

That's what drives Michelle Wang, an international beer ambassador in Shanghai who travels constantly to introduce Chinese brewers and investors to key people around the world, and vice versa. She produces the annual Craft Beer China conference and has launched Chinese beer magazines in two languages (way back in 2012–2013) and a digital platform for beer news that will soon add commercial and technical courses for the country's brewing industry.

She's the first Chinese national to speak at the European Brewers Forum and the (US) Brewers Association's Craft Beer Conference.

The normally humble Michelle made me chuckle when she confessed, "[BA president] Bob Pease said it was the best speech he had on that day."

Of women in Chinese beer, she observes that women in tier-one cities are independent, well educated, and keen to try new things, including heavy and full-flavored beers, some of which are developed and made by female brewmasters and research and development professionals.

Michelle's own professional aim, she tells me, is to "build the bridge between the East and West beer industries, help the Chinese brewers open their view and mind, and let more Western industry friends understand more about Chinese people and culture."

She did all of that and more for me one delightful afternoon when we happened to both be in Beijing. I had a few hours free and she was covering an informational meeting for potential investors in the Hot Beer craft brewery, which hosted it.

Michelle's friend, the owner, sent his very obviously displeased driver to collect and return me to my hotel. The assembled businesspeople invited me to introduce myself then bombarded me with questions in Mandarin that I wasn't prepared to answer about the international beer market. Mostly, this unexpected accostal entertained me, as did the semiformal presentation of floral bouquets and gifts of rotgut baijiu liquor to Michelle, myself, and a female board member at Lenovo in attendance. File this fun memory under, "Well, that doesn't happen every day."

It also doesn't happen every day that a blonde US brewster heads to Vietnam to work at a craft brewery, but that's what Allison Higi did a few years ago. While a great many American women are crossing large bodies of water to take jobs in the beer industry of late, most of the ones I know settle in Stockholm or Paris or Brussels, not Hanoi.

Allison *has* tremendously enjoyed some of her international stints. Vietnam is not one of them.

"In my head I compare international brewing to being a modern-day explorer. It is performing demanding physical labor in harsh environments paid with the rewards of outrageous stories, PTSD, and a complete reexamination of one's definition of the word culture. For every fun, adventurous story I have to tell, there is a dark story I'm not telling."

In Vietnam, Allison had a hard time sourcing ingredients in a country with no indigenous beer ingredients or potable water. "All ingredients must be imported through one of the most difficult and corrupt customs authorities in the world," she e-mails.

That said, she found it interesting to brew a lot of low-ABV and low-IBU pilsners, blonde ales, and cream ales using exotic ingredients such as dragon fruit and Buddha's-hand citrus fruit suited to the jungle climate, which locals would drink a touch warm or over ice. With few government regulations, she could flex her creativity like never before.

India also lacked native ingredients and clean water, but Allison at least had an easier time accessing them. Well-established fermentation science schools meant "a wealth of biochemical brewing understanding," and British colonialism meant more pub ales in Mumbai and comfort with diverse styles. However, the caste system coupled with strict alcohol production and sales laws put craft beer a bit out of reach for most.

"Craft beer," she writes, "was very much a casual yet upper-class product."

Working beer jobs in Munich for fifteen years, Cincinnati expat Kirsten Rhein need not worry about ingredients. She's owned and brewed at a Bavarian craft brewery or two, and she's also made the rounds at some very wealthy old companies, at varying times handling sales, exports, marketing, or brand identity for Schneider Weisse, Spaten, Löwenbräu, and Franziskaner.

"A lot of people ask me what it's like to work at the historic breweries Spaten, Franziskaner, and Löwenbräu," she writes of the sister breweries owned by AB InBev. "The brewery is really cool as there are many modern parts but also super old historic parts. I highly recommend taking our brewery tour where you get to see the centuries-old cellars as well as the best panoramic view of the Alps."

Kirsten claims the title as the first American woman to earn a brewmaster certificate from Germany's Doemens Academy, quite possibly the most difficult brewing program in the world. As a longtime Munich-area dweller whose digital connectivity and extremely outgoing personality has earned her more international beer friends than anyone I know, she's always happy to act as social connector or cruise director for anyone who wanders her way.

From 2014 to 2018, Kirsten's visitors included groups of Pink Boots members and friends who traveled through each autumn to meet and learn from the who's who of Bavarian beer women. The two most constant hosts along the way have been Sister Doris and Moni and Gisi Meinel, who welcome the annual exchange with brewsters—something almost no one would have thought about fifteen years ago.

"The narrative is being rewritten now," begin the Meinels, who get the nearly unique opportunity to bring their family's masculine seventeenth-century legacy into the more feminine twenty-first.

"It's up to men *and* women now," they conclude, "to rewrite the beer narrative."

32 | RAGING BITCHES

BACK IN OLDEN DAYS—a.k.a. before Facebook—you may have been able to get away relatively unscathed if you released a beer with a name or label designed for the male gaze. Though customers and readers of beer mags might have rolled their eyes, social media wasn't curled up ready to publicly pounce on beers with sexualized or controversial branding such as Leg Spreader ESB, Thong Remover Tripel, Mouth Raper IPA, or Raging Bitch Belgian IPA (the last of which, to be fair, I personally find inoffensive and pretty clever to boot).

But there is something icky and perverse about craft brewers perpetuating the same sexual stereotypes and caricatures that craft rose up to counter after decades of having macrobrewers shove Swedish bikini models and Saint Pauli girls down our throats. "One of the things that I loved is how we were turning away from bikini babes," Irene Firmat says of the early craft beer community.

Though I think this wave might be starting to crest now that everyone's being asked to reexamine their biases and corporate culture, Irene offered this opinion to explain how some of the guys who were supposed to save us from the Bud girl pinups are still making dick and fart jokes at women's expense. "I think it's becoming very macho, very frat boy," she said.

We can talk another time about how that mentality emerged alongside the testosterone-fueled hop wars that caused beer bros of the mid-2010s to measure their manhood in International Bitterness Units or how a surge of swaggering young brewers used their Mr. Beer Kits and Kickstarter money to flood the Main Streets of America around the same time. Or how the same upsurge of brewery investment ushered more women into the fold and potentially caused some skinny-jean-clad entrepreneurs to dig in their brewing boots and misogynistically name and label their beers as an "f-you" to the outcry, brandishing their can real estate as a weapon.

What's more important than the why is the what now.

I welcome the watchdogs who have the modern technological tools to call out the creeps. But the line is and always will be moving, and what offends one person makes another laugh. As a Gen Xer who first studied feminism in the 1990s, I wrestle with the polemic over women bearing their breasts for Instagram clicks. But after spending decades contemplating the role of gender in beer, I've settled on beer writer Carla Jean Lauter to speak my feelings best.

"It's critical to vet ideas with diverse stakeholders before putting them on the market," she says. "It's one thing to make jokes with your buddies in the garage and another to let that 'joke' carry your brand message. Like it or not, the message that half-baked concept sends is 'my product is not for you.' So then why are you in business?"

Some, like Stone cofounder Greg Koch, learn that lesson quickly. Someone in his social media department, tweeting as the voice of the brewery's offshoot brand, Arrogant Bastard, wrote in 2018, "Put me in your mouth, make an 'mmm' sound, swallow. Express appreciation and ask permission to do it again. Hint: only wussies do the 'ask permission' part."

You'd think that Tweeter might have learned a lesson from the debacle three years prior that compelled Bud Light to apologize and yank a slogan that encouraged drinkers to consider "removing no from your vocabulary."

Carla, who has taken it upon herself to police Twitter for red flags, caught the tweet and responded with something along the lines of "WTF??"

At least if Stone's anonymous social media scribe was unaware of the despicable history of rape inferences in beer advertising, Greg was on it. He pushed through a lengthy self-flagellating apology and promised that going forward a woman would handle all Arrogant Bastard tweets.

Though she acknowledges the retraction, Carla says the incident serves as a cautionary tale for breweries that lack diverse representation in their ranks.

"You have to run this by people other than the jockiest jock at the table," she says. "It's indicative of a culture that doesn't understand."

Most breweries caught making inappropriate comments about women seem to understand even less than that. I've observed most of them choosing to double down on their misogyny by defending their remarks and sometimes attacking their attackers—at least as long as they think they can get away with it.

Carla points to the West Sixth brewery in Indiana whose Sex and Candy can depicted a cartoon of a woman's private parts. When she called them out for it on Twitter, they criticized her. They stood their ground for a year. Then they gave in and changed the label because, as Carla says, "They were still getting crap about it."

As Julia Herz wrote in a column for the BA in 2016, she agrees that alienating half of one's potential customers is shortsighted, and she's glad to see checks and balances like these in play. She says vocal consumers are forcing many brands across many industries to "grow a conscience."

"Integrity is the metaphorical yardstick for the average craft brewer and beer lover," she wrote.

As women's viral voices grow louder, they're using private forums like the one hosted by Pink Boots to highlight problematic people, places, and things in the beer world. While Pink Boots as an organization is happy to provide this platform for discussion, it fields its own increasingly virulent criticism for adhering to a strict policy of neutrality from those who'd like it to back their concerned members.

I see the potential for conflicts of interest and all forms of retaliation in this suggestion. Former Pink Boots president Laura Ulrich, for example, works . . . at Stone.

More than that, however, is Pink Boots's commitment to staying out of it and keeping it positive. "We're not going to be the moral police," Laura says. "What I find offensive you might not find offensive. It's too much of a slippery slope."

After years of declining to get involved in these subjective matters, the BA did update its advertising and marketing code to address members' complaints over beer marketing with "sexually explicit, lewd, or demeaning brand names, language, text, graphics, photos, video, or other images."

As of 2017, the BA no longer announces any beer names deemed offensive if that beer wins a GABF or World Beer Cup award, and the producing brewery is barred from using the competitions' intellectual property to promote its win.

Before she lost her job to BA's COVID layoffs, Julia explained that "even one sexist label, logo, or beer ad dilutes the integrity of our beloved beverage."

Flying Dog, which famously produces the sexually suggestive Pearl Necklace Chesapeake Stout and the aforementioned Raging Bitch IPA, pulled out of the BA in protest. The owner of the Maryland brewery told *Brewbound*, "It's anti-free enterprise. It's interfering with their competitors' business. It's thinking for consumers. Americans hate thought police, and they hate censorship."

While Flying Dog thinks the code goes too far, Carla feels it doesn't go far enough. Though it's given her more leverage to complain when a brewery's branding doesn't meet the BA standard, she wishes the trade organization would do more than scold a brewery for doing wrong. "They have the role of being thought leaders," she says.

A year after the BA's move, the powerful Campaign for Real Ale (CAMRA) group, which labors to save England's traditional ale culture, took a bigger step by barring beers and ciders with "discriminatory" branding from entering its competitions or festivals.

Carla is reevaluating the nickname she gave herself when she started writing about beer in 2007: Beer Babe. Though she and others like myself who've christened ourselves or our groups with titles like Beer for Babes, Beer Wench, and Beer Fox have done so to rock our bad-assery, Carla is one who's feeling the time may have passed for this type of self-expression. While Carla says she didn't get pushback until the #MeToo movement, I heard misgivings right away when I interviewed select women for a column I wrote about calling my women-in-beer education group Beer for Babes in 2010. Generally, Gen Xers and boomers liked it; millennials didn't. Like me, Carla considers "Babe," when used in this context, a term of endearment. That said, she makes the point that people's attitudes toward those positions have changed.

To wit: the message that male beer writers have received from their reading public recently is if you can't say something everyone agrees on, don't say anything at all. In retrospect I regret writing an article saying I hoped Bill Metzger, who published the national *Brew News* chain of brewspapers, would professionally survive after he wrote and published a bizarre fictional piece that he called satire and the rest of the world called sexist and borderline scary.

He didn't.

But I think critics went too far in calling for former *Brewbound* editor Chris Furnari's job when he derided a certain class of female beer influencers on the media platform's podcast in 2019. Critiquing a website's list of beer Instagramers to follow, he commented that much of the list comprised "chicks who basically take photos of themselves in like low-cut tops with beer," to which cohost Justin Kendall replied, "Some of these photos of the women, their face isn't even in the photo."

Justin kept his job. Chris, until recently a *Forbes* colleague who commissioned me to write stories for the business-to-business cannabis website he edited, didn't. The loudest argument against Chris came from people who questioned why he felt privileged enough to act as arbiter of women's personal choices. The loudest argument to bolster the influencers was that empowered young women have the right to own their own sexuality and flaunt it how, where, when, and to whomever they want.

There's plenty to unpack here that we don't have space to get into but my other main question is why did mob mentality decide Chris should get punished for upholding these traditional feminist principles? When Justin talked about the women cropping their own heads out of the pictures, I couldn't shake the image of adolescent me learning about discrimination in advertising by following a teacher's instructions to flip through magazines and pick out all the female forms that had gotten separated from their heads.

Here I salute Janet Johanson, founder of the BevSource contract brewing facility, for complaining about men who make snap judgments about her and then admonishing herself for "doing the same fucking thing" to others.

I, too, do the same fucking thing.

Shortly after I published a treatise in *Forbes* on the topic of beer influencers' tatas, I ended up on a press trip to Scotland with one of the shapely Instagramers Chris had named (by handle only) in his podcast. I didn't know who she was until midway through the trip. But she knew me.

The unspoken relationship between us made things awkward. But I respect her intellect, professionalism, and beer knowledge, and as I watched her pose for shoots all over Edinburgh and Aberdeen, I felt shame for judging her before I knew her.

When we got home, I asked her to participate in another *Forbes* story, this one about #MeToo in the craft movement, and she agreed. I'm reprinting an excerpt here.

> *The Enemy Within*
> Women don't always take other women's backs, and as the craft beer community expands and morphs, we receive more opportunities to debate what constitutes gender discrimination and learn from one another in the process.
>
> Melis Papila has a figure many women would envy. So she shows it off in her Instagram feed where she regularly poses with beers from around the world. While she says most commenters applaud her lack of inhibition, she faces so much backlash from other women in the industry (including me, admittedly), three female head brewers and a replacement brewer pulled out of a TV show appearance to protest her inclusion.
>
> "I didn't represent women in the beer industry because of my Instagram account," she relays. "I'm not unfamiliar with sexism but internalized misogyny and sexism is something I started seeing or at least noticing when I began working in the beer industry."
>
> Far from knowing nothing about beer, as critics assume, Papila does marketing for a large San Diego brewery. But, she says, the "unfortunate incident . . . made me question whether I belonged in this community."
>
> "I was of course afraid to speak up but I'm glad I've continued to share my beer adventures on my Instagram," Papila says, referencing her decision to out the critical brewsters. "There was an overwhelming amount of positive support [in the comments] and other women opening up about their own experiences."

With her long blonde hair, dark lipstick, and clothes that show off her curves, forty-two-year-old Janet Johanson says she "doesn't look the part" of a brewer and gets reminded of that all the time by both women and men. She recounts a story about meeting a fellow Minneapolis brewster, who after a few minutes of chatting, exclaimed, "Oh you really do know what you're talking about!" Janet left the conversation worried she unknowingly puts on the persona of a bimbo.

Kristi McGuire felt the hot sting of reprobation from her own sex when she launched High Heel Brewing, one of a handful to make beer specifically targeting women. These endeavors never go well.

Critics (again, like myself) take to their beer columns and their social media accounts, like the two-time contributor to the Growler, Kaleigh Dunn, to shriek, "Does that mean I have been drinking 'dude beer' all along? Am I ruined because of it? Has it been hurting my delicate, flowery liver? What will happen to my ovaries because I've been drinking dude beer?!"

Look, time and again, marketing experts warn manufacturers against blatantly marketing their products to women. It's a very small segment of the population that gets gushy over a pink beer. Most just get pissed off. And even if people buy it once as a novelty or a gift, are you really going to load up your pantry with it?

But Kristi's perry-ale hybrid and assertively hopped IPA weren't pink, and they weren't dumbed down. They were simply a seemingly misguided attempt for a veteran female brewer to celebrate female beer drinkers and producers by shining a glowing light on their existence.

Sure, some chick beers, as they're sometimes derisively called, can scream condescension, gimmickry, exploitation, and even naked commercialization of our bodies. I'd drop the Polish beer fermented with the "vaginal lactic acid of beautiful women" into that last category.

Who's the market for vagina beer, anyway?

But Kristi, as they say, is the real deal. She's not only spent decades developing and marketing beers for Alaskan and ABI, she completed the Master Brewers program at UC Davis and earned the title of Associate with Distinction at the rigorous Institute of Brewing in London. Also, her perry (pear cider) took gold in the American fruit beer category at GABF.

Ultimately, none of that mattered. She left High Heel Brewing to her female business partner and went back to Alaska. As for the argument that she segregated and patronized women, Kristi says that's fair fodder for discussion. "Have the conversation," she says. "But have it in a way that's not so extreme."

Despite #MeToo, beer women were not having a public conversation about the pervasive discrimination, harassment, and rape they endure on the job until 2021. That's when former Boulevard Brewing microbiologist Keke Gibb exposed the company for protecting a well-known, long-time predator. At the same time, Notch Brewing brewmaster Brienne Allan blew the topic wide open with thousands of women submitting harrowing stories in response to her simple Instagram question about others' experiences with sexism. Across the country, breweries fired accused perpetrators, and founders—from the aloof to the abusive—stepped down in ignominy. As Brienne revealed, everyone has a story. Patrons telling beertenders to smile. Account managers announcing the arrival of a female sales rep by exclaiming, "Tits and tattoos, it must be a beer chick." My ex-fiancé's good-ole-boy distribution manager telling him to "control his woman" because that manager found himself on the losing end of an argument with me. A longtime sales rep getting groped and then raped by her boss, the owner of a brewery, inside the brewery.

What stops them from speaking out? Fear of being ignored, retaliated against, or ostracized as a troublemaker or a snowflake who can't handle the heat.

Single mom and sales rep Natalie Phillips accused her former boss Fred Lee, the owner of Columbus, Ohio's now-closed Actual Brewing, of repeatedly making lewd suggestions, touching her inappropriately, and then eventually raping her after a few rounds of drinks. When she reported it to her manager, she says he blew her off. She says it wasn't until the male brewmaster quit to protest the lack of action being taken that the brewery's board finally paid attention.

Having no idea what to do, the board sent her home on paid leave that dragged on for months. Frustrated, Natalie quit, filed a report with the police, and participated in an awareness rally organized by other local industry women who supported her claims of Fred's reputation for harassment and in some cases even refused to sell his beer because of it.

The rally made the press. Fred, who denies the allegations, lost his brewery to bankruptcy. Natalie's police report, closed by the assigned detective for "lack of evidence," went nowhere. Natalie left the public side of the business.

Her story isn't unique. Women flee the industry all the time to get away from these patterns of abuse, and when they speak of unequal treatment, they tend to minimize it as something that only comes from ignorant contractors or festivalgoers.

But on the rare occasion that someone like Natalie speaks up, women tend to respond by whispering their stories through back channels. "I've had women message me from as far away as Australia telling me their story," she says. "I praise all the women. I want them to know they're not alone."

33 | THAT'S RIGHT, THE WOMEN ARE SMARTER

IT WASN'T SO LONG AGO that outside of the United Kingdom, Germany, and Belgium, craft beer was an almost exclusively American thing. I remember being weirded out meeting the owner of a craft beer bar from Sweden during Philly Beer Week then hearing the hype when one then two then three Italian craft beers landed here at Marc Vetri's dearly departed *birreria*, Amis. I think word of craft breweries in France and Spain wafted this way next, with rumors they were putting out some stellar craft ciders.

But I never heard about women as part of these endeavors. When stories about brewsters in New Zealand and South America and Israel and Rwanda started populating my news feeds, I felt like I'd been catapulted to another world.

Last time I checked it's still sort of the same world but it is different. It's one where professional female brewers across the globe are both looking into their own national brewing traditions and outward to the States for guidance on how to cultivate a livelihood through their craft. As a source for education, networking, and support, the Pink Boots Society acts as an outstanding ambassador for brewing quality and career advancement for women.

Anita Lum, who used to head the membership committee, says she fielded inquiries from foreign countries all the time. She answered a lot of e-mails asking how to become a member. She most recently got one from New Zealand and received a nice handful from South America. She answered them in Spanish and says to me, "Some day I'll go visit them."

To my surprise, this isn't a recent phenomenon.

Anita wrote up an illustrative story in her personal notes from 2010:

> Just recently a lady wrote me from Argentina. She was ecstatic to find
> the existence of Pink Boots Society and was asking for "permission"
> to be the point of contact for South American members. Carolina
> (who appeared in chapter thirty-one) went on to tell me how she
> was formerly a chemical engineer and that she has been working in
> the brewing industry since 1996 holding various positions including
> laboratory coordinator and senior analyst. In 2004 she started train-
> ing homebrewers and craft brewers in beer tasting and in 2005, she
> and her husband opened a business in Buenos Aires to supply the
> Argentine craft beer market with malts. I look forward to helping
> Carolina stay connected with PBS here in the states. And I wonder
> where else we will have a "sister" in the beer industry write from next!

––––––––––

Denise Ratfield, who cochaired the first few International Women's
Collaboration Brew days on behalf of Pink Boots, deepened her relationships
with foreign brewers as a result. She appointed herself a "craft concierge and
beer ambassador" to set up brewery visits, meetings, and collabs for industry
folk visiting from Australia and New Zealand. So it was only natural that when
Kiwi brewsters wanted to celebrate their emerging community and start a Pink
Boots chapter in 2014, they asked Denise to come represent.

I remember feeling curious and excited before she left, considering this
would be the first official Pink Boots visit to a foreign country. The New
Zealand press wrote up the highlights of her itinerary: first, a collaboration
brew with two women from New Zealand and Australia, followed by the
launch of the country's national Pink Boots Society chapter at the Beervana
festival. She planned to pour a beer she brewed back home in San Diego,
at the Pink Boots Society (pop-up) Bar, serving an array of women-brewed
beers to festivalgoers.

In what I thought was an appropriate educational touch, she brought along
some US rarities fermented with *Brettanomyces* yeast to share with the uniniti-
ated because she'd read on Twitter that in New Zealand "brett is the new hops."

In 2018, Teri spent several weeks in Australia at the invitation of Pink Boots members there. She kept a very busy schedule brewing with people all over the country and speaking at a meeting held during BrewCon 2018. She praised the country, with three hundred members in chapters in every state at the time, for having one of, if not the most active Pink Boots Society organizations in the world.

As Pink Boots president, Laura Ulrich traveled to Ecuador for the first continentwide women's brewing conference. She was thrilled to participate, especially because she laments that the organization doesn't have materials translated into Spanish to pass along to women who want to join but don't have a local chapter. A priority for Laura is to fund scholarships earmarked for the Spanish or Latin American chapters.

Though Pink Boots's national structure doesn't set aside any of its many annual scholarships for specific geographies, it does award them to deserving women around the world. The first scholarship it offered, in fact, went to Swedish brewer Jessica Heidrich. The scholarship allowed her to take the online Concise Course in Brewing Technology from Siebel in 2013.

With no brewing schools in Sweden, the homebrewer-turned-pro whose homebrewing skills won her the title of Swedish Brewing Champion four times had nowhere to go to up her game.

"Jessica feels her lack of formal brewing education puts her at a disadvantage among her male counterparts, and her salary is suffering because of it," the Pink Boots blog explained in announcing her win.

"Always as a woman you have to be not 'as good.' You have to be better," she says.

When she said this, Herlinda and I were drinking soup and coffee with her on the back deck of a beer cafe on a brisk, beautiful October day on a forested little island a few boat connections away from where Herly and I were staying in downtown Stockholm.

When Jessica applied for the scholarship, she'd wanted to open her own brewery. The course gave her more confidence in her abilities, and with her husband, she opened Hop Notch Brewing in the same building as the cafe. Her husband prepped a session IPA, an Amarillo IPA, and an exquisite sour brown currant ale for us to try while she explained them and I hurried to scribble notes fast enough to avoid missing our boat back to our hotel.

"You will never regret education," she says, reflecting on her Siebel course. "You talk so much better with knowledge."

Colleen Rakowski is an American in Europe. Brussels, to be precise, brewing and blending at Cantillon, one of the most beloved sour breweries in the world. She probably wouldn't have gotten herself here if it hadn't been for her inquisitiveness, gumption, and Pink Boots scholarship.

She didn't know much, if anything, about beer when she started bartending at Free Will Brewing, outside of Philly. But she did everything it took to learn, from tasting beers with brewer Hannah Ghiolde to passing the BJCP exam to showing up early for shifts to trail the cellarmen and brewers to making herself the resident expert on the brewery's new filtration system.

As a twentysomething, she forced herself to work up the nerve to apply for the scholarship for the UC Davis intensive short course in brewing science. She came back from the one-week course with a new confidence to ask permission to pursue learning opportunities that made her more valuable in her job. She kept asking, and she kept getting promoted.

On a vacation to Belgium, she gathered up all her courage and walked into revered Cantillon owner Jean-Pierre Van Roy's office to proclaim, "I want to do an internship here. He said OK. I said for ten days. He said, 'OK, come in the fall.'"

That tactic worked again when, two weeks into her internship, she told him she wanted to work for him full time. Again, he said OK.

She'd been there a year and a half when she said to me in awe, "The scholarship launched my career into what it is."

A Pink Boots scholarship also launched Denise Jones's career into what it is. Even though she's a widely respected brewing vet, she got her first job as a distiller during a Pink Boots bus tour to Germany that a Pink Boots scholarship paid for.

Earlier in the trip to meet all manners of female brewers in Germany, she'd chatted with Sabine and Thomas Weyermann about the possibility of working for them as master distiller. One night at dinner she got a text from Thomas asking her to come fill the position. It was one of those nights when everyone had gotten into the spirit of too much Bavarian beer.

"I thought to myself, 'I'm pretty drunk. I'm going to put the phone down and look at it in the morning and see if it says the same thing,' and it did. Ten days later I moved to Germany."

Indirectly, I benefited from Denise's scholarship, too. With a few days to kill between work trips in the summer of 2017, I took the train to Bamberg to see Denise. There, the two of us, along with Kirsten Rhein, sipped Schlenkerla three feet the source. I interviewed Sabine, who generously lent Denise, Gregor, and me the company car to tour the Bavarian countryside. We stopped in to have lunch with the Meinel sisters and spend a few hours getting to know Sister Doris, with Gregor serving as interpreter.

Most of these encounters made it into the book, which means by extension, you, dear reader, have benefited, too.

34 | SISTERS ARE BREWING IT FOR THEMSELVES

THE BEER-HISTORY WORLD is nervously holding its breath for the day Sister Doris decides to retire. Not only is the seventy-year-old sister a European brewing nun, she's *the* European brewing nun. As in the *last one* (that anyone knows of). When she dies, a twelve-hundred-year-old tradition will die with her.

Some prominent beer women express dismay that she hasn't tried harder to bring more postulants into the fold. But Sister Doris seems happy. Not one to dwell on secular symbolism or sentimentality, she tells me, "All of my wishes have come true."

Through the Pink Boots's Germany tours, Teri Fahrendorf had the privilege, as I did, to meet with Sister Doris and the Meinel sisters—the first women to inherit their family's brewery since its founding in 1688—on the same trip.

When I asked how she felt theoretically holding beer that represented women's brewing past in one hand and the future in another, Teri answered, "As Americans, we've lost touch with that lineage. When I was a young woman you didn't realize you could be a brewer. You didn't have any idea."

Global beer sales are predicted to reach $711 billion by 2025, and the vast majority of the planet's population has no idea this monumental statistic bears a man's face atop a woman's body. The lack of credit or even recognition that women receive for their backbreaking labor to birth and raise the behemoth beer industry traces its parentage to the origination of the patriarchy back in hunter-gatherer days; the invention of hierarchical states in Mesopotamia, Egypt, and across the globe; the rise of religion from pagan times through modern Christianity; and the feminization of poverty plus the almighty profit motive that we humans haven't endeavored to replace as our galvanizing motivation since time immemorial.

It's because of old-guard brewsters such as Teri and new-school ones such as Whitney Burnside, innovators such as Rose Ann Finkel, farmers such as Hillary Bakker Barile, social media whizzes such as Chris Crabb, and so, so, so many others that women can stand on one another's shoulders once again. They power through indignities and archival silences and doors that slam in their faces to set examples and unearth the examples that have been quietly set before them. Through it all, they persevere.

"Wow, this is another world," Irene Firmat remembers marveling with a fellow craft brewing trailblazer decades after opening Hood River/Full Sail as the 151st operating brewery in the United States. "We're really in some ways passing the torch. I hope we do a good job."

It only takes a count of the nation's 8,500 functioning craft breweries and the nearly half of them who have at least partial female ownership to assure Irene that yes, in fact, you did. I daydream about how those young adventurers would react to hearing that half a lifetime later, Smithsonian craft beer curator Theresa McCulla would collect and publicly display their quotidien tools at nothing less than the National Museum of American History. Yet despite women's reentry into beer, Theresa knows their reality is much more robust than the record.

"Craft brewing has begun a new chapter of the history of women in beer," she says. However, "people aren't included for all kinds of reasons and that's why it's so important to think about including all sorts of voices."

The modern chapter is indelibly writing beer women onto its pages. Since around 2013, no day has gone by that I haven't read a newspaper or magazine article about a female brewer or, more recently, the herstory of beer.

At first, the majority of brewer profiles appeared lumped together in local articles that breathlessly turned their subjects into zoo-like spectacles by proclaiming that golly, women drink AND make beer, and here are a few in our area!!! The stories have evolved into deeper dives that mine the historical lineage of brewsters, probe the perceived links between brewsters and witches (often inaccurately), and interview female professionals in-depth about their take on some aspect of brewing or another.

In late 2020, blogger Jeff Alworth gave Suzy Stern Denison a heart wrenchingly overdue mainstream beer media debut by publishing a lengthy interview he conducted with her. A few weeks later, I read a semiprominent beer writer refer to "Jack McAuliffe's New Albion Brewing," and a few weeks after that a highly influential Pacific Northwest brewster asked if I'd heard of Suzy because she hadn't prior to Jeff's post. One step forward, two steps back.

Suzy dropped out of the beer world in 1982 after Jack walked away from his dream, leaving her more than $10,000 in debt. She never spoke to him again. Today, she tells me she has no regrets and harbors no resentment.

"I know what I contributed," says the opinionated and usually upbeat eighty-seven-year-old.

Sometime between moving to Seattle and making a career for herself as an English-as-a-Second-Language teacher and instructor teaching yoga to senior citizens, the optimistic octogenarian who habitually boards airplanes to visit grandchildren, foreign countries, and dear old friends Jane Zimmerman in Sonoma County and Don Barkley in Mendocino County, rediscovered beer.

But only as a drinker.

These days, she speaks eloquently about the beverage and frequents only the best Seattle breweries. (Reuben's Brews is her favorite.) On the rare occasion her connection to New Albion comes up, she says, "For the most part people aren't all that interested. 'I know about New Albion. Here's a free beer.' But one time, this guy, oh my god he was practically on his knees worshipping me! When that happens that's sort of fun."

I'm struck by the similarities between Suzy and most beer women I know. Extraordinarily practical. Clear-eyed, no nonsense, and usually pretty blunt. Very talkative and incisively articulate. Beyond brilliant. Absolutely engaged, including in old age. Endlessly hardworking. Uninterested in needlessly calling attention to themselves. And always, without exception, focused on forward-thinking and looking forward, even when paying homage to the past.

Thanks to them, I believe this book has no end.

ACKNOWLEDGMENTS

PER GLINDA, the good witch of the North, it's always best to start at the beginning. I reckon, with no better idea how to acknowledge the principal people who helped weave this book together, I'll heed her counsel. So where'd I leave that damn magic wand?

In sincerity, I am unspeakably grateful.

To:

My immediate family—my mom, brother, and sister-in-law, for never ceasing to support me. My immediate extended family—Uncle Manny, the Roths, the Meisters, and my late grandfathers, Lou and Lee, for the same.

Herlinda Heras, for being my biggest booster, cruise director, chef, and chauffeur; for taking her job as official project photographer so seriously; and for forever forcing me to do things I don't want to do. Jodi, Chris, Jack, and Lana Thompson, for living the dream and, obviously, barn raising the LTD lanai. Remember, there is no beer maximum but there is always a beer minimum.

Robin Shreeves, for rescuing me when I couldn't research fast enough, and Jadon Flores, for pitching in for free. Mr. Frog. Jadon knows why. Teri Fahrendorf, for guiding a generation of women in and to beer and for guiding me into this project.

Linda Balliro, for providing serious sanity when I needed it and for steering me to Kara Rota, the best editor at the best publishing house in the world. Violet Lange, Michael Feinberg, Dana Watson, and Michael Hochman for saving my life. To my best local friends for your unending laughter and loyalty, including but not limited to Jax Cusack, Yvonne Appeltans, Stephanie Bittner, Denise Spaulding, Cheryl Madden, and Joy Kennedy. Chicagoan Jessica Best gets an honorary title.

My mentors, Gary Monterosso, because beer (and everything else); Lew Bryson, because whiskey; Dr. Pat, because all the ancient things. Curators Tiah

Edmunson-Morton and Theresa McCulla for caring about women's voices and supplying me with centuries' worth of information whenever and however frantically I needed it.

Tom Acitelli, for originally connecting me to Suzy, and to Josh Noel, Lauren Clark, Stephen Beaumont, Stan Hieronymous, and Jeff Alworth for your authorly advice. Thank you so, so, so very much to Kristi Switzer and Clare Pelino for your generous guidance through the publishing process and Joanne Jordan and the ladies at Food Shelter for their assistance.

Everyone who gave me feedback on renditions of cover designs but especially Melissa Allen, the designer whiz at MAD Creative and one of my oldest, goofiest, and wisest friends. Eric Rayman, a hot-shot publishing attorney who answered his own phone on a Friday afternoon and had comments on my contract by Sunday.

Every single person who trusted me to grant an interview or contribute in any way to this book. Some of you very patiently answered repeated questions and others shared very personal thoughts. I cannot emphasize this enough, and I want to thank all of you individually but then I'd have to cut a lot more words from the copy.

Some whose deserving names don't appear enough or at all within these pages are mad scientists Lauren Limbach of New Belgium and Birgitte Skadhauge of Carlsberg; brewsters extraordinaire Tamar Banner and Vilija Bizinkauskas; Chuckanut co-owner Mari Kemper and White Labs co-owner Lisa White; coauthor of my next book, Pete Slosberg (shh, we haven't announced anything yet . . .); Rich Wagner for giving me World War II info that no one else could; Wild Bill Owens and his trusty ADI director of ops, Christy Howery; Jessi Flynn, managing director of Kweza Craft Brewery in Rwanda; Richard Cox of UNC Greensboro for info on North Carolina; Tom Conrad of Up Close Tours; witchy U. of Illinois curators Cait Coker and Ruthann Miller. Gregg Hinlicky and Jamie Bogner, who gave me their blessings to repurpose my witchcraft and women-in-history articles from *NJ Brew* and Craft Beer & Brewing magazines, respectively.

BA chief economist Bart Watson and Rosen Group for stats, stats, and more stats, along with the plethora of BA staffers who've helped along the way; beer historian Martin Stack; Drew Beechum from the Maltose Falcons; Katie Wiles at CAMRA; Helga and Christine at the Library of the Finnish Literature

Society; Daimon San and Marcus Consolini at Daimon Brewery; Janet Olson at the Frances Willard House Museum and WCTU Archives.

And in public relations, too many here to thank but most notable among them are Peter Breslow and his team, mostly because he makes me laugh and because he took me to Surly, twice; the Craigs—Hartinger and Alperowitz; Jessica Lyness because where else but McMenamins would you get to drink a straight-up righteous cocktail around a fire next to a donkey with a rainbow unicorn horn affixed to its head . . . while no one else seemed to notice??

Tony Forder, Gary Rosen, and Mark Haynie for championing my beer career. My original journalism pre-editors, Bruce Weber, and Sarah Rutledge Fischer, who taught me the word heteronormative. Megan Parisi and Laura Ulrich just because.

To everyone who forms an integral part of this story: your name may not appear in these pages but you are very much here in spirit. Anne Becerra, Nicole Erny, Mirella Amato, Lauren Limbach, Julie Verratti, Veronica Vega, Aimee Garlit, Zalika Guillory, and Birgitte Skadhauge, plus way, way, way too many more to mention.

And, of course, Steven B. Karpo, because I like him.

NOTES

Preface

As French writes: Marilyn French, *From Eve to Dawn, A History of Women in the World: Revolutions and Struggles for Justice in the 20th Century* (New York: Feminist Press at The City University of New York, 2008), 98–100.

"By the time of Ramses II": French, *From Eve to Dawn*, 98–100.

Women, too often illiterate: Rodney G.S. Carter, "Of Things Said and Unsaid: Power, Archival Silences, and Power in Silence," *Archivaria: The Journal of the Association of Canadian Archivists* 61, September 25, 2006, https://archivaria.ca/index.php/archivaria/article/view/12541/13687.

"Her [public] family story": Tiah Edmunson-Morton, "'Maybe You've Heard of Her Husband? Finding Louisa Weinhard.' The Zoom 2020 PCB-AHA Presentation," August 20, 2020, thebrewstorian.tumblr.com/post/627030027326865408/maybe-youve-heard-of-her-husband-finding-louisa.

Chapter 1: The Rebeginning

The partners welcomed visitors: Tom Acitelli, *The Audacity of Hops: The History of America's Craft Beer Revolution* (Chicago: Chicago Review Press, 2013).

The Associated Press reported that New Albion: Acitelli, *Audacity of Hops*.

In 1979, their output covered their expenses: Acitelli, *Audacity of Hops*.

With the exception of one blog post: Jeff Alworth, "Brewing Pioneers: Suzy Denison," November 25, 2020, beervanablog.com/beervana/2020/11/25/brewing-pioneers-suzy-denison.

a book or two that mention: Acitelli, *Audacity of Hops*.

Chatper 2: Planting the Seed

In Ancient Brews—Rediscovered and Re-created, *Dr. Pat*: Patrick McGovern, *Ancient Brews—Rediscovered & Re-created* (New York: W.W. Norton & Company, 2017).

Residue analysis conducted in 2015: Li Liu, et al., "Fermented Beverage and Food Storage in 13,000 Year-Old Stone Mortars at Raqefet Cave, Israel: Investigating Natufian Ritual Feasting," *Journal of Archaeological Science: Reports* 21, October 2018, 783–793.

"Ancient Israelites . . . proudly drank beer": Michael H. Homan, "Did the Ancient Israelites Drink Beer?" *Biblical Archaeology Review* 36:5 (September/October 2010).

"It is impossible to apply": John Arnold, *The Origin and History of Beer and Brewing* (Chicago: Alumni Association of the Wahl-Henius Institute of Fermentology, 1911).

Marilyn French, claims the word brew *derives*: French, *From Eve to Dawn*.

Chapter 3: Rainbows End down That Highway

Rainbows End down That Highway: Grateful Dead, "Estimated Prophet."

"I think tiny breweries like DeBakker and New Albion": Acitelli, *Audacity of Hops*.

Chapter 4: The *Hymn to Ninkasi*

"You are the one who holds": Ian S. Hornsey, *A History of Beer and Brewing* (Cambridge, England: Royal Society of Chemistry, 2007), 89.

"distinguished them from savages": Tom Standage, *A History of the World in 6 Glasses* (New York: Bloomsbury, 2005).

The Oxford Companion to Beer *tells that Ninkasi*: Ian Hornsey, "Ninkasi," in *The Oxford Companion to Beer*, ed. Garrett Oliver (Cary, NC: Oxford University Press, 2011).

"The house where beer is never lacking": Jean Bottero, *The Oldest Cuisine in the World: Cooking in Mesopotamia*, trans. Teresa Lavender Fagan (Chicago, IL: University of Chicago Press, 2011).

At first, elite women: Scott Rank, "Mesopotamia: Overview and Summary," History onthenet.com, July 2, 2018. https://www.historyonthenet.com/mesopotamia.

"In early Sumerian myths": French, *From Eve to Dawn*.

"Exploiting the name of the goddess": Deborah Scholionkov, "The Beer That Made Sumerians Famous," *New York Times*, March 24, 1993, 46.

The U.S. Brewing Industry: Data and Economic Analysis *guidebook*: Victor J. Tremblay and Carol Horton Tremblay, *The US Brewing Industry: Data and Economic Analysis* (Cambridge, MA: MIT Press, 2004).

"Passionate isn't the right word": Carole Ockert, "Carole Ockert Oral History Interview," interview by Tiah Edmunson-Morton, Oregon Hops and Brewing Archives, Special Collections & Archives Research Center, Oregon State University Libraries, March 1, 2014, audio, media.oregonstate.edu/media/t/0_7k3hutyq.

Chapter 6: Of Goddesses and High Priestesses

"discerning clientele" from the "leisure class": William Bostwick, *The Brewer's Tale: A History of the World According to Beer* (New York: WW Norton, 2015).

Seventy varieties, in fact: Joshua J. Mark, "The Hymn to Ninkasi, Goddess of Beer," *World History Encyclopedia*, 2011, https://www.ancient.eu/article/222/the-hymn -to-ninkasi-goddess-of-beer/.

The rarer the spice: Bostwick, *Brewer's Tale*.

Depending on the grains: Hornsey, *History of Beer and Brewing*.

Babylonians named their beers very literally: Bostwick, *Brewer's Tale*.

Though some archeologists remain skeptical: Claudia Glatz, Elsa Perruchini, et al., "Babylonian Encounters in the Upper Diyala River Valley: Contextualizing the Results of Regional Survey and the 2016–2017 Excavations at Khani Masi," *American Journal of Archaeology* 123, no. 3 (July 2019), 439–471.

Chapter 8: Brew Like an Egyptian

Beer, as in Sumer and Babylonia: Garrett Oliver, ed., *The Oxford Companion to Beer* (New York: Oxford University Press, 2011).

A thirty-five-hundred-year-old medical text: Kim Ryholt, "The Papyrus Carlsberg Collection: Home," 2008, https://pcarlsberg.ku.dk/.

History's first beer tax: Jay R. Brooks, "The Geek Shall Inherit the Earth," *Beer Advocate*, March 2007, https://www.beeradvocate.com/articles/629/the-geek-shall-inherit -the-earth/.

No one can definitively explain the shift: French, *From Eve to Dawn*.

"In societies where a man names his family": French, *From Eve to Dawn*.

"One of them paying her tribute to nature": Bostwick, *The Brewer's Tale*.

"Although beer was produced daily [by women]": Helen M. Strudwick, ed., *The Encyclopedia of Ancient Egypt* (London: Amber Books, 2016).

According to the Atlantic, *this gentleman*: Megan Garber, "Discovered: The Tomb of an Ancient Egyptian Beer Brewer," *Atlantic*, January 3, 2014, theatlantic.com/international /archive/2014/01/discovered-the-tomb-of-an-ancient-egyptian-beer-brewer/282801.

Chapter 9: The Great Eastward Migration

According to Tom Acitelli, they served their first beer: Acitelli, *Audacity of Hops*.

Time magazine included Newman's ale: "Small Is Tasty," *Time*, July 25, 1983.

The region's first craft brewery to incorporate: Lauren Clark, *Crafty Bastards: Beer in New England from the Mayflower to Modern Day* (Wellesley Hills, MA: Union Park Press, 2014).

Thanks to David's travels: Clark, *Crafty Bastards*.

Chapter 10: What's Past Is Prologue

"all labor devolves anyway upon the women": Arnold, *Origin and History*.

"In Africa, fermented alcoholic drinks": Patrick McGovern, "Uncorking the Past: Alcoholic Fermentation as Humankind's First Biotechnology," in *Alcohol and Humans: A Long and Social Affair*, ed. Kimberley Hockings and Robin Dunbar (Cary, NC: Oxford University Press, 2019).

Women, particularly those of the Zulu: "Godchecker.com—Your Guide to the Gods," Godchecker, Accessed May 5, 2021, Godchecker.com.

Inkosazana, another fertility goddess: "Inkosazana," Sacred Texts, accessed May 5, 2021, https://www.sacred-texts.com/afr/rsa/rsa08.htm.

In Tanzania, both women and men: Matthew Van Dis, "Ulanzi: The Magical Drink of Tanzania," Where Is MVD? Travel Blog, last modified June 2, 2016, whereismvd.weebly.com/blog/ulanzi-the-magical-drink-of-tanzania.

"The finding of barley was a surprise": Adam Hoffman, "5,000-Year-Old Microbrewery Found in China," *National Geographic*, last modified May 23, 2016, nationalgeographic.com/culture/article/5000-Year-Old-Microbrewery-Found-In-China.

"the rice from a sober grain": Reina Gattuso, "The Return of Japan's Female Sake Brewers." *Gastro Obscura*, last modified December 10, 2019, https://www.atlasobscura.com/articles/women-sake-brewers-in-japan.

"First," yells the brewster: Gattuso, "The Return of Japan's Female Sake Brewers."

"He saw the golden Inca throne": French, *From Eve to Dawn*.

Chapter 11: Relax, Don't Worry, Have a Homebrew

Relax, Don't Worry, Have a Homebrew: Charlie Papazian, Association of Brewers and Great American Beer Festival founder.

Lauren Clark says Jim Koch bought his homebrew: Clark, *Crafty Bastards*.

Though Nancy Crosby cofounded it: BJCP Board of Directors History, last updated June 6, 2016, https://www.bjcp.org/boardhistory.php.

Last year, women held a staggering eleven: Current Governing Committee Members, American Homebrewers Association, accessed 2020, https://www.homebrewersassociation.org/membership/aha-governing-committee/.

Chapter 12: It's a Sahti Paati

Osmotar, the beer-preparer: Elias Lonnrot, *The Kalevala, the Epic Poem of Finland (Volume I)*, trans. John Martin Crawford (Lector House, 2019).

Translating folklore expert Satu Apo's analysis: Satu Apo, *The Power of Liquor: Cultural Models of Finnish Drinking* (Helsinki: Finnish Literature Society, 2001).

Likewise, Lithuanians, Latvians, and Prussians: Jay Brooks, n.d., https://brookstonbeer bulletin.com/.

Archaeologists have discovered an altar stone: Chas Saunders and Peter J. Allen, "Ragutis (Lithuanian mythology)," Godchecker, last updated May 10, 2019, https://www .godchecker.com/lithuanian-mythology/RAGUTIS.

And in Norse mythology, Ægir, god of the seas: Daughter RavynStar, "Wave Maidens," Journeying to the Goddess, last modified June 7, 2012, https://journeyingtothegoddess .wordpress.com/2012/06/07/wave-maidens/.

"They were portrayed as beautiful maidens": Patricia Monaghan, *The New Book of Goddesses and Heroines*, 3rd ed. (Woodbury, MN: Llewellyn Publications, 1997).

"The belief was that if a woman": Lars Marius Garshol, *Historical Brewing Techniques: The Lost Art of Farmhouse Brewing* (Boulder, CO: Brewers Publications 2020).

Jackson calls sahti "a glass of anthropology": Michael Jackson, ed., *World GT Beer* (Philadelphia: Running Press Book, 1984).

Chapter 14: B(eer) Is for Barbarians

It seems, says Max Nelson: Max Nelson, *The Barbarian's Beverage: A History of Beer in Ancient Europe* (London: Routledge, 2008).

Ian Hornsby ponders: Hornsey, *History of Beer and Brewing*.

Chapter 16: The Fatherland

German monasteries and what we now call convents: Richard W. Unger, *Beer in the Middle Ages and the Renaissance* (Philadelphia: University of Pennsylvania Press, 2013), 52.

Religious orders in Germany: Unger, *Beer in the Middle Ages*.

While monks got most of the attention: Arnold, *Origin and History*.

They, too, sold their excess ale: "German Beer's Sacred Roots," Prost Brewing, last modified May 24, 2013, https://prostbrewing.wordpress.com/2013/05/24/german -beers-sacred-roots/.

Nuns were encouraged to refine their techniques: "German Beer's Sacred Roots."

Nuns also contributed to a body of knowledge: "German Monks, German Nuns, & German Beer," Prost Brewing, last modified November 18, 2013, https://prostbrewing .wordpress.com/2013/11/18/german-monks-german-nuns-german-beer/.

Not the nuns: French, *From Eve to Dawn*.

Protestants were lashing back: French, *From Eve to Dawn*, 100.

It's likely that, intentionally or not: Nelson, *The Barbarian's Beverage*, 100.

One such rule from Ireland: Nelson, *The Barbarian's Beverage*.

Inconsistent facts swirl around her: "German Beer's Sacred Roots."

The first large-scale use of hops: "German Beer's Sacred Roots."

Hildegard documented her own: "German Beer's Sacred Roots."

by the time the use of hops spread to northern Europe: "German Monks, German Nuns."

hops had become the main factor: Bostwick, *Brewer's Tale*.

Hildegard herself enjoyed the beverage: "German Beer's Sacred Roots."

married German women of the Middle Ages homebrewed: "Brewing: Traditionally the Woman's Job," Prost Brewing, last modified September 6, 2013, https://prostbrewing .wordpress.com/2013/09/06/brewing-traditionally-the-womans-job/.

Governing bodies took great interest in beer: "German Monks, German Nuns."

For a while, nobles didn't concern: Arnold, *Origin and History*.

Brandenberg, for example: "History of Beer in the 15th Century: Timeline," Alcohol Problems And Solutions, last modified April 22, 2016, https://www.alcoholproblem sandsolutions.org/history-of-beer-in-the-15th-century-timeline/.

As a precursor to the famous Reinheitsgebot: "History of Beer in the 15th Century."

Bavaria's brewing guilds: "History of Beer in the 15th Century."

"The modern world was formed": French, *From Eve to Dawn*, 98.

"advanced scientific rationality with messianic zeal": French, *From Eve to Dawn*,100.

Holistic family production faded: French, *From Eve to Dawn*, 98.

This was a time of tremendous poverty: French, *From Eve to Dawn*, 114.

A century later, most guilds: French, *From Eve to Dawn*, 114.

Women had no choice but to drop out: French, *From Eve to Dawn*, 114.

Chapter 17: Boom and Bust

"The craft, or microbrew, market had grown": Tina Grant, *International Directory of Company Histories* Vol. 33 (Farmington Hills, MI: St. James Press, 2000), via FundingUniverse, http://www.fundinguniverse.com/company-histories/pyramid -breweries-inc-history/.

"the realm of 'juiciness' a decade": Jeff Alworth, "Portland's BridgePort Brewery Has Closed after 35 Years," Beervana, last modified February 12, 2019, https://www .beervanablog.com/beervana/2019/2/12/oregons-oldest-brewery-bridgeport-has-closed.

Chapter 19: Alewives Unflattered

"As brewing became more profitable": Judith M. Bennett, *Ale, Beer and Brewsters in England: Women's Work in a Changing World, 1300–1600* (New York: Oxford University Press, 1999).

married women generally dominate the rolls: Elizabeth Ewan, *'For Whatever Ales Ye': Women as Consumers and Producers in Late Medieval Scottish Towns* (East Lothian, Scotland: Tuckwell Press, 1999).

"commented in disgust that it seemed": Ewan, 'For Whatever Ales Ye'.

Kathleen Biddick writes: Kathleen Biddick, "Medieval English Peasants and Market Involvement," *Journal of Economic History* 45, no. 4 (1985): 823–31.

"Hucksters were disliked by authorities": Ewan, 'For Whatever Ales Ye'.

"The introduction of hops completed": Sarah Hand Meacham, *Every Home a Distillery: Alcohol, Gender, and Technology in the Colonial Chesapeake* (Baltimore: Johns Hopkins University Press, 2009).

"If women had once independently brewed": Bennett, *Ale, Beer and Brewsters*.

"Within both the rhetoric of social order": Elizabeth Ewan, *Twisted Sisters: Women, Crime and Deviance in Scotland since 1400* (East Lothian, Scotland: Tuckwell Press, 2002).

"The loud, jostling and competitive atmosphere": Ewan, *Twisted Sisters*.

"[These] cultural ideas about women": Christopher Mark O'Brien, *Fermenting Revolution: How to Drink Beer and Save the World* (Gabriola, BC, Canada: New Society, 2011).

"brewers often cheated with impunity": Bennett, *Ale, Beer and Brewsters*.

"Her face bristles with hair": Bennett, *Ale, Beer and Brewsters*.

Chapter 21: Strange Brew

"If alehouses were 'the devil's schoolhouse'": Bennett, *Ale, Beer and Brewsters*.

The Welsh/Irish barley goddess Ceridwen: Patti Wigington, "Cerridwen: Keeper of the Cauldron," Learn Religions, accessed May 5, 2021, https://www.learnreligions.com/cerridwen-keeper-of-the-cauldron-2561960.

"Ceridwen owned the 'witches' cauldron": "Beer Gods & Goddesses," Brookston Beer Bulletin, last modified August 26, 2013, https://brookstonbeerbulletin.com/beer-gods-goddesses/.

The sixteenth-century Book of Taliesin *chronicles*: Charlotte E. Guest, *The Mabinogion* (Mineola, NY: Dover Publications, 1998) 471–491.

Habonde, the Welsh goddess of abundance: Myth Woodling, "Amalthean Horn," Aradia Goddess, accessed May 5, 2021, http://www.jesterbear.com/Aradia/Amalthean Horn.html.

Welsh pagans would light the hearth: "Goddess Habonde," Journeying to the Goddess, last modified July 9, 2012, https://journeyingtothegoddess.wordpress.com/2012/07/09/goddess-habonde/.

Irish Catholics still regard Saint Brigid: n.d., https://brookstonbeerbulletin.com/.

Her story resembles that of the goddess Brigit: "Goddess Brigit," Journeying to the Goddess, last modified February 1, 2012, https://journeyingtothegoddess.wordpress.com/2012/02/01/goddess-brigit/.

Two Sisters Brewing in Kildare: "Two Sisters Brewing," Two Sisters Brewing, accessed May 5, 2021, https://twosistersbrewing.com/.

scholar Peter Burke's theory: Peter Y. Burke, *Eyewitnessing: The Uses of Images as Historical Evidence* (Ithaca, NY: Cornell University Press, 2008).

witch trials rarely mentioned a cauldron: Marian F. McNeill, *The Silver Bough: Scottish Folklore and Folk-Belief* (Ash, England: William Maclellan, 1957).

witches tended to be poorer than their accusers: Alan Macfarlane and James Sharpe, *Witchcraft in Tudor and Stuart England: A Regional and Comparative Study* (Abingdon, UK: Taylor and Francis, 1970).

England's population grew rapidly: Marianne Hester, *The Witchcraft Reader* (Oldridge, Darren, London, New York: Routledge, 2002).

"took her cursing bone and made her way": McNeill, *Silver Bough*.

Chapter 23: Coming to America

Henry Badcock, bequeathed her: Rich Wagner, *Philadelphia Beer: A Heady History of Brewing in the Cradle of Liberty* (Charleston, SC: The History Press, 2012).

"Hath put himself an apprentice": Morris family papers (Collection 2000E), The Historical Society of Pennsylvania.

"were hasted ashore and made to drink": William Bradford, *Of Plimouth Plantation*, State Library of Massachusetts, 1650, accessed May 6, 2021, https://www.mass.gov/info-details/bradfords-manuscript-of-plimoth-plantation.

"Nor," she wrote, "do I presume": Sarah Hand Meacham, *Every Home a Distillery: Alcohol, Gender, and Technology in the Colonial Chesapeake* (Baltimore: Johns Hopkins University Press, 2009).

Even though women ran: Meacham, *Every Home a Distillery*.

"When money got involved": Gregg Smith, *Beer in America: The Early Years—1587–1840: Beer's Role in the Settling of America and the Birth of a Nation* (Boulder, CO: Brewers Publications, 1998).

Settlers established the first licensed tavern: Clark, *Crafty Bastards*.

That's nineteen years after Spanish explorer Pedro Menendez de Aviles: "A Spanish Expedition Established St. Augustine in Florida," America's Library, accessed May 5, 2021, http://www.americaslibrary.gov/jb/colonial/jb_colonial_augustin_1.html.

When American schoolchildren learn: Meacham, *Every Home a Distillery*.

"This included four days of prayer": Tiah Edmunson-Morton, "LibGuides: Beer Research Guide: Women," Oregon State University, last updated April 23, 2021, https://guides.library.oregonstate.edu/c.php?g=991302&p=7439341.

"some strong beer and cider": Meacham, *Every Home a Distillery*.

Some wealthy Colonial women took a nip: Meacham, *Every Home a Distillery*.

She proved herself: "History of the Town of Haddonfield," Haddonfield History, accessed May 5, 2021, https://haddonfieldhistory.org/about/history-of-the-town-of-haddonfield/.

immortalized in the poem "Elizabeth": Henry Wadswoth Longfellow, "The Theologian's Tale; Elizabeth," Henry Wadsworth Longfellow, A Maine Historical Society Website (public domain, n.d.).

Elizabeth kept herself very busy: "Elizabeth Haddon," History of American Women, last updated August 4, 2008, https://www.womenhistoryblog.com/2008/08/elizabeth -haddon-estaugh.html.

"distillation, tho[ugh] long practiced": Ambrose Cooper, *The Complete Distiller (1757)* (Whitefish, MT: Kessinger Publishing Legacy Reprints, 2010).

"Everything was coming together": Smith, *Beer in America.*

Chapter 24: From the Back Office to the Boardroom

The Brewers Association says craft brewery output: "National Beer Sales and Production Data," Brewers Association, accessed May 6, 2021, https://www.brewersassociation .org/statistics-and-data/national-beer-stats.

Lest you think that's a biased generality: Sarah Oliver and Meredith Conroy, *Who Runs? The Masculine Advantage in Candidate Emergence* (Ann Arbor, MI: University of Michigan Press, 2020), https://cawp.rutgers.edu/research/candidate -recruitment.

Chapter 25: Rivers of Lager Flow Toward Temperance

Tiah notes in a blog post about Frederika: Tiah Edmunson-Morton, "Fredericka Wetterer: Eagle Brewery, 1879-1884, part 1," Oregon Hops & Brewing Archives, March 31, 2018, https://thebrewstorian.tumblr.com/post/172448934536/fredericka -wetterer-eagle-brewery-jacksonville.

By 1859, Rich Wagner reports: Wagner, *Philadelphia Beer.*

"It was part of the rise of working-class leisure": Christine Sismondo, *America Walks into a Bar: A Spirited History of Taverns and Saloons, Speakeasies and Grog Shops* (New York: Oxford University Press, 2014).

"Beer gardens became playgrounds": Maureen Ogle, *Ambitious Brew: The Story of American Beer* (Boston: Mariner Books, 2007).

Despite their disdain for beer halls: "The 1800s: When Americans Drank Whiskey Like it Was Water," *Paste,* accessed May 5, 2021, https://www.pastemagazine.com/drink /alcohol-history/the-1800s-when-americans-drank-whiskey-like-it-was/.

"In cities it was widely understood": Daniel Okrent, *Last Call: The Rise and Fall of Prohibition* (New York: Scribner, 2010).

left "this work with God and the women": Mark Lawrence Schrad, *Smashing the Liquor Machine: A Global History of Prohibition* (Cary, NC: Oxford University Press, 2021).

"The sight of the community's most respectable ladies": Schrad, *Smashing the Liquor Machine.*

"'Axes were placed in the hands of the women'": Schrad, *Smashing the Liquor Machine.*

"The sight of these women kneeling": Schrad, *Smashing the Liquor Machine.*

"will quickly learn the impossibility": Schrad, *Smashing the Liquor Machine.*

"With ribaldry and sneers the liquor men": Schrad, *Smashing the Liquor Machine.*

"The merging of Anthony's campaign": Okrent, *Last Call.*

Next she convinced Congress: Okrent, *Last Call.*

Half of the nation's public school students: Okrent, *Last Call.*

Her second husband divorced her: Schrad, *Smashing the Liquor Machine.*

beer was not, in fact, "healthful": Schrad, *Smashing the Liquor Machine.*

"the predatory white man's liquor trade": Schrad, *Smashing the Liquor Machine.*

The march toward temperance took hold: Schrad, *Smashing the Liquor Machine.*

"In the two decades leading up to Prohibition's enactment": Okrent, *Last Call.*

"Our German women do not want": Okrent, *Last Call.*

"forces best not written about": Okrent, *Last Call.*

"Is it not sufficient political achievement for women": Okrent, *Last Call.*

because of "political exigency": Okrent, *Last Call.*

"If Southern [White] men are not careful": Ida B. Wells, Editorial, *The Free Speech*, May 21, 1892, accessed May 6, 2021, https://www.digitalhistory.uh.edu/disp_textbook.cfm?smtid=3&psid=3614.

"On this liquor question there is room": Frances Ellen Watkins Harper, *Sowing and Reaping: A Temperance Story* (Salt Lake City: Project Gutenberg, public domain, reprinted in 2004), accessed May 6, 2021, https://www.gutenberg.org/ebooks/11022.

"Harper's leadership as the most prominent": Ann D. Gordon, Bettye Collier-Thomas, John H. Bracey, Arlene Voski Avakian, and Joyce Avrech Berkman, eds., *African-American Women and the Vote, 1837–1965* (Amherst, NY: University of Massachusetts Press, 1997).

"The failures of white WCTU members to answer": The Director, "FEW-Harper-1885-1," Frances Willard House Museum and Archives, July 24, 2020, https://franceswillardhouse.org/the-activism-and-artistry-of-frances-ellen-watkins-harper/.

The year after Frances Willard's death: Okrent, *Last Call.*

"Even a group as powerful, wealthy, and self-interested": Okrent, *Last Call.*

Chapter 26: The Customer Is Sometimes Right

the only one sanctioned by the AHA: Gail Ann Williams and Steve Shapiro, "Education a Focus for Queen of Beer Competition," American Homebrewers Association,

January 31, 2020, https://www.homebrewersassociation.org/homebrew-community
-culture/pink-boots-and-queen-of-beer-celebrate-the-homebrew-path-to-going
-pro.

she *"didn't have balls"*: Reuters Staff, "'Blokes-only' rule leaves New Zealand woman
brewer flat," *Reuters,* January 12, 2012, https://www.reuters.com/article/newzealand
-beer-idINL3E8CC66J20120112.

Chapter 27: Prohibited from the Halls of Power No More

"In essence, it became the woman's job": Dylan Garret, "The Underground Spaces Where
Drinking While Female Was a Radical Act," *Wine Enthusiast,* March 8, 2020,
https://www.winemag.com/2020/03/08/ladies-drinking-rooms-history/.

"cheap booze and suggestive women": "Queens of the Speakeasies," Prohibition: An
Interactive History, The Mob Museum, accessed May 6, 2021, https://prohibition
.themobmuseum.org/the-history/the-prohibition-underworld/queens-of-the
-speakeasies/.

"Young women who ventured into these": Mary Murphy, "Bootlegging Mothers and
Drinking Daughters: Gender and Prohibition in Butte, Montana," *American Quarterly* 46, no. 2 (1994), 174–94.

"The joint has been doing": *Greensboro Patriot,* March 3, 1909.

"women assistants in the rum-running profession": "'Bootleggerette' Is Captured with
Cargo of Whisky," *Greensboro News Record,* January 4, 1933.

A 1929 police blotter printed: "Speakeasy Patrons Start a Squabble; Police Stage Raid,"
Greensboro News Record, July 23, 1929.

"Women in the 1910s had drunk quietly": Catherine Gilbert Murdock, *Domesticating Drink: Women, Men, and Alcohol in America, 1870–1940* (Baltimore: Johns
Hopkins University Press, 2002).

"fond of sports suits, wears purple": Okrent, *Last Call.*

By the end of 1933 Pauline's group: Okrent, *Last Call.*

"What have you done to my wife, Mrs. Sabin?": Grace Cogswell Root, *Women and
Repeal: The Story of the Women's Organization for National Prohibition Reform*
(New York: Harper, 1934).

"They are not fit to guide automobiles": Murdock, *Domesticating Drink.*

Chapter 28: Big Boss Ladies and the Family Ties That Bind

"We recognize we have the opportunity": Tara Nurin, "The Four Sisters Who Run
America's Oldest Brewery Double Down On Supporting Female Brewers," *Forbes,*
March 5, 2020, https://www.forbes.com/sites/taranurin/2020/03/05/the-four

-sisters-who-run-americas-oldest-brewery-double-down-on-supporting-female
-brewers/?sh=4e809df462a6.

"If I don't leave now": Steven Burns, "One Last Pint: Laura Bell On Leadership & Change In Craft," City Tap Kitchen & Craft, May 9, 2018, https://www.citytap.com/news -item/one-last-pint-laura-bell-on-leadership-change-in-craft-beer/.

Chapter 29: Don't Worry, Darling, You Didn't Burn the Beer

"I tried to get them to look": Arthur O. Murray, "Brew Mistress," *Business North Carolina*, July 2002.

"Honestly, in my wildest dreams": Murray, "Brew Mistress."

"Two of the men asked me to fetch": Harriet Sherwood, "How Victorian Female Brewers Broke the (Pint) Glass Ceiling," *Guardian*, September 6, 2020, https://www .theguardian.com/lifeandstyle/2020/sep/06/how-victorian-female-brewers-broke -the-pint-glass-ceiling.

At the conclusion of World War II: Laurel White, "Breaking the Pint Glass Ceiling: Female Brewmasters Pouring into State Craft Beer Scene," *Cap Times*, last modified February 11, 2015, https://madison.com/ct/business/breaking-the-pint-glass -ceiling-female-brewmasters-pouring-into-state-craft-beer-scene/article_3a2ac015 -f362-56ac-a730-9b7ba07a68d9.html.

Gulf's personnel and safety director: J. M. Delmar, "Women *Can* Replace Men in a Brewery," *American Brewer*, August 1943.

"Now that the war in Europe has ended": *American Brewer* 78, no. 5, May 1945, 21.

Although Miller claims it invented "lite": E. J. Schultz, "MillerCoors Exec Discusses the Way Forward for Light Beer," *Ad Age*, last modified October 13, 2014, http://adage .com/article/cmo-strategy/millercoors-exec-discusses-forward-light-beer/295381; "Did Miller Just Say It Invented Light Beer?" *Truth in Advertising*, last modified October 28, 2014, https://www.truthinadvertising.org/miller-just-say-invented-light -beer; Annie Gabillet, "Cheers! A Look Back at Beer Advertising for Women," *Popsugar*, last modified April 7, 2014, https://www.popsugar.com/love/photo -gallery/19010605/image/19010616/OMG-ve-discovered-nonfattening-beer.

Regional breweries such as George J. Renner Brewing: Ogle, *Ambitious Brew*, 230.

What seems strange about Miller's spurious claim: Ogle, *Ambitious Brew*, 230.

In five years, the brewery's sales shot up: Ogle, *Ambitious Brew*, 232.

"The right to enjoy this beverage": "Beer belongs – enjoy it! 20 quaint scenes from the '40s & '50s," *Click Americana*, accessed May 7, 2021, https://clickamericana .com/topics/food-drink/beer-belongs-enjoy-it-americas-beverage-of-moderation -1940s-1950s.

"*Whether being served while friends picnic*": "How Art Helped Convince Post-WWII America That 'Beer Belongs,'" *Craft Beer*, last modified December 6, 2019, https://www.craftbeer.com/craft-beer-muses/american-ad-campaign-beer-belongs.

On the surface, these: White, "Breaking the Pint Glass Ceiling."

More often than not they sized: "Cheers! A Look Back at Beer Advertising For Women," *Popsugar*, accessed May 5, 2021, https://www.popsugar.com/love/photo-gallery/19010605/image/19010718/woman-just-cant-resist-Bud.

In 2007 ad critic Bob Garfield: Bob Garfield, "Heineken 'DraftKeg': The Most Sexist Beer Commercial Ever Produced?" *Ad Age*, August 27, 2007, https://adage.com/article/ad-review/heineken-draftkeg-sexist-beer-commerical-produced/120078.

I do have to hand it to AB InBev: "Leadership Team," Anheuser-Busch InBev, accessed May 7, 2021, https://www.ab-inbev.com/who-we-are/people.

In 2016 MillerCoors announced: Shareen Pathak, "Bottoms Up: One Exec's Quest to Turn Down the Bro in Beer Marketing," *Digiday*, September 12, 2016, https://digiday.com/marketing/bottoms-one-execs-quest-turn-bro-beer-marketing/.

In 2019 Budweiser made a splash: Hidrėlėy, "Budweiser Adapts Its Sexist Ads from the 50s and 60s to 2019," Bored Panda, last modified March 11, 2019, https://www.boredpanda.com/modernized-vintage-sexist-beer-advertisements-budweiser/.

Chapter 30: Beyond Beards, Beyond Breasts

It announced three initiatives: "Diversity, Equity and Inclusion (DEI) Update," Pink Boots Society, June 19, 2020, https://www.pinkbootssociety.org/category/dei/.

Chapter 32: Raging Bitches

"*Put me in your mouth*": Edith Hancock, "'I f*cked up' — Stone Brewing boss forced to apologise twice after consent tweet went viral," *The Drinks Business*, March 2, 2018, https://www.thedrinksbusiness.com/2018/03/i-fcked-up-stone-brewery-boss-forced-to-apologise-twice-after-sexist-tweet-went-viral/.

compelled Bud Light to apologize: Jessica Glenza, "Bud Light sorry for 'removing no from your vocabulary for the night' label," *Guardian*, April 29, 2015, https://www.theguardian.com/business/2015/apr/29/bud-light-slogan-no-means-no.

He pushed through a lengthy: Hancock, "'I f*cked up.'"

"*Integrity is the metaphorical yardstick*": Julia Herz, "Embracing Diversity in the Beer Biz," Brewers Association, November 21, 2016, https://www.brewersassociation.org/brewing-industry-updates/embracing-diversity-beer-biz/.

After years of declining: "Brewers Association Marketing and Advertising Code," Brewers Association, accessed May 7, 2021, https://www.brewersassociation.org/brewers-association-advertising-marketing-code/.

"It's anti–free enterprise": Justin Kendall, "In Defense of Free Speech, Flying Dog Terminates BA Membership," July 14, 2017, Brewbound, https://www.brewbound.com/news/defense-free-speech-flying-dog-terminates-ba-membership/.

A year after the BA's move: "CAMRA bans discriminatory beers at its flagship festival," June 8, 2019, CAMRA, https://camra.org.uk/press_release/camra-bans-discriminatory-beers-at-its-flagship-festival/.

In retrospect I regret: Tara Nurin, "Publisher's Odd Anti-#MeToo Rant Raises Question of How Writers Should Cover Beer," *Forbes*, February 12, 2019, https://www.forbes.com/sites/taranurin/2019/02/12/publishers-odd-anti-metoo-rant-raises-question-of-how-writers-should-cover-beer/?sh=43a7f294f5cb.

"chicks who basically take photos": Tara Nurin, "Brewbound Editor Leaves After Publicly Disparaging Female Influencers' Instagram Accounts," *Forbes*, July 25, 2019, https://www.forbes.com/sites/taranurin/2019/07/25/brewbound-editor-leaves-after-publicly-disparaging-female-influencers-instagram-accounts/?sh=3c4a698e2be6.

Shortly after I published a treatise: Nurin, "Brewbound Editor Leaves."

"Women don't always take": Tara Nurin, "The #MeToo Movement Is Coming To Craft Beer ... Will It Arrive Before All the Women Leave?" *Forbes*, March 6, 2020, https://www.forbes.com/sites/taranurin/2020/03/06/the-metoo-movement-is-coming-to-craft-beer--will-it-arrive-before-all-the-women-leave/?sh=24821f0c17ac.

Chapter 33: That's Right, the Women Are Smarter

That's Right, the Women Are Smarter: Harry Belafonte, "Man Smart (Woman Smarter)."

"Jessica feels her lack": Sibyl Perkins, "Jessica Heidrich wins first PBS scholarship," Pink Boots Society, April 9, 2013, https://www.pinkbootssociety.org/2013/04/09/jessica-heidrich-wins-first-pbs-scholarship.

Chapter 34: Sisters Are Brewing It for Themselves

Global beer sales are predicted: "Global Beer Market Report 2020 with Impact of COVID-19 in the Medium Term," Research and Markets, last modified October 19, 2020, https://www.globenewswire.com/news-release/2020/10/19/2110117/0/en/Global-Beer-Market-Report-2020-with-Impact-of-COVID-19-in-the-Medium-Term.html.

It only takes a count of the nation's: "BA Diversity Benchmarking Study, 2018," Brewer's Association, https://www.brewersassociation.org/educational-publications/sustainability-benchmarking-reports/.

In late 2020, blogger Jeff Alworth: Alworth, "Brewing Pioneers."

INDEX

ABOUT THE AUTHORS

Tara Nurin is the beer and spirits contributor to *Forbes* and an adjunct Beer 101 instructor at Wilmington University. She has been the Libations columnist for *New Jersey Monthly*, the women-in-beer columnist for *Ale Street News*, and the cohost of the *What's on Tap* weekly beer TV show. Her work has been published in more than fifty newspapers, magazines, and digital platforms such as *Food + Wine*, *USA Today*, and *Wine Enthusiast*. She is certified by the Beer Judge Certification Program and serves as a frequent expert and host in the media and in educational programming.

Foreword author **Teri Fahrendorf** is a brewer and founder of the Pink Boots Society, an organization that supports women in the brewing industry. She is notable for being one of the first women in craft brewing and her beers have been widely awarded in competitions such as the Great American Beer Festival.